# ESSAYS IN THERAVADA BUDDHISM

*Writings of an Incendiary Western Monk*

Paññobhāsa Bhikkhu (a.k.a.
John David Reynolds)

ISBN: 9798519788915

Cover art and rhinoceros sigil by Deide Hamlin
Library of Congress Control Number: 2018675309
Printed in the United States of America

*To RON SHERMAN*
*guru to a troubled teenager long ago*

# CONTENTS

# PREFACE, BY WAY OF INTRODUCTION

Hello, and welcome to this book. I have been writing for many years, overflowing with strange ideas, although aside from a translation of some ancient Buddhist texts that I had published for free distribution, back when I was a monk living in Burma, this is my first book, and I hope there will be ideas of value to you in the following pages. If you are a thoughtful person with an interest in Buddhism or Eastern philosophy/spirituality, then I am confident that you will find plenty of food for thought.

I maintained the Nippapanca Blog from June 2012 to June 2016, which was mostly writings on Buddhist philosophy and ethics, but I also veered occasionally into all sorts of topics viewed from a Buddhist perspective; everything I view intellectually has some Buddhist perspective lurking around *somewhere* nearby. And assuming that Buddhist philosophy, Dhamma, accurately describes the human condition, then everything I view even intuitively and nonverbally has some Buddhist perspective at the heart of it. Dhamma, or Dharma, is practically by definition the way to knowing reality, or highest truth.

After leaving the Theravada Buddhist Sangha, after thirty years as a monk, I decided to take down the obscure little blog and edit the weekly essays into more accessible books. This volume consists of essays, most of them originally posts on the Nippapanca Blog, that deal specifically with the theme of Theravada —the most conservative and closest to ancient Indian culture, the culture in which the Buddha himself lived, of all the traditional schools of Buddhism in existence today. My tastes are eclectic though, so I bring in ideas from outside the mainstream of Theravada—from other schools of Buddhism occasionally, and sometimes from western spiritual traditions, western philosophy, and my own nondenominational personal experience.

A friend and supporter suggested a title for this book: *Real Buddhism: Why 99% of What You Hear from a Modern "Buddhist Teacher" Is False—and What You Can Do About It.* If people interpret this book in this way, fine, I guess; although if I really try to write a book with a title like that it will be a more organized, specific manifesto than what you are holding now. This book is just a collection of ideas, written by a western Theravada Buddhist monk, attempting a fresh, and possibly an original, perspective on a very ancient Buddhist tradition. Ancient, but in its deepest respects also timeless and always new.

Some of the essays in this collection are original translations from Pali into English, generally with some explanatory commentary following them—"The Elephant," "When Godhika Took the Knife" (an ancient tale of a monk who became enlightened while committing suicide), "Pointless Potthila," "The Spike," "The Outsider" (a strange account of an enlightened non-Buddhist), and "The Story of the Elder Protector of Vision" are examples of this type. Others discuss some rather obscure and arcane monastic themes, particularly the essays with titles beginning with "Technical Matters," which may be of specific interest to monks, although I hope I have written plainly and engagingly enough that anyone who is not a total beginner to Buddhism will be able to fathom and appreciate them without difficulty. They do shed considerable light on the lifestyle of a Theravadin monk, in ancient as well as modern times. Other essays are more blatantly philosophical, dealing with topics including mysticism ("Notes on Mysticism"), dogmatism ("Buddhism Meets Monty Python"), karma ("The Autopilot"), meditation ("On the Four Stages of Meditation"), dependent co-arising, and insight. Other essays deal with the history and evolution of Buddhism, such as the very first essay "On the 500-Year Lifespan of Buddhism," "Bodhisattas and

Bodhisattvas" (on the evolution of the Bodhisattva concept), and "The Great Schism." Other essays address modern social issues in Theravada Buddhism, including "The New Bhikkhunis," "Four Western Theravadas," and "Reflections on American 'Protestant Theravada.'" And one essay in particular, I think, "One of Many Middle Paths," deals ostensibly with the Buddhist ideal of the Middle Way, but applies it to the everyday mental life of a Buddhist, or just spiritual, practitioner. Thus I trust that this book will have something to say worthy of consideration by any thoughtful reader.

These essays were written not only on various topics but in various places. The earliest were composed in Bellingham, Washington, USA, as I was moving from place to place, house sitting and couch surfing (or rather floor surfing), trying to live at the time as a "free range monk" in the west. Many others were written in a cave in Burma, or else under a thatched little shelter in front of that cave, surrounded by trees, rocks, wild chickens, and owls. A few others were written when I was living in a bamboo hut in the central highlands of Bali, on the edge of an old Chinese cemetery. It appears that my days of living in caves and huts are over now, and the final touches, like this Preface, are written sitting at a nice desk in a clean and comfortable little apartment in South Carolina.

For those of you who are not already conversant in Theravada Buddhist terms, and are new to this school of Buddhism, I offer here some introductory explanation. Theravada, or "Doctrine of the Elders," is based on ancient Indian culture extending all the way back to the time of Gotama (Gautama) Buddha, before Buddhism spread to places like China and Tibet. The texts or "scriptures" are composed in the Pali language, in contrast to the Sanskrit (or Chinese, etc.) used by later schools; and the original Buddhist language, spoken by the Buddha himself, was probably very similar to Pali. Consequently some words you will find in this book may appear unusual: Pali "Dhamma" instead of Sanskrit "Dharma," kamma instead of karma, Nibbāna instead of Nirvana, and so on. Also, you may notice in the Table of Contents a few essays on Abhidhamma, which is the third and last section of the early Buddhist scriptures; it is an attempt by early

Buddhist philosophers to systematize the teachings found in the Suttas (Sanskrit *sutras*), and which some traditionalists like the Burmese Buddhists consider to be the most important part of the entire Pali Tipitaka, or Theravada Buddhist Canon. I use "Theravada" as a noun describing the system itself, and "Theravadin" as an adjective, in accordance with Pali grammar. I do not consider orthodox Theravada, or any other school of Buddhism, to represent perfectly what the historical Buddha originally taught, as you may see in the essays which follow, although I think it is clear that Theravada comes much closer than the other schools in most respects, coming closer to the Buddha historically and culturally. But, as Buddhist philosophy declares, everything is impermanent and subject to change, including Buddhism itself.

This relative faithfulness to the culture of the time of the Buddha certainly has its advantages, but also its disadvantages. Theravada today fits very well in traditional cultures based on classical India, like Sri Lanka and Myanmar, but not so well in the west. It was designed primarily as a monastic system of renunciation, austerity, self-discipline, and deep contemplation, which does not convert well to being practiced by modern western people with jobs and worldly lives to live; and so, as will be addressed more in books to be published after this one, some sort of modification must take place if Theravada is to be more prevalent and to prosper in the west. Modifications are already taking place, some good, some not so good. But as I say, that issue is just touched upon in this volume, and will be discussed more fully in other books.

Those other books, also collections of selected essays from the Nippapanca Blog, will feature, in addition to the issue just mentioned, a more wide-ranging field of topics, including western philosophy, spirituality in general, and a fair amount of social commentary—observations on postmodern western culture from a person who had been outside of it for literally decades. Many people in the west are like the almost-proverbial frog who will allow itself to be cooked to death when it sits in water that is slowly brought to a boil, because the changes are too gradual to notice as something important; but I plunged headfirst directly into a very different culture than the one I left in 1991—different in many ways even though very similar in others—and so I am like a frog dropped into already hot water and noticing it very intensely. Also I bring thirty years of introspection and contemplation of Buddhist philosophy with my views on my native yet greatly changed culture.

If this experiment prospers, that is if people read the book and others that will follow on this theme, then I will very probably write some from scratch—including the whole surreal drama of renouncing the world, being ordained as a Theravada Buddhist monk, moving to Burma/Myanmar, and meditating and sweating in Burmese caves for many years, as well as the possibly just-as-strange events of my attempts at living as a "free range monk" in the secular west. The experiences of my life, a modern westerner disenchanted with western life who goes halfway around the world and practices austerities like an ancient Indian renunciant, are weird enough to at least have some mind-blowing entertainment value. At the very least.

I have tried to track down any copyrighted material in this book, but may possibly have overlooked something. Much of the writings in this book were composed while I was living in caves and huts in Southeast Asia, and many quotations that I used were from old personal notebooks in which I had written down ideas that intrigued me. All translations from ancient Pali are my own, unless otherwise specified, and any errors are also my own.

I give special thanks to the generous people who have been helping me make this huge transition from monk to nobody, or rather to someone with no status in particular. I also cannot hope to convey my gratitude to the kind-hearted and generous Burmese Buddhist folks who supported my existence for so many years, in Asia and also in America. Special gratitude flows to my sweetheart Deide, who not only has been of great help to me in the preparing of this book, but who has been of great help with regard to pretty much everything in my life lately. May all of you be as well, peaceful, and happy as Samsara and the First Noble Truth of Buddhism ("to exist is to suffer") will allow.

Mettā
David Reynolds, alias Paññobhāsa
Greenville, South Carolina
9 June 2021

# ON THE 500-YEAR LIFESPAN OF BUDDHISM

*(NOTE: I wrote the bulk of this article way back in 2012, about a politically incorrect prophecy attributed to the Buddha, as recorded in the canonical ancient Pali texts. Subsequent to that time, a few years ago, when I was in Burma last time in fact, I mentioned the strange case of the 500-year lifespan of Buddhism to a very intelligent Burmese monk named Sayadaw U Vimala, who gave an interpretation not included in the old essay, so I update it here. Venerable U Vimala's interpretation may be the most attractive, or the least unattractive, interpretation to many people over this controversial issue, so I suppose it is good to add that ingredient to the stew. Also I have made a few minor stylistic changes, just because I'm fussy. Enjoy.)*

There is a very politically incorrect story in the Pali Buddhist texts, in the tenth chapter of the Vinaya Cullavagga, describing how the Buddha's aunt/stepmother Mahāpajāpati Gotamī approaches the Buddha and asks him for permission to become the first ordained Buddhist nun (bhikkhunī). She asks three times. The Buddha, evidently considering this to be a very bad idea, sternly refuses all three times. Mahāpajāpati Gotamī goes away weeping. Later she begins following the Buddha and standing outside his door with dust on her body and tears on her face, grieving because women are not allowed to be ordained as nuns. The Buddha's cousin and faithful attendant, the venerable Ānanda

Gotama, who in the texts is often portrayed as having a tender spot in his heart for women, then remonstrates with the Buddha on Mahāpajāpati Gotamī's behalf. After being sternly refused like Mahāpajāpati was, he employs persuasive arguments that the Buddha cannot deny, for example that women are just as capable of attaining enlightenment as men are. Finally the Buddha relents, but gives Ānanda a sort of "OK, but *now* you've done it" speech:

> *"If, Ānanda, women had not gone forth from the home into homelessness in the Way and Discipline made known by the Tathāgata, then the Holy Life would last a long time; the true Way would last for a thousand years. But since, Ānanda, women have gone forth from the home into homelessness in the Way and Discipline made known by the Tathāgata, now, Ānanda, the Holy Life will not last for a long time; now, Ānanda, the true Way will last for only five hundred years."*

The purpose of this article is not to discuss the controversial issue of the recent attempted revival of the Order of Theravada Buddhist nuns. I've already written some of my ideas on that subject in other essays (like "The New Bhikkhunis," and "Appendix on Bhikkhunis and Equality," included in this volume). The main purpose of this essay is to address the strange prophecy made by the Buddha in the above text, that Buddhism would survive for only 500 years—not 500 years from now, mind you, but 500 years from the time of the Buddha; and if that is the case, then Buddhism should have died out around 2000 years ago. There are a number of possible explanations for this prophecy, and I will consider some of the most obvious ones.

**1. The Commentarial explanation.** According to the medieval commentaries, which happen to represent the official "party line" of orthodox Theravada Buddhist tradition, when the Buddha said that *Saddhamma* would survive for five hundred years what he really *meant* was that *Saddhamma* would survive for five *thou-*

*sand* years. As far as I know, the commentator made no serious attempt to explain why the Buddha would say 500 if he really meant 5000. (This would be a rather misleading way of speaking to the venerable Ānanda, who of course would have no commentary to refer to for cases when the Buddha says X when he really means Y—the commentaries are indispensable for pointing out such cases.)

This explanation may seem rather unlikely to Western Buddhists, but it is accepted without question by most Burmese Buddhists, for example, including most Burmese scholar-sayadaws. No doubt the commentator was faced with the dilemma of an old text which could not be doubted saying something which could not be believed, as the commentary was compiled and edited more than 500 years after the time of the Buddha. Theravadin tradition goes further with the legend of the 5000-year reign of the true Dhamma: at the end of this period all the relics of the Buddha enshrined in pagodas, etc., throughout heavens and earth will leave their places and assemble in midair over the site at Bodh Gaya where the Buddha first realized enlightenment, will assume the form of the Buddha, will perform the "twin miracle" of spraying water and fire simultaneously, and will deliver a final sermon—at the end of which the dispensation of Gotama Buddha will be at an end. The dispensation of Gotama Buddha will end with this sermon because no human will be present to hear it and be inspired by it—only gods and goddesses will attend. Thousands of years later another Buddha, Metteyya, will rediscover Dhamma and set the wheel rolling again.

**2. The Buddha didn't really say it.** This explanation would probably be the preferred choice for most skeptical Western Buddhists, and I must admit I prefer it also, although the notion that the scriptures are not 100% authentic and reliable is unthinkable for millions of faithful Asians, plus a fair amount of Western fundamentalists. One plausible theory is that the Order of nuns was not very popular with many of the monks in very ancient times, nor very well established, so the "prophecy" was added at an early

Great Council as a moral lesson of some kind. If this theory is correct, then it is interesting that ancient Buddhist monks were so modest and unassuming about the future popularity of the Buddhist system.

**3. The Buddha really did say it, but was mistaken.** This one also is a non-starter for millions of faithful Asians, plus a fairer amount of Westerners than with the previous one. The idea that the Buddha was omniscient at least to the point of knowing anything he wanted to know is accepted by most Buddhists; that he could say what is not true, deliberately or accidentally, is considered an impossibility. However, as I've pointed out elsewhere, there is evidence in the Pali texts themselves that enlightened beings, and even the Buddha himself, can occasionally be mistaken. And of course there is plenty of evidence from other traditions that great sages can make great errors in their predictions. Probably the most famous is the apparent belief of Jesus of Nazareth that the world would come to an end, or at least Judgement Day would come, very soon, probably within a few decades of his own time. The belief that the End is Near has been assumed as gospel truth by Christians ever since.

It does not *necessarily* imply a logical contradiction for a fully enlightened being to say something that is not empirically true; it may be that full enlightenment involves an awareness of Ultimate Truth that is not entirely relevant to the conventionally true mass delusion of Samsara. (See my essay "Buddhism Meets Skepticism, originally posted July 28, 2012, on the old blog, for a slightly more detailed discussion of these points.) Even so, it does strike me as rather unlikely that the Buddha would predict that the existence of nuns would shorten the lifespan of Buddhism to only 500 years. It just doesn't sound convincing for some reason.

**4. The Buddha did really say it, and was right.** This strikes me as the most intriguing of the possible explanations—that the true Way, the *Saddhamma*, really did last only 500 years, and that what we've been calling Buddhism ever since has been some kind of cheap imitation.

The Theravadins might derive some grim satisfaction from the idea that Mahayana arose about 500 years after the time of the Buddha, but still it would seem that virtually all Buddhists would prefer to believe that they themselves are following the "real deal" and not some pale shadow of the truth. (Incidentally, at least one Mahayana tradition has its own interpretation of the case—that there would be *five* 500-year periods of Buddhism: the first period being a time of genuine, pure Dharma; the second being a time of lesser purity but still strong practice; the third mainly being strong in Buddhist scholarship; the fourth degenerating into more superficial levels of practice and learning, and the fifth being characterized mainly by debate and dissension. If this is the case then we are at or very near the end of the last period.) Even if this fourth explanation were true, that real Buddhism no longer exists, it would not necessarily mean that people calling themselves Buddhists could not become liberated at all, as Buddhism does not necessarily have a monopoly on liberation. It would just suggest that they were not attaining this in the exact way that Gotama Buddha advised.

Interestingly, a plausible variation on this theme has been stated by the not particularly Buddhist spiritual teacher Paul Lowe: according to him (and I do not know how he arrived at this idea), for 500 years after the time of the Buddha there was an unbroken lineage of enlightened teachers and disciples; that is, there was always at least one teacher with at least one enlightened disciple, with this lineage continuing all the way back to the Buddha himself. After 500 years the lineage was broken, although since then there have been other enlightened lineages arising and passing away. Possibly the amazing profusion of great Zen masters in medieval China would represent such a later resurgence of liberating wisdom. I could only begin to guess at what lineages, if any, are going strong nowadays. Among some of the Tibetans maybe? Perhaps some obscure Theravadin forest tradition?

**5. The Buddha did really say it, and was not mistaken, but meant it only figuratively.** This possibility was brought to my attention by a very intelligent Burmese monk who, although reluctant to disbelieve anything in the Pali texts, nevertheless was quite capable of critical thought, and of wanting things to make good sense. So his explanation was this: When the Buddha said his teachings would survive for a thousand years if bhikkhunis were not ordained, but only five hundred if they were, he simply meant that because of bhikkhuni ordination the teachings of Buddhism would last only half as long, with the actual numbers given being purely arbitrary. This is possible, I suppose, although if that were the case he could have said simply that it would last only half as long; and the fact remains that the actual passage in the Vinaya has him saying very clearly that Buddhism would last only five hundred years as a result of ordaining nuns. So I am skeptical of this explanation, though it at least has the virtue (to devout Buddhists at least) of not considering the Pali texts or the Buddha himself to be wrong, and thus may appeal to dedicated westerners with little use for the medieval commentarial tradition or the new western tradition of rejecting out of hand whatever doesn't appeal to the western ultraliberal Buddhist mind.

~ ~ ~

This issue of the strange prophecy leads to the interesting either/or dichotomy of Eastern and Western Theravada Buddhism: the Eastern Buddhists being psychologically compelled to accept it all as infallible dogma, and the Western Buddhists casually dismissing any parts they don't want to believe. Another rather bizarre example of the former extreme is a case I came upon in Burma. There was a great and brilliant scholar-monk named Mingun Tipiṭakadhara Sayadaw, who I was told was mentioned in the *Guinness Book of World Records* for his prodigious memory: he had memorized by heart the entire 40-volume Sixth Council edition of the Pali Tipiṭaka, plus several other works like commentaries and Pali grammars. He knew the Pali texts inside and out, and had received a long list of ecclesiastical titles for his scholarship. So he well knew that, according to these texts, the Buddha was tall, but not phenomenally so; people would often meet the Buddha and mistake him for an ordinary monk, for example. *But*, the commentarial tradition asserts that Gotama Buddha was 4 1/2 times the height of an ordinary person, i.e. approximately 25 feet (8 meters) tall. Being exceedingly devout, the venerable sayadaw was not able to doubt even the commentarial tradition; consequently, also being brilliant, he came up with the following way of reconciling the data: According to him, people were more honest and virtuous in the Buddha's time than they are nowadays. Because of this, the gods loved humanity more. Thus the gods responsible for influencing the weather caused the rain and sun to occur more seasonably, yielding greater benefit to the crops in farmers' fields. The more greatly benefited crops were more nutritious...the result being that in the Buddha's time *everybody* was much larger than they are today, averaging somewhere around 20 feet in height.

At the other extreme, many Buddhists of the West reject not only talking animal stories, the theory of a flat earth floating on water, eclipses of the sun and moon being caused by a demon named Rahu, etc., but even such fundamental principles of Dhamma as the value of seeking out and examining unpleasantness, No Self, karma conditioning our reality, or even the possibility of realizing Nibbāna Itself. Dhamma can thereby become something completely integrated into worldly, materialistic Western culture. The result can be not only a pale shadow of Dhamma, but a pale shadow of a dismembered fragment of it.

Consequently, some Middle Way between unquestioning dogmatism and casual rejection of the parts we don't like may be in order—the consideration of Dhamma not in terms of acceptance or rejection, belief or disbelief, but in terms of "I don't know. I'll consider it." So long as we adjust the box to fit Buddhism, as Easterners tend to do, or adjust Buddhism to fit the box, as Westerners tend to do, we are still stuck in the box of our own limitations, our own limited beliefs. The point is to get out of the box; and outside of the box is "I don't know." By accepting this universal "I don't know" we attain what ancient Greek philosophers called *ataraxia*, the peace of mind which comes from suspension of judgement. I think in Christianity it's called "the peace that passeth all understanding." But we can still use the box to keep our junk in.

# NOTES ON MYSTICISM (WITH RESPECT TO VEN. ÑĀṆAVĪRA)

*(This is one of the first essays I ever wrote for publication on the Internet. It also marks the beginning of my history of getting into occasional hot water for writing what certain people would rather not see, in this case followers of the philosopher-monk venerable Nyanavira. One of the first people to express real enthusiasm about my first blog was eager, at first, for my writings to be better known, and wanted to publish some of them into a book; although he was a follower of Nyanavira and a major contributor to a website dedicated to his honor. So when, almost right off the bat, I published a post criticizing some of Nyanavira's ideas, it resulted in awkwardness, friction, and the setup for eventual washing of hands in disgust. The thing is, though, that through perverse karmic random chance, this was always one of the first essays I had wanted to write for publication. So it goes.)*

It is just a little ironic that some of the stuff I have written has been published by Path Press on their website pathpress.org, as the original purpose of Path Press, I think, was to promulgate the writings of a Buddhist philosopher named Bhikkhu Ñāṇavīra. Ñāṇavīra was a highly intellectual English monk who practiced in Sri Lanka, and who committed suicide in 1965 due to a distracting chronic health problem. I read his work as a junior monk in Burma, but was not greatly impressed by his interpretation of Buddhism in general, or of Right View in particular. For one, he seemed to insist on an elaborate, rationalistic Right View that he had devised for himself, influenced much by Existentialist philosophy (he especially liked Kierkegaard), asserting, essentially, that anyone who disagreed with his interpretation had wrong view, and thus had little if any hope of becoming enlightened. At the time that I read him he seemed hyper-intellectual, intolerant, and rather arrogant. The last statement of his that I saw was at a used bookstore in Mandalay several years ago; there was a copy of some selected letters of his (an old Buddhist Publication Society booklet) on the shelf, so I picked it up and opened it at random just to see what my gaze would land upon. It was a statement to the effect that Aldous Huxley could never hope to be any better than a second-rate thinker. The statement seemed to imply that the writer, Ñāṇavīra himself, was a first-rate one qualified to pass such a judgement. It struck me as uncomfortably arrogant, partly because I like Huxley, and I put the book back on the shelf.

Although he has quite a few followers to this day, and has much to say that is interesting and thought-provoking, the only noticeable effect he had on my practice was to encourage me to read Gibbon's *The Decline and Fall of the Roman Empire* again. At the time I was scrupulous about reading "worldly" literature, but Ñāṇavīra, an intelligent man and a serious monk besides, considered it to be an excellent reflection on Dhamma, and had read it himself more than once, so that was good enough for me.

We do have certain traits in common, like a failure to have much appreciation for Abhidhamma philosophy or the commentarial tradition, a preference for interpreting Dependent Co-arising as simultaneous and not sequential in time (as he astutely points out, the texts say, "This arising, that arises," not "This *ceasing*, that arises"), a tendency toward rejecting orthodox interpretations of Dhamma in favor of our own systems, and, unfortunately, a tendency toward intellectual arrogance. I did not acquire these traits from him, however.

I do think that he made certain fundamental mistakes, not the least of which being that he considered the so-called "core texts" (first four books of Vinaya, first four Nikāyas, and first several books of the fifth Nikāya) to be absolutely reliable records of the Buddha's teaching. Thus he built up a mind-boggling superexistentialist interpretation of Dhamma on an authority that could easily be called into question. It has always struck me as odd that such a brilliant person (educated at Cambridge, no less) could have accepted texts which include fairy tales, talking animals, fire-breathing dragons, and devotionalistic miracle stories, as well as texts in which the Buddha is essentially boasting about how wonderful he is and encouraging others practically to worship him. It seems to be the same gamble made by Burmese sayadaws and the Abhidhamma scholars that Ñāṇavīra derided; they devote their academic lives, and sometimes their spiritual lives, to building up and mastering a system based upon a foundation of axioms that on close examination prove to be largely a dogmatic wild guess. All their brilliance and logic are in a way debased by expending them on something not necessarily valid. Of course the expounders of religious and philosophical systems other than Buddhism also do the same thing.

But the main issue I would like to discuss here is Ñāṇavīra's open disdain for anything mystical. Sometimes it seems that it was sufficient for him to reject an idea simply by labeling it "mysticism." Ñāṇavīra was a supreme rationalist who believed that any valid system of thought must be "of a piece," and that mysticism violated Aristotle's "Laws of Thought," which may be briefly summarized as:

1. A equals A. (The Law of Identity)
2. A is not equal to not-A. (The Law of Noncontradiction)
3. Anything must be either A or not-A. (The Law of Excluded Middle)

Ñāṇavīra insisted that mysticism necessarily maintains something like, "The world is *and* is not real," which is a logical absurdity and necessarily false. One of his followers, in a book on Buddhist existentialism, even went to the extreme of refusing to translate the name of the highest formless contemplative state, *the sphere of neither perception nor nonperception*, I assume because it sounded too monstrously illogical to admit it publicly as a teaching of Gotama Buddha. Consequently, of course, Ñāṇavīra and his followers have interpreted Dhamma along rationalistic, non-mystical lines.

Several years ago I wrangled with a very hard-headed Englishman who had taken Ñāṇavīra's teachings, at least some of them, to heart and had zero use for my mystical approach to Dhamma because he saw it as self-contradictory. In response I unearthed the following ancient document:

### The Bumpkin: A Pseudoplatonic Dialogue

SOPHIST (pointing to an empty Coca-Cola bottle): What is that—is it glass, or is it a bottle?

BUMPKIN: Well, it's glass *and* it's a bottle.

SOP: Oh I see! So "glass" and "bottle" are synonyms. When I say "glass" I mean "bottle," and when I say "bottle" I mean "glass." Isn't that so?

BUM: Of course not.

SOP: What!? So when I say "glass" I don't really mean "bottle," and when I say "bottle" I don't really mean "glass"?

BUM: Naturally.

SOP: So "glass" means something other than "bottle," and "bottle" means something other than "glass"?

BUM: Quite so.

SOP: And so they are not the same?

BUM: Right.

SOP: Ah, I think I understand now. *Part* of this is glass, and the other part is a bottle. Right?

BUM: No, the whole thing is glass.

SOP: And the whole thing is a bottle too?

BUM: Naturally.

SOP: Wait a minute…let me get this straight—You say that the whole thing is glass, *and* the whole thing is a bottle. But we have already determined that "bottle" means something other than "glass." So if we say that the whole thing is glass and the whole thing is a bottle, it is the same as saying that the whole thing is glass *and* the whole thing is other than glass. Isn't that so?

BUM: Eh…I guess so.

SOP: *Doublethink*! You are saying that it is A *and* not-A, which is logically inconsistent and impossible! You have violated the laws of thought!

BUM: Well...er...huh?

*(The ancient manuscript is fragmentary and breaks off here.)*

Now clearly, glass and bottle are not the same; they do not even imply each other, as one may have a glass ashtray or a plastic bottle. The glass and the bottle are qualitatively different. Yet at the very same time they are the very same object, and are completely mutually inclusive. If one takes away the bottle, the glass also is taken away; and if the glass disappears, so does the bottle. The solution to this mystery is is that glass and bottle are at *two different levels of truth.* The glass is the *substance*, or *essence* of the bottle, and the bottle is the *form*, or *appearance*, of the glass. We have two levels of reality involved here—the level of essence and the level of form. They are the same in a sense and different in a sense, but this is not pernicious doublethink as the sense is not the same; there are two senses which are not mutually exclusive. (Similarly, to say that Agathon is taller than Diocles but shorter than Theophilus, and thus is both tall and short at the same time, is not muddle-headed self-contradiction as his tallness and shortness are in two different relations which are not mutually exclusive.)

The thing is this: If one allows that the above line of reasoning concerning the Coca-Cola bottle is valid, not self-contradictory doublethink, then one has in effect flung the door wide open to nondualistic mysticism, as its fundamental premise can be based upon exactly the same kind of reasoning (assuming that a nondualist bothers to rationalize it; usually they don't). Thus, at the experiential level consciousness is the *essence* of mental states (and experience as a whole), while mental states are the *form* of consciousness (and experience as a whole). Water and waves—the same yet different. Likewise, at the universal level Nibbāna-dhatu, the Dharmakāya, Brahman, Tao, the Spirit of God, or whatever one wishes to call it is the *essence* of the samsaric world, and Saṁsāra is the apparent *form* of Nibbāna. And hence the paradoxical Mahayanist claim that Nirvana and Samsara are obviously in a sense different, yet nevertheless exactly the same and completely mutually inclusive. The difference between the two levels is the difference between the two kinds of truth described in Buddhist philosophy—ultimate truth and conventional truth. They are simultaneous, and superimposed. We do not progress from conventional truth to ultimate truth, from Samsara to Nirvana; ultimate truth and Nirvana are already present at the beginning of the Path, but we just don't notice, somewhat like a fish doesn't notice being wet.

One further consideration is that anything that is infinite and formless transcends the boundaries of "is" and "isn't," of existence and nonexistence. As the philosopher Hegel pointed out in his logical dialectic, absolute, infinite Anything is absolutely indistinguishable from absolute, infinite Nothing, as both are devoid of any determinate content. Only differentiation of some sort can create a duality between these two extremes. Thus consciousness without mental states, or the ultimate essence of the world, cannot be said to exist or not exist, or both, or neither. Yet we have to choose some dualistic terminology in order to speak. So, it's a matter of personal choice: If one prefers "is" one may call it "Brahman," say, and be a Hindu; and if one prefers "isn't" one may call it Nibbāna or Nirvana and be a Buddhist. Whichever works for you. Take your pick.

Venerable Ñāṇavīra was right in insisting that in order for a philosophical system to be logically valid and self-consistent it must be "of a piece." But the "piece" may not be a flat, two-dimensional surface; the "piece" may be a cube instead of a square.

On the other hand, metaphysical speculations such as these are probably unnecessary, and may be a waste of time.

# THE ELEPHANT

In the Pali Udāna, the Book of Inspired Utterances, there is a discourse with the obscure name Paṭhamanānātitthiya Sutta, the First Discourse on Various Sectarians (Udāna 6:4). Although the name of this ancient sutta is relatively unknown even in Buddhist countries, it contains one of the most famous parables of all time, the Simile of the Blind Men and the Elephant.

*Thus have I heard: At one time the Blessed One was residing in Sāvatthī, in the Jeta Grove, at Anāthapiṇḍika's Park. Also at that time many philosophers, priests, and wanderers of various sects were staying in Sāvatthī, favoring various views, entertaining various beliefs, endorsing various opinions, dependent, living in dependence, upon various views.*

*There were some philosophers and priests with a doctrine and a view like this: "The world is eternal. Only this is true; anything otherwise is wrong."*

*And there were some philosophers and priests with a doctrine and a view like this: "The world is* <u>*not*</u> *eternal. Only this is true; anything otherwise is wrong."*

*There were some philosophers and priests with a doctrine and a view like this: "The world is finite. Only this is true; anything otherwise is wrong."*

*And there were some philosophers and priests with a doctrine and a view like this: "The world is infinite. Only this is true; anything otherwise is wrong."*

*There were some philosophers and priests with a doctrine and a view like this: "The vital essence is the same as the body. Only this is true; anything otherwise is wrong."*

*And there were some philosophers and priests with a doctrine and a view like this: "The vital essence is one thing, the body is another. Only this is true; anything else is wrong."*

*There were some philosophers and priests with a doctrine and a view like this: "A fully enlightened being exists after death. Only this is true; anything else is wrong."*

*And there were some philosophers and priests with a doctrine and a view like this: "A fully enlightened being does not exist after death. Only this is true; anything else is wrong."*

*There were some philosophers and priests with a doctrine and a view like this: "A fully enlightened being does and does not exist after death. Only this is true; anything else is wrong."*

*And there were some philosophers and priests with a doctrine and a view like this: "A fully enlightened being neither does nor does not exist after death. Only this is true; anything else is wrong."*

*They, fallen to disputing and quarreling, deeply engaged in argument, kept stabbing each other with verbal daggers—"The Way is like this, the Way is not like that!" "The Way is not like that, the Way is like this!"*

*Then a number of monks, having dressed in the morning time and having taken their alms bowls and outer robes, entered Sāvatthī for alms. Having gone for alms in Sāvatthī, after their meal, returning from almsround they approached the Blessed One. Having approached the Blessed One, and having paid respect, they sat down at one side. Sitting at one side those monks said this to the Blessed One: "At present, venerable sir, many philosophers, priests, and wanderers of various sects are staying in Sāvatthī, favoring various views, entertaining various beliefs, endorsing various opinions, dependent, living in dependence, upon various views.*

*"There are some philosophers and priests with a doctrine and a view like this: 'The world is eternal. Only this is true; anything otherwise is wrong'...*[repeat the entire list of various views]*...They, fallen to disputing and quarreling, deeply engaged in argument, keep stabbing each other with verbal daggers—'The Way is like this, the Way is not like that!' 'The Way is not like that, the Way is like this!'"*

[The Buddha:] *"It once happened, monks, that in this very city of*

*Sāvatthī there was a certain king. Now, monks, that king called a certain manservant—'Come now good fellow manservant, however many there are in Sāvatthī who have been blind from birth, collect them all in one place.' 'As you say, Lord,' replied, monks, that manservant to the king, and however many there were in Sāvatthī who were born blind, he got all of them and then approached the king. Having approached him, he said this to the king: 'Lord, all those in Sāvatthī who were born blind have been collected together.' 'Well then my good man, show to those blind from birth an elephant.' 'As you say, Lord.' replied, monks, that manservant to the king, and he showed to those blind from birth an elephant.*

*"To some blind from birth he showed the elephant's head—'You born blind, an elephant is like this.'*

*"To some blind from birth he showed the elephant's ear—'You born blind, an elephant is like this.'*

*"To some blind from birth he showed the elephant's tusk—'You born blind, an elephant is like this.'*

*"To some blind from birth he showed the elephant's trunk—'You born blind, an elephant is like this.'*

*"To some blind from birth he showed the elephant's body—'You born blind, an elephant is like this.'*

*"To some blind from birth he showed the elephant's foot—'You born blind, an elephant is like this.'*

*"To some blind from birth he showed the elephant's thigh—'You born blind, an elephant is like this.'*

*"To some blind from birth he showed the elephant's tail—'You born blind, an elephant is like this.'*

*"To some blind from birth he showed the brushy tip of the elephant's tail—'You born blind, an elephant is like this.'*

*"Then, monks, the king approached those who had been blind from birth. Having approached them, he said this to those blind from birth: 'You born blind, an elephant has been viewed by you?' 'As you say, Lord. An elephant has been viewed by us.' 'Then tell me, you born blind, what is an elephant like?'*

*"Monks, those blind from birth by whom the elephant's head had been viewed spoke thus: 'An elephant is like this, Lord, just like a water pot.'*

*"Monks, those blind from birth by whom the elephant's ear had been viewed spoke thus: 'An elephant is like this, Lord, just like a winnowing tray.'*

*"Monks, those blind from birth by whom the elephant's tusk had been viewed spoke thus: 'An elephant is like this, Lord, just like a big peg.'*

*"Monks, those blind from birth by whom the elephant's trunk had been viewed spoke thus: 'An elephant is like this, Lord, just like a plowbeam.'*

*"Monks, those blind from birth by whom the elephant's body had been viewed spoke thus: 'An elephant is like this, Lord, just like a large storage bin.'*

*"Monks, those blind from birth by whom the elephant's foot had been viewed spoke thus: 'An elephant is like this, Lord, just like a column.'*

*"Monks, those blind from birth by whom the elephant's thigh had been viewed spoke thus: 'An elephant is like this, Lord, just like a big mortar.'*

*"Monks, those blind from birth by whom the elephant's tail had been viewed spoke thus: 'An elephant is like this, Lord, just like a pestle.'*

*"Monks, those blind from birth by whom the brushy tip of the elephant's tail had been viewed spoke thus: 'An elephant is like this, Lord, just like a broom.'*

*"Saying, 'An elephant is like this, an elephant is not like that!' 'An elephant is not like that, an elephant is like this!' they punched each other with their fists. And with that, monks, the king was made glad.*

*"Even so, monks, these wanderers of other sects are blind, eyeless; they do not know the Goal (attha), and do not know what is not the Goal. They do not know the Way (dhamma), and do not know what is not the Way. They, not knowing the Goal, not knowing what is not the Goal, not knowing the Way, not knowing what is not the Way, are fallen to disputing and quarreling, deeply engaged in argument, and keep stabbing each other with verbal daggers—'The Way is like this, the Way is not like that!' 'The Way is not like that, the Way is like this!'"*

*Then the Blessed One, having comprehended this matter, on that occasion uttered this inspired utterance:*

*It is known some philosophers and priests are attached with regard to these things,*
*Fellows who see just a single side, take up a position, and contend.*

Although this parable is one of the most well known stories in all of Buddhist literature, familiar to both Buddhists and non-Buddhists, the deep moral of the story is almost universally missed, again by both Buddhists and non-Buddhists. The moral of the story, clearly, is that one-sided points of view do not comprehend the whole truth, and thus are not entirely correct and should not be clung to or depended upon. This sort of misguided adherence to a limited point of view is not only the basis of fanaticism but is also the very essence of all error and delusion.

*The trouble is that every point of view is necessarily limited, for the simple reason that it is a point of view.*

So as early schools of Buddhism, including Theravada, developed their own interpretations of Dharma and systematized them, they necessarily developed their own points of view by attempting to walk the razor's edge between the particular extreme views pointed out as invalid by the Buddha, such as eternalism ("we have an eternal soul") and annihilationism ("when you're dead you're dead"). But, as the invalid view about the neither existence nor nonexistence of an enlightened being after death implies, or other ancient texts indicate by declaring even existence and nonexistence, or unity and plurality, to be unacceptable extremes, such attempts still result in limited points of view, and consequently in a blindly, partially groped elephant.

And so it is evident that Theravada became yet another sect pretty quickly in its history, with its own versions of "Only this is true; anything otherwise is wrong." Thus we see in Burma, for example, the followers of the Mahasi system holding the elephant's trunk and declaring that an elephant is like a plowbeam, and the followers of the Pah Auk system holding the elephant's ear and declaring that an elephant is like a winnowing fan (and intelligently explaining why the Mahasi people couldn't possibly understand what an elephant is really like), with some of the Mahayana Buddhists holding the elephant's head and looking down on the Buddhists of the "Lesser Vehicle" for failing to realize that an elephant is just like a water pot. Meanwhile, the Christians are at the other end holding on to the elephant's tail and insisting that the only way to be saved is to believe in the gospel truth that an elephant is like a pestle, or a broom (the Catholics and the Protestants are not in agreement on this issue), with every other philosopher and priest, including the priests of Scientism, holding some part or other of the elephant and making authoritative assertions about it. Those who show some flexibility and are willing to vary with regard to which of the elephant's members to grope are often ostracized for being erratic and unreliable, and soft-headed besides.

Yet examining various systems, each with its own necessarily limited perspective, may lead to valuable insight. For example, if one reads the spiritual literature of the world, one may see that the great saint and sage Ramana Maharshi worshiped a hill; the extremely advanced Indian guru Neem Karoli Baba worshiped a deified monkey; Saint John of the Cross and his mentor Saint Teresa of Avila, both of whom apparently were adept meditation masters who had attained mystical union with "God," worshiped the Virgin Mary and believed that a cracker they ate at certain ceremonies was literally the flesh of a Hebrew carpenter who created the universe; and even the greatest sages of South Asian Theravada Buddhism have accepted the idea of a flat earth floating on water, with a 10,000,000 mile high mountain in the center, with the sun and moon, each only a few hundred miles in diameter, orbiting the central mountain...and so on. It seems that extremely wise people can endorse some very strange points of view.

But endorsing a point of view is not necessarily the same as clinging to it. I love repeating the following words of Arthur Schopenhauer:

> *And what I have described here with feeble tongue, and only in general terms, is not some philosophical fable, invented by myself and only of today. No, it was the enviable life of so many saints and great souls among the Christians, and even more*

> *among the Hindus and Buddhists, and also among the believers of other religions....[I]t has been known directly and expressed in deed by all those saints and ascetics who, in spite of the same inner knowledge, used very different language according to the dogmas which their faculty of reason had accepted, and in consequence of which an Indian, a Christian, or a Lamaist saint must each give a very different account of his own conduct; but this is of no importance at all as regards the fact. A saint may be full of the most absurd superstition, or, on the other hand, may be a philosopher; it is all the same. His conduct alone is evidence that he is a saint; for, in a moral regard, it springs not from abstract knowledge, but from intuitively apprehended, immediate knowledge of the world and of its inner nature, and is expressed by him through some dogma only for the satisfaction of his faculty of reason.**

I used to have great difficulty in accepting the possibility of this; if an enlightened being can still go along with absurd mythologies and narrow-minded dogmas, then what good is enlightenment? Isn't enlightenment the cessation of delusion? I've gradually come to consider that a truly objective, objectively true view of the world is just another absurd myth. Maybe it doesn't exist any more than does the 10,000,000 mile high Mt. Meru.

It seems to me that what the Buddha tried to do was to present a way of being which led to this immediate, comprehensive, intuitive knowledge of reality with an absolute minimum of theoretical points of view which could be clung to and argued over; thereby making Buddhism, to use another elephant simile, like the footprint of the elephant, which can contain all other footprints within its great span. All limited views would thus fit within it. However, for the mind of later Buddhist philosophers this created an unacceptable vacuum, a lack of anything to chew on, creating feelings of disorientation and distress like those of a fish deprived of water. The dogmas the Buddha tried to set aside were reestablished shortly after his disappearance from this world, in a form subtle enough that Buddhist philosophers could declare them to be not limited points of view, but Truth. The ancient admonitions to harbor no view (*diṭṭhi,* literally, "what is seen") came to be interpreted as admonitions to harbor no *wrong* view—thereby leaving the door wide open to the harboring of Right View or orthodox Buddhist View, which were determined to be synonymous. The Buddhist philosopher Nagarjuna tried to rectify this situation by returning to the philosophical Emptiness of the Master, but was rejected by the older schools, and unnecessarily elaborated upon by the newer ones.

Bearing all this in mind, it is presumably a good idea carefully to investigate and consider many points of view, but not to take any of them very seriously. This includes our own religion, Scientism, political correctness, common sense, and everything else.

* From Schopenhauer's *The World as Will and Representation*, translated by E. F. J. Payne (Dover 1969), p. 383.

# BODHISATTAS AND BODHISATTVAS

One of the most common answers to the question "What is the difference between Theravada and Mahayana?" is the answer "The Bodhisattva concept." Mahayana teaches that one should not try to become enlightened as soon as possible, as Theravada advises, but should strive to become a fully enlightened Buddha, or even postpone enlightenment indefinitely until all beings are liberated from the wheel of Samsara. This answer with regard to the difference, however, is not 100% accurate. There are other differences too of course—for example Mahayana metaphysics are rather more sophisticated and, I think, more profound—but Theravada has a Bodhisattva concept also, or rather a Bodhisatta concept.

Before going any further in that regard I'd like to discuss briefly what the term Bodhisatta means. The term *bodhisattva* was translated from *bodhisatta* in Pali, or perhaps more likely a Buddhist Prakrit language very similar to Pali. The term is a combination of two words, *bodhi* and *satta*; the first part is the same in Pali and Sanskrit and means "awakening" or "enlightenment." The second part, *satta*, is not so certain. In Sanskrit the word *sattva* means "creature" or "being"; thus Bodhisattva means "Enlightenment Being." But this is not necessarily what the word originally meant. It does seem a little odd that a being who is not yet enlightened, and in Mahayana Buddhism may not even be trying to become enlightened any time sooner than the end of the Universe, would be called an Enlightenment Being. The word *satta* in Pali has more than one possible meaning, and its rendering into Sanskrit as *sattva* could possibly be a mistranslation.

Mistranslations from an older language like Pali into Buddhist Sanskrit have happened before. For example, in the doctrine of the Two Truths, ultimate and conventional, the very ancient term *sammuti*—"convention, consent, tradition"—somehow got converted into the Sanskrit word *saṁvṛti*, which means "covering" or "concealing." Thus from *sammuti sacca*, conventional truth, arose *saṁvṛti satya*, concealing truth (although the philosophical implications are practically the same).

Getting back to *satta*, however, in Pali it can also mean "seven" (in Sanskrit, *sapta*), but I think we can easily rule out "Enlightenment Seven."

Also, *satta* can be a past participle of the verb *sapati*, "to curse," but "Enlightenment-Cursed" also appears very unlikely.

Yet *satta* in Pali may also be a past participle of the verb *sajjati*, forming an adjectival noun. *Sajjati* means "to be attached to," "to be hung on to." Thus the original meaning of the word *bodhisatta* may have been "One who is committed to enlightenment" or "One who is bound for enlightenment." This would seem to make more sense, and is apparently more in harmony with the older Theravadin conception of the idea.

In orthodox Theravadin tradition a bodhisatta is indeed one bound for enlightenment, or rather bound for full-blown Buddhahood. He is one who is destined to become a fully enlightened Buddha, one who rediscovers Dhamma after it has been lost to the world, and then teaches it, thereby reintroducing Dhamma (and Buddhism) into the world. He reaches this state by bringing various qualities called *pāramī*, including generosity, truthfulness, loving-kindness, and so on, to perfection over a period of incalculable eons, lifetime after lifetime. According to the commentarial literature there are certain other requirements for a true bodhisatta: for example he should already have a mastery of *jhāna*, or deep contemplative states, and he must also make a vow to become a Buddha in the presence of one who already is a Buddha—and receive a prophecy from that Buddha assuring him that he will ultimately succeed. "Our" Buddha Gotama reportedly received his prophesy from a Buddha named Dīpaṅkara more than 2 incalculable eons in the past, on a different world.

Looking at the most ancient texts available, it seems likely that originally there was no difference between Buddhas and ordinarily enlightened Arahants. "Buddha" literally means awakened or enlightened, and Arahants are certainly that, otherwise they wouldn't be Arahants. And the Buddha himself is sometimes called an Arahant, as in the famous formula *namo tassa bhāgavato arahato sammāsambuddhassa*—Reverence to him, the Blessed One, the Worthy One (Arahant), the Truly, Fully Enlightened One. I feel that in all probability the Buddha, like Jesus also, was saying essentially, "Look, I'm a human being like you, and I did it. If I can do it, you can do it too. You can be like me."

However, it is human nature to glorify great leaders, political, military, cultural, or spiritual. So as Buddhism developed into a popular religion followed largely by simple and not very spiritually talented folks, the Buddha became more and more glorified, and eventually even worshipped. For many this worship replaced the way of life taught by the master, as also happened with Christianity. Jesus became the Son of God, and Buddha became higher than any god, including the Mahā-Brahmā, who allegedly descended to earth to worship Buddha. Sakka the King of Gods reportedly became one of the Buddha's chief followers.

The Buddha's glorification involved an ancient genre of literature called Jātaka, which described the Buddha's former lives as a Bodhisatta, often in moral tales portraying talking animals, similar to the fables of Aesop. Many of these stories were common Indian legends which were appropriated and modified by the Buddhists. Anyhow, the idea developed that the Buddha heroically strived for many eons to perfect himself to the point of Buddhahood, sometimes as an animal, sometimes even in hell... which implied that he was somehow more noble, more wise, and more enlightened than even his most successful disciples. Thus the discrepancy between an "ordinary" enlightened being and the extraordinary Buddha; and thus also the genesis of the Bodhisatta/Bodhisattva concept.

I am no expert on Mahayana Buddhism, but I have been led to understand that Mahayana Buddhists are supposed to shun ordinary enlightenment as something selfish and perhaps even cowardly (running away from Samsara), and to strive to become fully enlightened Buddhas—or even to forgo enlightenment altogether until all other beings in the Universe have also been liberated. One of the four main vows made by Mahayanist Bodhisattvas is, "Beings are numberless: I vow to save them."

It seems to me, though, that this idea involves some faulty logic. According to Buddhist philosophy, this Universe (or, if you prefer, this endless series of Universes) has no creator and no beginning; so it has existed already for an infinite length of time, and there are *still* an infinite number of suffering, unenlightened beings. This would seem to suggest that there will *always* be an infinite number of suffering, unenlightened beings. If an infinite length of time has already passed and the number of suffering beings is still numberless...

It may be that the vow mentioned above is a noble gesture of rejecting enlightenment since everyone can't have it. It would, however, seem to be practically the exact opposite of what Gotama Buddha reportedly taught, as indicated by the oldest Buddhist texts we have. The time for enlightenment is Now.

There is another approach to the apparent dilemma which I came across in a profound Chinese Zen text called the Sutra of Hui Neng, also called the Platform Sutra.* It has been a long time since I read it, but if I remember correctly Hui Neng, the Sixth Chinese Patriarch of Zen, says essentially that once you become enlightened you look around and see that everyone else is enlightened too. In other words, when you see with perfect eyes all that you see is perfect. "To the pure man all things are pure." As Benedict Spinoza said in his *Ethics*, "By reality and perfection I mean the same thing." This world of suffering is a creation of our own delusion. Consequently, the only way to liberate all beings would be to liberate ourselves; then we see that, ultimately, there are no beings to liberate.

There is another way of looking at the issue: I have found that the directions for Bodhisattvas in Mahayana texts like the Diamond Cutter Sutra are very similar in details to descriptions of the psychology of a sage in ancient Theravada texts like the Sutta Nipāta. It could be that once one realizes a certain stage of wisdom, labels such as "Arahant" and "Bodhisattva" no longer stick. One has gone off the scale, and quibbles about what label to apply become irrelevant.

* I used to think that the Sutra of Hui Neng was, finally, a Buddhist text whose authenticity was relatively certain, as it is reportedly a verbatim transcript of a Dharma talk given by the Patriarch, recorded by a professional scribe who attended the talk. I figured one couldn't be more trustworthy than that, and I trusted this for years. Then I came across a different translation at a library in Rangoon, written by a fellow named Yampolsky, of Columbia University. In his introduction he made a number of very interesting and disillusioning statements. First he declared that his translation was based on a recently discovered manuscript of the Sutra which is older than the traditionally accepted version and differs from it in many respects. Then he went on to deduce that the Sutra doesn't really represent a discourse of Hui Neng, but is a forgery written by one of the Patriarch's disciples, which then underwent extensive modification over many years...although it was in all likelihood originally based on the teachings of the master. Not only that, but he further wrecked the illusion by hypothesizing that Hui Neng probably wasn't really the Sixth Patriarch at all, and that the story of his receiving the emblems of the Patriarchate secretly from the Fifth Patriarch, and so on, are apocryphal. The real Sixth Patriarch was presumably the timid senior monk belittled in the story, who wrote inferior poetry on the monastery wall; but his school, "the gradual school" of the north, died out, so no one could contest the claims of the forged Sutra declaring that Hui Neng was secretly the Sixth Patriarch. This would explain, among other things, why the lineage ended with the Sixth, with no Seventh. It all goes to show the hopeless unreliability of

"authentic" sacred scriptures, and the unscrupulousness even of dedicated spiritual practitioners when it comes to recording them. The moral of the story is that the *effect* of a text—its *usefulness* in expanding consciousness, or at least in knocking us out of ruts—is of real importance, not its supposed authenticity or even its factuality.

# TECHNICAL MATTERS: THE ANCIENT BUDDHIST STAR CALENDAR

*(This is possibly the most technical essay that I have written, full as it is with Pali and Sanskrit names, Greek letters, and astronomy jargon. It is, though, an interesting look at how ancient Indians looked at the night sky and used what they saw to measure the passage of time. It may be of interest mainly to forest monks and people who wish to understand ancient Indian culture in general, but those of you who simply find weird information interesting may forgive the Greek letters and consider much, or at least some, of this to be interesting.)*

There is an obscure rule of monastic discipline which states that any monk who lives in a forest must know how to use the night sky as a calendar. So, wanting to follow the rules correctly and also wanting to live in a forest, I tried to learn this ancient art. One of the first things I learned is that almost nobody knows it any more, and that information on the subject is hard to come by. I eventually found an old Burmese Sayadaw who specialized in Indian astronomy and had written at least one book on the subject, but it turned out that the Indian astronomy studied by Burmese monks is medieval, not ancient, and thus not the form of it that was mentioned in the ancient Buddhist texts. So, being stubborn and fussy, I kept searching.

Finally I came across an old book at a bookstall on a sidewalk in Rangoon—it was a medieval Indian astronomy text called the *Surya Siddhanta*, translated in the 1800's by a Christian missionary named Ebenezer Burgess. The text itself was practically unreadable: an English translation of Sanskrit poetry teaching Ptolemaic astronomy with the sun, planets, and stars going around the earth, circular orbits adjusted by epicycles, etc. Who wants to take the trouble of grinding through poetically complicated trigonometry calculations based on an astronomical system that has been obsolete for centuries? Certainly not me. BUT, some of the editorial notes to this edition discussed the Indian astronomical calendar as it existed in very early times, which was exactly what I was looking for. The information in this article is based mainly on those editorial notes, plus information in the Pali texts themselves and my own attempts to make good sense out of all of it.

The ancient Indian calendar, accepted and used by ancient Indian Buddhists, may be interesting to some people, especially to Buddhists with a desire to understand such things (like strict Theravāda monks living in forests), so I am happy to share my knowledge on the subject, incomplete as it is. Anyone able to fill in blanks or to correct mistakes in my interpretation is welcome to contact me, so that any future version of this article may be more informative and useful.

* * *

The Indian calendar, and consequently the calendars of other cultures based on classical India, appears to be prehistoric in origin, possibly going back to the pre-Vedic culture of the Indus Valley civilization, one of the earliest advanced urban civilizations known to archeologists. The ancient Chinese and ancient Arabic systems bear remarkable similarities with the Indian, and they are all probably related.

This calendar is *lunisolar* in that it is based upon the position of the full moon among the stars. A month is a lunar month, lasting 29 or 30 days; and although in later centuries the system was adjusted so that the months followed a standardized system of alternation between 29 and 30, with the full moon day always on the 15th waxing and the new moon day alternating between 14th and 15th waning, in the Buddha's time the full moon day was determined primarily by just looking: if it looked full, it was full. Likewise for the new moon. As a result of this, different communities might have a day or two of difference between their observance of the full moon and new moon days; and the Pali rules of discipline give guidelines with regard to proper protocol when monks disagree on which days to observe them. (Nowadays, because of the later standardized system accepted by the Pali commentaries, sometimes the phases of the moon as officially determined in Theravāda Buddhist countries like Burma are obviously off by a day or two.) On the other hand, even as far back as the 5th century BCE the designated half moon days were already standardized to be always on the 8th day of the waxing and waning moons, regardless of how the moon actually looked.

Because a year of 12 lunar months is only 354 days long, in order to keep the year in sync with the sun and stars an extra "intercalary" month is added every two or three years. In the Buddha's time it apparently could happen at any time of year when the full moon appeared in the same group of stars twice in a row, but in the texts there is a case of a king declaring an intercalary month in Āsāḷha (around July, at the beginning of the monsoon season at the time), and it may be because of this that in Burma, at least, the extra month is always added at this time.

As the month depends upon the full moon's position among the *nakkhatta* or asterisms (sometimes called "lunar mansions"), the 27 asterisms recognized in the Buddha's time will be described here. (In later times a 28th one was added to fill a perceived gap, plus maybe to make certain calculations easier, but it is unrecognized in the Pali; its Sanskrit name is *Abhijit.*) I am very rusty on my astronomy jargon, and forget the proper words for explaining the positions of stars in the sky, so the positions of the stars will be described as though one is looking up at them with one's back to the North Star, so the series of asterisms progresses from right to left. A star map would be helpful to anyone wishing to learn these asterisms, plus of course plenty of real-life gazing at the night sky.

1. **Assayuja** (in Sanskrit, *Aṣvinī*, "The Horsemen")—β and γ Arietis (The second- and third-brightest stars in Aries, forming a close, diagonally-slanting couple. Some later systems include the brighter α Arietis also, but the original version of the asterism was almost certainly a pair, as the Aṣvins were twins in Indian mythology much like Castor and Pollux in the Greek myths, plus often the Sanskrit name has the dual suffix, representing "twoness." Why the asterism did not originally include the more obvious pair α and β Arietis is somewhat of a mystery.)

2. **Bharaṇī** (*Bharaṇī*, "The Bearer")—35, 39, and 41 Arietis (A small triangle of dim stars over the back of the Ram, supposedly representing the female pudendum. In the West it is also called Musca Borealis, or "The Northern Fly.")

3. **Kattikā** (*Kṛttikā,* "The Cutter")—η Tauri plus 5 others, a.k.a. the Pleiades (A well-defined group in Taurus, supposed to look like a straight razor by the ancient Indians; it looks somewhat like a tiny version of the Big Dipper. Originally, in very ancient times, this was the first asterism in the series.)

4. **Rohiṇī** (*Rohiṇī,* "The Red One")—α (Aldebaran), θ, γ, δ, and ε Tauri, a.k.a. the Hyades (The head of the Bull, another well-defined group in Taurus resembling a sideways V; it includes the reddish Aldebaran, the brightest star in Taurus, after which the asterism derives its name.)

5. **Magasiraṁ** (*Mṛgaśīras* or *Mṛgaśīrṣa,* "The Head of the Stag")—λ, $\phi^1$, and $\phi^2$ Orionis (A small triangle of faint stars serving as the head of Orion in the Western system.)

6. **Addā** (*Ārdrā,* "The Moist One")—α Orionis, a.k.a. Betelgeuse (The upper shoulder and brightest star in Orion. It may be called The Moist One because it rose in the sky at the beginning of rainy weather.)

7. **Punabbasu** (*Punarvasu*, "The Twice-Resplendent")—β and α Geminorum, a.k.a. Castor and Pollux (The two brightest

stars in Gemini.)

**8. Phussa** or **Tissa** (*Puṣya,* "The Nourisher")—The nebular cluster Praesepe plus δ and γ Cancri (A triangular configuration in Cancer supposed to resemble a cow's udder, a woman's breast, or (by some authorities) a bow and arrow, with the whitish blob of Praesepe in the middle pointing to the right, serving as the milky teat or the arrow, respectively.)

**9. Asilesā** (*Āśḷeṣā,* "The Entwining One")—ε, δ, σ, η, and ρ Hydrae (A somewhat flattened ring-like asterism serving as the head of Hydra in the Western system, almost at the same meridian as, but lower than, Phussa.)

**10. Maghā** (*Maghā,* "The Bountiful")—α (Regulus), η, γ, ζ, μ, and ε Leonis (The head and elbow of the Lion; forming a well-defined group of stars resembling a hook, sickle, or backwards question mark, with Regulus, the brightest star in Leo, at the bottom or south end.)

**11. Pubba-Phaggunī** (*Pūrva-Phalgunī,* "The Fore Ruddy One")—δ and θ Leonis (The front, or right end of an almost perfect rectangle of stars forming the haunches of the Lion, and in the Indian system supposed to resemble the head end of a bed.)

**12. Uttara-Phaggunī** (*Uttara-Phalgunī,* "The Hind Ruddy One")—β (Denebola) and 93 Leonis (The back, or left end of the same rectangle in Leo, forming the foot end of the bed.)

**13. Hattha** (*Hasta,* "The Hand")—δ, γ, ε, α, and β Corvi (Essentially the constellation Corvus, a conspicuous group of stars shaped somewhat like a hand with the fingers together.)

**14. Cittā** (*Citrā,* "The Bright One")—α Virginis, a.k.a. Spica (A beautiful white star, the only bright star in Virgo; so probably its beauty and solitariness are what gave the Virgin its name.)

**15. Sāti** (*Svātī,* "The Lovely One")—α Boötis, a.k.a. Arcturus (A bright star in Boötes, rather far north of the ecliptic and

Western zodiac.)

**16. Visākhā** (*Viśākhā,* "The Out-Branching")—α and β Librae (The two brightest stars in Libra, "branching out" from the Scorpion with one branch leading up to Sāti and the other leading over to Cittā.)

**17. Anurādhā** (*Anurādhā,* "Success")—δ, β, and π Scorpionis (A north-south row of brightish stars at the head of the Scorpion.)

**18. Jeṭṭhā** (*Jyeṣṭhā,* "The Eldest")—α (Antares), σ, and τ Scorpionis (A row of three stars in the body of the Scorpion, with the bright, reddish Antares in the center.)

**19. Mūlaṁ** (*Mūla,* "The Root")—λ and υ Scorpionis *or* λ, υ, χ, ι, θ, ε, ξ, μ, and ε Scorpionis (The sting *or* the entire tail of the Scorpion; possibly called The Root because it is the beginning of the series giving birth first to The Eldest and eventually leading to the branches ending in The Lovely One and The Bright One.)

**20. Pubbāsāḷha** (*Pūrva-Aṣāḍhā,* "The Fore Invincible One")—δ and ε Sagittarii (The front or right half of a regular parallelogram of stars in the body of the Archer, supposed to resemble, as in the case of Pubba-Phaggunī, the front end of a bed or couch.)

**21. Uttarāsāḷha** (*Uttara-Aṣāḍhā,* "The Hind Invincible One") —σ and ζ Sagittarii (The back or left half of the same parallelogram in Sagittarius, not very easy to make out because so cluttered with similar-looking stars; the easiest way to see the Asāḷha asterisms is to locate Sagittarius and then seek out the parallelogram of brightish stars in the group.)

**22. Savaṇa** (*Śravaṇa,* "The Listening")—α (Altair), β, and γ Aquilae (A row of the three brightest stars in Aquila, at the head end of the Eagle; imagined as looking like an ear to the ancient Indians, relatively far north of the ecliptic; relatively easy to find if one seeks the very bright Altair.)

**23. Dhaniṭṭhā** (*Śraviṣṭhā* or *Dhaniṣṭhā,* "The Wealthiest")—β, α, γ, and δ Delphini (Essentially the constellation Delphinus, looking much like a little Dolphin near Savaṇa, and supposed to look like an ear ornament adorning the aforementioned ear in the Indian reckoning.)

**24. Satabhisaja** (*Śatabhisaj*, "Having One Hundred Doctors") —Described as λ Aquarii plus approximately 100 faint stars in the knee and water stream of Aquarius (The constellation Aquarius looks rather like a crude stick figure of a man lying on his side with his head to the left, and with a cloud of very faint stars below it; presumably these are the doctors attending the sick man, although the sick man seems the more reasonable figure for the asterism; either way, the position in the sky is the same.)

**25. Pubba-Bhaddapadā** (*Pūrva-Bhādrapadā* or -*Proṣṭhapadā*, "The Forefeet of the Ox")—α and β Pegasi (The two bright stars on the right side of a large, conspicuous rectangle called the Square of Pegasus, just to the right of Pisces.)

**26. Uttara-Bhaddapadā** (*Uttara-Bhādrapadā* or -*Proṣṭhapadā*, "The Hind Feet of the Ox")—γ Pegasi and α Andromedae (The two bright stars on the left side of the Square of Pegasus.)

**27. Revatī** (*Revatī*, "The Prosperous One")—ζ Piscium and 31 other stars in Pisces (A roughly circular asterism composed of more or less dim stars in the area between the two fishes, with ζ, zeta, being the southernmost of the group. In medieval times an Indian astronomer calculated that very, very long ago there was a conjunction of the sun, moon, and all the planets at the meridian containing ζ Piscium, and it was assumed that our universe must have begun with such a conjunction, so the conclusion since then has been that our world cycle or eon began with the sun in this asterism; and so in Theravada Buddhist countries like Thailand and Burma the new year officially begins when the sun passes through the meridian of this star in Pisces. Indian astronomy in the Buddha's time was not nearly so sophisticated that it could back up such an extrapolation, however.)

The first star named after each asterism above is called the junction star: After the Buddha's time, when Indian astronomy became advanced enough to predict conjunctions (of the moon, planets, etc.) with a fair degree of accuracy, it became necessary to narrow down an asterism to a single point in the sky so that the exact time and place of the conjunction could be determined. Eventually, at least in some systems, the asterisms themselves were reduced to a single star each. But in the Buddha's time astronomy was used mainly just for determining the time of year, and proper times for conducting certain ceremonial rituals. Junction stars seem to have been a much later innovation.

As there are 27 asterisms and only 12 months, the asterisms are combined into 12 groups, the month being determined by the group in which the full moon appears. There is some disagreement in the ancient Vedic literature over how the asterisms are grouped together, however. The Pali months are listed below, with the corresponding asterisms listed by their corresponding numbers in the preceding list:

1. **Citta** *or* **Citra** (Apr-May) 14, 15
2. **Vesākha** (May-Jun) 16, 17
3. **Jeṭṭha** (Jun-Jul) 18, 19
4. **Āsaḷha** (Jul-Aug) 20, 21
5. **Sāvaṇa** (Aug-Sep) 22, 23 *or* 22, 23, 24
6. **Bhaddapada** *or* **Poṭṭhapada** (Sep-Oct) 24, 25, 26 *or* 25, 26, 27
7. **Assayuja** *or* **Paṭhama-Kattika** (Oct-Nov) 27, 1, 2 *or* 1, 2
8. **Kattika** (Nov-Dec) 3, 4
9. **Māgasira** (Dec-Jan) 5, 6
10. **Phussa** (Jan-Feb) 7, 8
11. **Māgha** (Feb-Mar) 9, 10
12. **Phagguna** (Mar-Apr) 11, 12, 13

One detail I was never able to determine was exactly *when* the transition occurs between one month and the next---does the moon actually have to reach the next group of asterisms? Is there an imaginary line equidistant between them that divides them? Later refinements of the system resulted in the sky being divided into 12 equal portions, which, however, causes some of the asterisms to be in the wrong month. The distance between Dhaniṭṭhā (23) and Satabhisaja (24), for example, is very great, so that the month Sāvaṇa could involve much more than 1/12 of the sky.

At the time that the canonical Rules of Discipline were composed the full moon day was the first day of the month; however, by the time of the commentator Buddhaghosa the full moon day was the last day of the month, and in the modern Burmese calendar the full moon day is the middle of the month. These alterations are largely due to a troublesome phenomenon called *precession of the equinoxes*. The Indian calendar, being based upon the observed movement of celestial bodies through the night sky, is based upon the sidereal year, the time it takes the earth to pass all the way round the ecliptic. On the other hand, the Gregorian calendar used in the West is based upon the seasonal year, the time it takes the earth to pass from, say, one winter solstice to the next. As it turns out, there is a discrepancy between these two ways of measuring the year, amounting to about one day every 70 years. Consequently, over the past 2500 years the Buddhist calendar has gotten about five weeks out of sync with the seasons. For example, the monsoon season officially begins in Āsaḷha, around the middle of July, but nowadays it actually begins around the start of June; and the coldest time of year by the traditional Buddhist reckoning is approximately the middle of February, but in modern South Asia it is more like the first half of January. The commentarial method of counting the full moon day as the last day of the month largely corrects the difference—except for the full moon day itself, which, unfortunately, is by far the most likely day on the Buddhist calendar for important events to occur, for example the beginning and end of the Rains Retreat.

Precession of the equinoxes is caused by a wobble in the earth's axis of rotation, rather like the wobble of a spinning top that is starting to slow down. One effect of this wobble is that the ecliptic now is tilted slightly differently than it was in ancient times. This may be why there is so little space between the meridians of the asterisms Phussa (8) and Asilesā (9); nowanights they are practically stacked one on top of the other. Another peculiarity of the precessional wobble is that the North Star in the Buddha's time, in Pali *Dhuvaṁ*, "The Everlasting One," was not the same North Star that we have today. 2500 years ago the North Star was β Ursae Minoris, or Kochab, at the opposite end of the Little Dipper from Polaris, "our" North Star. Which just goes to show that nothing really lasts forever.

# THE NEW BHIKKHUNIS

*(This is, I think, my first attempt at addressing what is probably the most contentious social/political issue in Theravada Buddhism over the past few decades, the attempted revival of the fully ordained Order of nuns. Actually it is more or less of a feminist issue. This is what happens when modern feminism meets ancient religious patriarchies.)*

When I was a junior monk studying the rules of monastic discipline the rules concerning bhikkhunis, or fully ordained Theravada Buddhist nuns, were attended to but not studied much, as it was common knowledge among my Asian teachers that the Bhikkhuni Order had become extinct hundreds of years ago, so the rules concerning them were purely academic. At the uposatha ceremony conducted on every full moon day and new moon day it is ancient tradition for the Sangha to acknowledge a designated monk's "exhortation" (Dhamma talk) to the bhikkhunis; and it is a common practice at monasteries throughout Burma simply to announce as part of the preliminaries to the ceremony, "There are no more bhikkhunis." In fact, I've been told more than once by Burmese monks that the only way the Bhikkhuni Order could possibly be revived would be for at least five fully ordained monks to spontaneously, instantaneously be transformed into women, as they would then be fully ordained nuns; if the transformation were gradual, like by surgery, it would be invalid, as a eunuch (castrated man) cannot be a monk, much less a nun, so any interval of time between complete man and complete woman would break the validity of the status of ordination. And five would be needed because any new nuns must be ordained by a Sangha of at least five fully ordained bhikkhunis—if the necessary five do not exist, the lineage is broken. This is what I was told, matter-of-factly, for years.

So it was a bit of a surprise last year, just a few months before I returned to America, when an Australian fellow told me about how the famous Ajahn Brahmavamso in Australia had become infamous by unilaterally taking upon himself the authority of Gotama Buddha and ordaining some new bhikkhunis. He had been censured by the Thai ecclesiastical council and by the abbots of other monasteries in the Ajahn Chah tradition, but he had refused to back down and had been essentially ostracized for what was considered to be an ecclesiastically illegal act. Monks who lived at his monastery were banned from staying at any other monastery in the same tradition, so most of the Sangha there bailed out to avoid the stigma. Or at least this is what I was told by that Australian fellow.

Then a few months ago, during a return visit to Burma, I heard a little more about the issue, and looked into a book of articles written on the subject of reviving the Bhikkhuni Sangha, the title of which I no longer remember. It seems that Ajahn Brahm wasn't the first, but that some monks in Sri Lanka started participating in bhikkhuni ordinations quite a few years ago. The book had a few articles attempting to explain the standard objections to modern bhikkhuni ordination, but it was in order to refute these objections, as the book was decidedly in favor of the idea, mainly, it seems, because of the politically correct issue of Gender Equality.

Before going any further I would like to assure one and all that I have no objection to the idea of gender equality. I consider women to be different from men but equal to them, especially in the realm of spirituality. It may even be that spiritually women have a slight advantage over men in general. I can't really say for sure, but I wouldn't be surprised. But this whole issue and controversy concerning bhikkhuni ordination strikes me as a case of Western Enlightened Political Correctness losing touch with practicality.

First of all, for the sake of gender equality efforts are being made to revive an Order which according to the Pali texts is necessarily to be discriminated against, and thus would *not* have gender equality. For example, according to the rules of monastic discipline *any* nun, regardless of her seniority, is required to pay respect to *any* monk, even though he may have been ordained that very same day. Thus any nun is automatically lower in precedence than any monk. Also, the rules in general are stricter for nuns than for monks (for example, there are four *pārājika* rules for monks, the breaking of any one of which entails immediate excommunication from the Sangha, while there are eight of them for nuns); and even the ordination ceremony for bhikkhunis, if done according to the book, requires them to answer several rather embarrassing questions concerning their private parts that bhikkhus are not required to answer. Consequently, the only way bhikkhunis will have equality with bhikkhus is by changing the ancient rules, which nobody really has the authority to do, or by breaking the rules, which is a strange way of reviving a tradition—not exactly starting the tradition "purely," on the right foot, it seems to me. Changing the rules is precisely what was suggested by that book I was looking at, but I'm sure that would go over in the Sanghas of Theravada Buddhist countries like a lead balloon.

Which brings up another difficulty: In order for there to be a major change in the ecclesiastical status quo there must be unanimous consent of the Sangha, or at least the agreement of a representative sample of the Sangha—and the overwhelming majority of the Sangha consists of conservative Asian types who no doubt would be very reluctant to make such a change. According to the Pali text, the Buddha himself considered bhikkhuni ordination to be a bad idea; and although Western scholars may doubt the authenticity of the passage (found in the Chapter on Bhikkhunis in the Vinaya Cūḷavagga), traditional Asian Buddhists tend to be psychologically incapable of doubting the legitimacy of their sacred scriptures, and will likely see the aforementioned Westerners as arrogant troublemakers flouting the teachings of Buddha. In fact I was told recently that it is more difficult for Western men to be ordained as monks in Thailand nowadays as a result of the Thai monks' reaction to "illegal" ordination of women in the West.

Of course one reason why the Order of Bhikkhunis became extinct in the first place is because the rules were so off-puttingly strict and discriminatory; although there were some practical reasons for this. In addition to the standard explanation that desire between monks and nuns within a community leads to problems, there is also the fact that Indian women often are obligated to marry men that they do not love, and in some cases have never even met. This resulted in many unhappy marriages in ancient India, and many women fled into a convent to escape an unhappy home situation. One reason why the rules of discipline are so hard on nuns is to weed out those women who did not have a true spiritual calling and were merely using the nun's life as an easy way of escaping an obnoxious husband. (There is also a rule stating that any married woman must be married for at least 12 years before she may be ordained, which I suppose gives her time to perform her "wifely duties" and possibly reconcile herself to married life before bailing out.) Things are very different for modern Western women, but changing ancient rules in the most orthodox, unchanging school of Buddhism is bound to lead to problems, possibly even to schism.

As I see it, there is *absolutely nothing* preventing any group of women from designing any set of rules they please, dressing however they please, calling themselves whatever they please, and seeking enlightenment however they think is best. They could design a system specifically for the modern West, which no doubt would work better than more or less illegally modifying an ancient Indian version which never was well suited to women anyway. It seems that the only thing that prevents this is a desire for the security of *Official Status*. That really seems to be the crux of it. And Official Status is essentially a worldly phenomenon which has no bearing on Enlightenment.

Women could design from scratch a system as strict and austere as they saw fit, and although they would not be technically ordained bhikkhunis, it would have almost no practical effect on their life of renunciation as far as the Sangha is concerned, as ordained women and unordained ones do not get treated very differently by monks—in fact unordained ones would seem to be treated a little more respectfully.

I have to admit that my Official Status as an ordained bhikkhu certainly has its advantages in Asia; in Burma I'm a Mahathera ("Great Elder") and the abbot of a forest monastery there. But here in America it doesn't seem to count for much. People don't care much if I'm a Mahathera, or if I was ordained this way or that way. So long as a group of nuns agrees to a code of mutual respect for, say, seniority within the system, possibly with a non-canonical, unofficial recognition from the Asian Sangha, then it would seem to be the obvious solution—so long as there is no need for worldly Official Status as fully ordained bhikkhunis.

I have considered that something similar could be done for men also, here in the West—establishing a kind of unofficial quasi-monkhood more adapted to Western society, as rules based on the ancient Ganges Valley do not seem to fit the culture very well. It could be a new subsystem endorsed by the Bhikkhu Sangha, or not. It wouldn't be exactly Theravada though, more like *Navakavada*; not the Doctrine of the Elders, but the Doctrine of the Juniors, the Newcomers. It would not be schismatic however, as the new Sanghas would not technically be ordained at all.

On the other hand, if modern women really insist on being officially, fully ordained bhikkhunis, then it seems that one prerequisite for this goal to be fully realized would be a Western-style Political Correctness propaganda media blitz throughout the Theravada Buddhist countries in Asia, for the purpose of changing the traditional way of thinking over there. It is feasible I suppose, if enough rich sponsors feel strongly enough about enlightening the Buddhist countries to get behind it. There does seem to be a certain audacity, even arrogance, to the idea of us worldly Westerners trying to enlighten the monks of a much more spiritually-oriented cultural system though. Oh well! We are what we are. Sometimes wisdom comes from the mouth of babes, or in this case, newcomers.

I've met maybe one or two modern bhikkhunis over the past several years, and so I have almost no direct experience with them, but from what I have heard they are very sincere, and are conscientiously striving on the Path to Enlightenment. The courage to go against the grain as they have helps to ensure this. I have no desire to discourage them or anyone else from striving for Enlightenment, or from renunciation. This sort of thing is what will save the world. However, I would point out that Waking Up is not a matter of what in Theravada is called *sīlabbata-parāmāsa,* adherence to rules and observances; and insisting upon the Official Status of ordination in a system which would have to be overhauled to be acceptable anyhow seems to be a pretty clear case of this kind of adherence. It really is not necessary. Or anyway, that is my opinion.

May nuns, monks, laypeople, and all beings be well in body, peaceful in mind, and Free.

***A "theela shin," or traditional Burmese Buddhist nun, in meditation***

# WHEN GODHIKA TOOK THE KNIFE

*(Seriously, this may be one of the weirdest discourses in the Pali Canon, for a number of reasons, not the least of which being that it is an account of a person becoming enlightened while killing himself. What follows is the discourse in full, translated by Yours Truly, with some commentary by same. It really is a strange one, and one of my favorites.)*

Well, let's face it: Pali Buddhist texts tend to be pretty dry. For one thing, they are so repetitive that even the official editions of the Tipitaka, in the original Pali language, contain plenty of abbreviations (called peyyāla) to shorten the redundant parts. The Pali texts were composed with ease of memorization in mind, and I can speak from experience when I say that when one is memorizing a text, repetitions are welcome, as they make the job easier. This however doesn't fully account for why Dhamma is told in such a repetitive way. If I see three cows in a field, a red one, a black one, and a spotted one, does it make sense for me to say, "Today I saw three cows in a field. What were these three cows like in that field? Listen, and I will tell you. Today I saw a red cow in that field; that was what the first cow was like. And today I also saw a black cow in that field; that was what the second cow was like. And today I also saw a spotted cow in that field; that was what the third cow was like. That was what the three cows were like that I saw today in the field." I think not. It doesn't work for me. Some discourses are unnecessarily expanded out to many times the length necessary to say what needs to be said. Sometimes it is rather tedious to read. I suppose this is one reason why Burmese laypeople usually prefer to read books written by modern Burmese monks, and why American laypeople usually prefer to read books written by modern Western lay teachers. Less tedious, even though the Dhamma therein may be secondhand at best.

Even so, the Pali texts are the closest documents we have to the Buddhism taught by Gotama Buddha himself, and the Tipitaka contains some real treasures—inspiring profundity as well as fascinating stories. Also if one looks one may find some refreshingly mind-bending strangeness. One may have to do some patient searching, however.

Some of you may have noticed that I like looking at Dhamma from unusual points of view. It helps to keep the Doctrine fresh and interesting, and also helps one to stay out of some of the deeper dogmatic ruts. So my favorite Pali Suttas tend to be unusual in some way or other. Some, like the Suttas of the Aṭṭhakavagga, or the Dīghanakha Sutta of the Majjhima Nikāya, are fascinating because they teach a profound and radically different sort of Buddhism than do most Pali texts. Others, like the Bāhiya Sutta of the Udāna, contain an extraordinary story of ancient India in addition to some deep philosophy. I like the following discourse because of its strange story (with an unexpected view of suicide) and also because it seems to endorse an interpretation of enlightenment which has become unorthodox and unacceptable to developed Theravadin tradition. It is from the Saṁyutta Nikāya (S.1.4.23).

### Godhika Sutta: *The Discourse on Godhika*

*Thus have I heard: At one time the Blessed One was living at Rājagaha, in the Bamboo Grove, at the squirrels' feeding place. And at that time the venerable Godhika was living at the Black Rock on the hillside of Isigili.*

*Then, venerable Godhika, living with unclouded mind, ardent, applying himself, attained to temporary liberation of mind. But then venerable Godhika fell away from that temporary liberation of mind. A second time, venerable Godhika, living with unclouded mind, ardent, applying himself, attained to temporary liberation of mind. But a second time venerable Godhika fell away from that temporary liberation of mind. A third time, venerable Godhika, living with unclouded mind, ardent, applying himself, attained to temporary liberation of mind. And still a third time venerable Godhika fell away from that temporary liberation of mind. A fourth time venerable Godhika... attained to temporary liberation of mind...and fell away from that temporary liberation of mind. A fifth time venerable Godhika...attained to temporary liberation of mind...and fell away from that temporary liberation of mind. A sixth time venerable Godhika...attained to temporary liberation of mind...and fell away from that temporary liberation of mind. A seventh time, venerable Godhika, living with unclouded mind, ardent, applying himself, attained to temporary liberation of mind.*

*Then this occurred to the venerable Godhika: "For the sixth time I have fallen away from temporary liberation of mind. Why don't I just take the knife to myself* [that is, why doesn't he just cut his own throat before losing it a seventh time]."

*Then Māra the Evil One, having known by his own mind the thought in the mind of venerable Godhika, approached the Blessed One. Having approached the Blessed One he addressed him in verses:*

*"Great hero, great in understanding,*
*Blazing with power and glory,*
*Gone beyond all enmity and fear,*
*Endowed with vision, I worship at your feet.*

*Your disciple, great hero,*
*O overcomer of death, is planning*
*And intending on death;*
*Prevent him, O bearer of radiant brilliance!*

*How indeed, Blessed One, can your disciple*
*—One who delights in your wise instruction,*
*One in training who has not fulfilled his intention—*
*Take his own life, you who are listened to by the people!"*

*By that time venerable Godhika had already taken the knife. Then the Blessed One, realizing "This is Māra the Evil One," addressed Māra the Evil One with a verse:*

> *"Thus indeed do wise men act;*
> *They do not yearn for life.*
> *Having pulled out craving with its root,*
> *Godhika is completely blown out."*

*Then the Blessed One called on the monks, "Come on, monks, let's go to the Black Rock on the hillside of Isigili, where the gentleman Godhika has taken a knife to himself."*

*"As you say, venerable sir," the monks replied to the Blessed One.*

*Then the Blessed One along with many monks went to the Black Rock on the hillside of Isigili. From a distance the Blessed One saw venerable Godhika lying on a bed with his body rolled over to one side. Then at that time a cloudiness, a darkness, was moving in the eastern direction, moving in the western direction, moving in the northern direction, moving in the southern direction, moving upwards, moving downwards, moving in every direction between.*

*Then the Blessed One called to the monks, "Monks, do you see that cloudiness, that darkness, that moves in the eastern direction, then moves in the western direction, then moves in the northern direction, then moves in the southern direction, then moves upwards, then moves downwards, then moves in every direction between?"*

*"As you say, venerable sir."*

*"That indeed, monks, is Māra the Evil One searching for the consciousness of the gentleman Godhika, thinking, 'Where is the consciousness of the gentleman Godhika established?' But with his consciousness unestablished, monks, the gentleman Godhika has completely blown out."*

*Then Māra the Evil One, having taken up a lute of yellow marmelos wood, approached the Blessed One. Having approached the Blessed One he addressed him with a verse:*

> *"Above, below, and across,*
> *In all the directions and everywhere between,*
> *I search but do not find*
> *Where that Godhika has gone."*

[The Buddha:]

*"This wise man endowed with wisdom,*
*A contemplative always delighting in contemplation,*
*Applying himself day and night,*
*Devoid of desire for life,*

*Having defeated the army of Death,*
*Not returning to another existence,*
*Having pulled out craving with its root*
*Godhika is completely blown out."*

* * *

*In his sorrow and affliction*
*The lute dropped from under his arm,*
*And that unhappy spirit* [Māra]
*Disappeared right then and there.*

Well, of course this is a strange story; it even has a visitation from the Buddhist devil in it. Some of it may be made more clear with some commentary provided by me.

Isigili Hill is nowadays, I think, called Sona Hill, not far from Rajgir in the Indian state of Bihar. Rajgir (Rājagaha) during the Buddha's time was capital of the kingdom of Magadha. Isigili Hill is considered to be sacred by Buddhists as well as Jains, as the Buddha and Mahāvīra, reputed founder of Jainism, both spent time there. Isigili means something like "Sage Swallower" because it has caves that have served for millennia as the abodes of spiritual renunciants. According to Buddhist tradition many paccekabuddhas (enlightened beings living solitary lives at times when Dhamma is unestablished in the world) had formerly lived on the hillside and in the caves. One other claim to fame for Isigili is that it is the reputed site of the murder of Mahā Moggallāna, one of the Buddha's two chief disciples. According to tradition, even though he was a fully enlightened being who was foremost among the Buddha's disciples for his psychic powers, he was literally beaten to a pulp by a group of enemies of Buddhism; when his assailants were finished not a single one of Moggallāna's bones remained unbroken. But that's another story.

Godhika's "temporary liberation of mind" (*sāmayikaṁ cetovimuttiṁ*) means essentially *jhāna,* an advanced contemplative state in which the thinking process has stopped, and the mind becomes clear and still. It is only a temporary liberation because it depends on delusion being stopped through the temporary stillness of mind; permanent liberation of mind occurs when one is completely detached from samsaric delusion even when one is thinking and moving around. This is a radically more subtle state than clarity relying upon simplicity and stillness.

According to the commentarial tradition, Godhika kept falling away from *jhāna* because of bad health; although it may be that he was simply high-strung, and his meditative attainments were consequently unstable. I think there are plenty of meditators like that, especially Western ones.

He decided to commit suicide before losing his clarity a seventh time because, again according to the medieval commentary, he reasoned that if he died with *jhāna* he would be guaranteed at least of rebirth in a Brahma Realm, a very exalted heaven. On the other hand, since he wasn't technically a saint yet, if he died without *jhāna* there would be no guarantee at all, and he could be reborn even in a lower realm. He decided to play it safe.

He probably cut his throat with the razor for shaving his head, one of the traditional eight requisites which any Theravada monk should own (i.e. three robes, a belt, a bowl, a razor, a needle, and a water strainer). The commentary states that he twisted his body in death because he wanted to assume the "lion's position," that is, lying on his right side with one foot atop the other, as this is considered the proper position for a sleeping monk. (Some of you may have noticed that statues of the Buddha in the "parinirvana mudra," or the position representing his death and final Nirvana, almost always have him lying in this position.) However, my guess is that he wanted to hold his bleeding throat over the side of the bed so as not to ruin it. It probably wasn't his bed, but one owned by the Sangha.

Māra the Evil One—the Buddhist devil—rushed to the Buddha

and spoke very respectfully to him because he was worried that Godhika might actually become enlightened if he died in his state, considering how resolute and unafraid of death he was. He knew he could't talk Godhika out of suicide, but that the Buddha could, theoretically. But of course it didn't work. The only way to escape the Buddhist devil is to become enlightened, as he holds the entire phenomenal universe, including the highest heaven realms, in the palm of his hand. In fact Māra himself, unlike Lucifer who reportedly lives chained up in the lowest pit of Hell, lives on a magnificent estate in the highest heaven in the so-called Sensual World. (Those of us who do not believe in devils may accept this part of the discourse as a metaphor.)

The Buddha and the monks went to Isigili to dispose of Godhika's body, probably by cremating it. There apparently was no great stigma associated with suicide in ancient India, unlike in the modern West. Nowadays taking one's own life is considered a terrible thing, and in America it is even against the law to attempt it. Those who do attempt it are not only criminals but are likely to be committed to a mental hospital. But even in the West long ago, before Christianity became the predominant tradition and while death was still considered to be a normal part of a violent world, suicide was considered to be socially acceptable and "politically correct." To give just a few famous examples, Demosthenes and Hannibal poisoned themselves; Cato the Younger, when he learned that Caesar's army had defeated the Republican legions, "opened his veins" and bled to death; Cleopatra had herself bitten by a snake; and her lover Mark Antony adopted the most honorable way for a Roman soldier to kill himself—he fell on his own sword.

But Christianity has long considered suicide to be a sin, the rejection of a divine gift from God; and not so long ago suicides were not even allowed to be buried in consecrated churchyards. Sometimes they would even be buried with a wooden stake through their chest to prevent them from becoming vampires or zombies. Dante gave them a special place in his Inferno, where they assume the form of thorny trees with blood for sap, and are denied even the ability to resume their original form on Judgement Day. This condemnation by Christianity, combined with the modern materialistic notion that death is the worst possible thing that can happen to a person, causes suicide to be viewed with severe disapproval in the West.

Sometimes suicide is looked upon not only with disapproval but with resentment. It is often called "the coward's way out"—which is ironic considering that the suicide has willingly brought upon himself that which the disapproving one fears more than all else. It is a similar kind of resentment that I have noticed a few times directed toward monks: in both cases, suicides and monks, the very thing that the other most valued was renounced and thrust away with both hands. Their own life, or their lifestyle, was in a sense spat upon. Or so they seemed to view it.

But even though Buddhism does not *necessarily* condemn the act of killing oneself, it is still the killing of a living being—oneself—and rarely solves the problem it attempts to solve. From the Buddhist point of view, unless the suicide becomes enlightened as Godhika did, he or she will simply be born again, and with essentially the same issues to contend with. We cannot really run from our problems because we take them with us when we run; we are the ones who generated them in the first place through our own karma, and we take our karma wherever we go, even into death. So it's best to face our issues and make peace with them as best we can; otherwise we will continue to be oppressed by them. Elsewhere in the texts the Buddha says that one shouldn't commit suicide unless one's business is done. (Which, however, was not the case with Godhika, as he didn't finish his business until after his neck was already carved.)

Also, when a person commits suicide, especially in a modern world that is not so stoic about death, he or she is usually in a state of utter despair, or some equally negative mental state; and it is considered very important to die with as conscious and expanded a mental state as possible, as that last thought in life largely determines one's momentum into the next stage, or whether there will even be a next stage. It has been wisely observed that death is the most important part of life, and that life is a decades-long preparation for it.

After Godhika's death Māra searched for his consciousness but failed to find it, because Godhika's consciousness had become "unestablished" (*appatiṭṭhitena viññāṇena*). I consider this to be interesting, and possibly very important philosophically. Venerable Bhikkhu Bodhi in the editorial notes to his translation of the Saṁyutta Nikāya assures the reader that, according to the commentary, Māra was searching for where Godhika had been reborn (reincarnated), and that "When the monk is said to attain final Nibbāna with consciousness unestablished, this should not be understood to mean that after death consciousness survives in an 'unestablished' condition...for enough texts make it plain that with the passing away of the arahant consciousness too ceases and no longer exists...." Yet there are very old texts which also may support the idea of consciousness surviving the death of an enlightened being. The most famous is probably the controversial verses found in the Kevaṭṭa Sutta of the Dīgha Nikāya, which begin "Consciousness unmanifest, infinite, shining all around" (*viññāṇaṁ anidassanaṁ, anantaṁ sabbatopabhaṁ*) which evidently is describing Nirvana. Instead of the consciousness of an enlightened being simply vanishing from existence, it may be more like an individual raindrop falling into and merging with the sea.

But it all depends on how one looks at it. How does one describe what no longer has boundaries? One can say that it no longer exists, as has become the orthodox approach in Theravada; or one can say that it has become unmanifest and infinite. They are both equally valid (or equally invalid) ways of describing what is now Completely Off the Scale.

This may be why again and again the Buddha absolutely refused to answer whether or not an enlightened being exists after death. Ultimately, one cannot really say whether or not he or she exists even before death. The duality of existence/nonexistence doesn't really apply.

Last and probably least, the marmelos wood of which Māra's lute was constructed comes from the marmelos tree, also called the bael tree or bilva tree (Pali *beluva*), which grows throughout the drier areas of South Asia. In India it is sacred to Shiva, and it bears a kind of fruit that does not taste very good unless it is candied—thus, marmalade.

## Appendix: The Verses of the Godhika Sutta Translated into Actual Poetry

The following are the same verses translated above, except in real metre. They were written by Henry Clarke Warren almost a century ago in his pioneering book *Buddhism in Translation*:

> *"Thou Hero Great, profoundly wise,*
> *Whose magic power full brightly shines,*
> *Who hast o'ercome all sin and fear,*
> *Thy feet I worship, Seeing One.*
>
> *"Thy follower, O thou Hero Great,*
> *Although o'er death victorious,*
> *Doth long for death, and plotteth it;*
> *Dissuade him, O thou Radiant One.*
>
> *"Pray, shall thy follower, Blessed One,*
> *Whose keen delight is in thy law*
> *With goal unreached, not perfect trained,*
> *So soon expire, O Chief of Men?"*
>
> *"Thus, verily, the valiant act,*
> *Nor think to hanker after life!*
> *Lo! Godhika uproots desire,*
> *And, dying, has Nirvana gained."*
>
> *"Always in meditation found*
> *That brave, strong man his best delight;*
> *Each day and night he practised it,*
> *And recked not, cared not, for his life.*
>
> *"Thus vanquished he Namuci's host;*
> *No more to rebirth he returns.*
> *Lo! Godhika uproots desire,*

*And, dying, has Nirvana gained."*

*The Demon sorely mortified,*
*Down from his side let fall the lute;*
*And in a sore, dejected mood,*
*He straightway disappeared from sight.*

(Māra's final verse to the Buddha, asking the whereabouts of Godhika's consciousness, was rendered by Warren in prose.)

# TECHNICAL MATTERS: EXCOMMUNICATION BY THEFT OF A PĀDA

Many of you know, and hopefully all of you who are Theravada Buddhist monks know, that there are four rules of monastic discipline which, if any one them is transgressed, result in a monk being automatically disqualified from the Bhikkhu Sangha for the rest of his life; re-ordination is not allowed in such a case. The four disqualifications, called *pārājika,* are 1) having S-E-C-K-S with somebody, "even with an animal"; 2) Intentionally stealing ("taking what is not given") anything valuable enough that one could be arrested for doing it; 3) Deliberately causing the death of another human being, which would include hiring an assassin, using black magic, and persuading someone to commit suicide; and 4) Deliberately lying about having attained "superhuman mental states," for example claiming to be enlightened, when one knows one is not, for the sake of becoming famous. Traditionally they are said to be listed in ascending order of seriousness.

There is an unofficial fifth *pārājika* rule that even many monks don't know about: If a monk somehow is castrated or "neutered," even if it is by accident, he automatically stops being a bhikkhu and cannot be re-ordained (unless he somehow regains what he lost).

The one rule in particular that I intend to discuss in this article is number two, intentional theft. At every monk's ordination the four *pārājikas* are explained to him, and he is told that if a monk steals a coin called a *pāda*, anything worth a *pāda*, or anything worth more than a *pāda*, he is excommunicated and, as a yellow leaf that falls from a tree cannot be rejoined to the tree and continue to live, he cannot be rejoined with the Sangha of monks. The exact wording of the rule, in English translation, is as follows:

> *"And whatever bhikkhu, with intention of theft, takes what is not given from a village or a forest, in such a manner of taking what is not given that the authorities, having caught a robber, would execute him or imprison him or banish him, saying "You are a robber, you are a fool, you are an idiot, you are a thief," then this bhikkhu, taking what is not given in such a manner, is also excommunicated and no longer a member of the Community."*

*Pārājika* rules being of such great consequence, there are extremely minute details in the books of discipline regarding what is and is not a theft entailing excommunication. For example, if a monk *starts* to steal something so that part of it has been lifted but part of it is still touching whatever it was resting on, then he has not yet committed *pārājika*, but is guilty of a lesser offense (called *thullaccaya*, a serious transgression) which may still be confessed and atoned for. Another example: If a monk steals something of little value, but worth more than a *pāda,* like honey, a little bit at a time, then whether or not he is guilty of *pārājika* depends on whether he does it according to an overall plan or whether he steals something less than a *pāda* again and again, each time with a fresh intention.

Sometimes the considerations can be very complicated. There is a story in the commentarial literature about a monk who picked up a roll of cloth at a crowded marketplace and made off with it. He was later struck with remorse and confessed the deed to a senior monk. The elder then went off in search of the owner of the cloth, and when he found him he asked a few questions. He returned to the penitent thief and told him that he had not committed *pārājika* at all because the owner of the cloth had dropped it and had given it up for lost—and thus technically the cloth was without an owner. The books of discipline, being essentially law books, contain many, many pages of such sample cases.

It was probably this need for crystal-clear certainty with regard to what is and is not an offense that caused the rule to be defined, even before the Canon had reached completion, in accordance with the value of a *pāda.* It was apparently a common coin in ancient India, and so was a convenient criterion.

The trouble is that we don't use *pādas* any more; and the value of one is questionable. Which is not so good in a case of such great consequence, potentially, to the Sangha.

The section of the commentary corresponding to this rule simply states that a *pāda* is one fourth part of a *kahāpaṇa* (in Sanskrit *kārṣāpaṇa,* a coin which was the standard unit of currency in northern India for centuries). Elsewhere in the commentary, if my memory serves me correctly (I'm too lazy to look it up), all the further information that is forthcoming is that the *kahāpaṇa* in question is the *nīla,* or blue, *kahāpaṇa.*

In the medieval to modern sub-commentarial literature, however, there is a statement that the *kahāpaṇa* which the fateful stolen *pāda* is one-fourth of is a coin consisting of five unhusked rice grains' weight of gold, five of silver, five of copper, and possibly five of iron (the authorities did not agree on the iron). Using the sub-commentary as an authority and calculating the value of a *kahāpaṇa* by the current value of gold and silver, some scholar monks determined that it was worth the modern equivalent of around US $60, and thus a *pāda* would be worth around $15. This was about 15 years ago when gold was approximately $600 per troy ounce; now it is more than 2½ times that much. A *kahāpaṇa* would now be worth about $150. So this is the official party line in Theravada Buddhism as far as I can tell. A monk can steal anything worth less than about $37 and not be excommunicated.

This strikes me as hardly likely for a number of reasons. First of all, $37 is a considerable amount of money, and it is hard to believe that a monk could walk into a store, steal a book worth $35, be arrested, convicted, and fined for shoplifting, and be called a thief, a fool, and a knucklehead besides by the judge—and *still* not be guilty of a *pārājika* offense.

Furthermore, the ancient texts give as examples such small things as several spoonfuls of honey or a piece of meat small enough to be carried off by a bird as grounds for excommunication.

Another consideration is that in the ancient rules for nuns there are two rules discussing a coin called a *kaṁsa*, or "bronze," which according to the texts themselves was worth four *kahāpaṇas.* According to the rules, heavy cloth to make a robe should be worth no more than four *kaṁsas*, and light cloth for same should be worth no more than two and a half. This would make a light summer robe worth approximately $1500, which doesn't seem very likely. The very fact that the coin was called a *bronze* indicates that it probably wasn't worth all that much, certainly not more than a coin containing gold.

Back in the days when I was avidly studying monastic discipline this issue seemed rather important, and I tried to get to the bottom of it. Finally I found the following information in a magnificent book called *The Wonder That Was India*, by A. L. Basham (Sidgwick and Jackson, London 1954):

> *A money economy only existed in India from the days of the Buddha. That coinage was introduced from the west cannot be proved with certainty, but the earliest clear references to coined money are found in texts looking back to a period shortly after the foundation of the Achaemenid Empire in Persia [c.550 BCE], which was the first great empire to mint an official coinage, and which for a time controlled the Panjāb. The Babylonians and Assyrians managed with unstamped silver shekels, but the Achaemenid emperors adopted stamped coinage from Lydia and the Greek cities of Asia Minor, which had already employed it for a century or two. If India did not learn the use of coinage from the Persians she invented it independently, but the coincidence is too striking to make this seem probable.*

> *The earliest Indian coinage consisted of flat pieces of silver or*

*bronze, of irregular shape, but fairly accurate in weight. They bore no inscriptions, but a number of punch-marks, the significance of which is not finally established, but which probably included the emblems of kings who minted the coins, and control marks of local officials and merchants. Inscribed coins were not regularly minted in India until the 2nd century B.C., and though literary evidence suggests that gold coinage may have existed earlier the oldest surviving gold coins, other than one or two very rare specimens, are those of Vīma Kadphises of the 1st century A.D.…(pp. 220-221)*

*Uninscribed, punchmarked coins were minted from the 6th century B.C. onwards, and were in circulation for many centuries. Among the earliest silver specimens are those in the shape of a small bent bar, the largest of which, the śatamāna, weighed 180 grains. Half, quarter and half-quarter śatamānas are attested.*

*The basic silver punchmarked coin of the usual type was the kārṣāpaṇa or paṇa, of 57.8 grains. The māṣa or māṣika weighed one-sixteenth of this, or 3.6 grains. Various intermediate weights are attested, as well as large silver coins of 30 and 20 māṣas and small half-māṣa pieces.*

*Punchmarked copper coins were generally based on a different standard—a māṣa of 9 grains and a kārṣāpaṇa of 144. Quarter-māṣas of copper, or kākiṇīs (2.25 grains) are attested, as well as large coins of 20, 30 and 45 copper māṣas.*

*Only one gold punchmarked coin is known, and it must be assumed that gold was very rarely minted before the beginning of the Christian era.…(pp. 504-505)*

Judging from the information above, it would seem that the coin described in the sub-commentarial literature has never been found and may never have existed, and that there were two main kinds of *kahāpaṇa* in ancient India, specimens of which abound in museums and can be purchased from coin dealers—which one would expect of a standard unit of currency which prevailed for centuries.

Since silver is more *blue* than copper, I assume that the *nīla kahāpaṇa* specified in the commentary is the silver one. So, if silver is one US dollar per gram, and there are 0.0648 grams to one grain, then a 57.8 grain *kahāpaṇa* would be worth US $3.74 by modern prices—and thus the criterion for excommunication by theft would be one-fourth of that: 93 cents. (This is assuming that the silver in ancient Indian coins was as pure as sterling silver nowadays.) Which still seems like rather a lot; thirty years ago when silver was just a few dollars an ounce a monk could be automatically defrocked for stealing anything worth more than about 18 cents.

This comes nowhere near to exhausting the issue of *pārājika* #2 in modern times. There are all sorts of new issues which simply didn't exist in the Buddha's day. For example there is the problem of copyright theft. Some of the photographs I put on my blog are downloaded from the Internet, and I can't be sure that they're not copyrighted. Also I'm not sure exactly what is legal or illegal in this regard. If a photo shows signs of being copyrighted I don't use it, but that is no guarantee. Fortunately a monk is not excommunicated unless he commits theft with conscious *intention to commit theft*. In Buddhism intention is the primary factor in ethics, and is the essence of karma itself.

# BUDDHISM MEETS MONTY PYTHON

*(I really meant no disrespect with this one, but we westerners just can't help but be skeptical sometimes.)*

Years ago when I was living in a desert in central Burma someone gave me a set of several books entitled The Great Chronicle of Buddhas. It is an English translation of a work written by the renowned Ashin Vicittasārābhivaṁsa, better known in Burma as Mingun Tipiṭakadhara Sayadaw, who was the reciter at the Buddhist Sixth Council held in 1956, who was a brilliant scholar with a long list of ecclesiastical titles, and who, I've been told, was listed in the Guinness Book of World Records for memorizing the entire forty-volume Pali Tipiṭaka by heart, not to mention several other books.

*The Great Chronicle of Buddhas* (translated by U Ko Lay and U Tin Lwin, Ti=Ni Publishing Center, Yangon 1992) is based upon the canonical Pali text *Buddhavaṁsa* and its official commentary. I found in these books information that was totally amazing to me, including, in volume I, part 2, the following details of the alleged life of Maṅgala Buddha, who arose 22 Buddhas before "our" Buddha Gotama:

Date of Birth: Two incalculable eons plus 100,000 world cycles before present

Place of Birth: The city of Uttara (in India, on a previous Earth)

Father's name: King Uttara

Mother's name: Queen Uttarā

Place of his Enlightenment: Uttara Park

Name of the woman who offered rice milk on the eve of his Enlightenment: Uttarā

Name of the village in which she lived: Uttara

Name of the ascetic who offered him grass with which to make a seat beneath the Bodhi tree: Uttara

His height: 88 *ratanas* or cubits (approximately 132 feet, or 40 meters)

His lifespan: 90,000 years

From the moment he took conception light radiated from his mother's body to a distance of eight cubits all around, which could not be overpowered even by the light of the sun. Not requiring other lights, the pregnant queen moved about by means of her own luminescence.

When Maṅgala renounced the household life, three *koṭis* of people (thirty million) renounced it also and practiced severe austerities with him.

The light from Maṅgala Buddha's body shone night and day throughout 10,000 world systems. During the 90,000 years of his life everything appeared golden in color, and the sun, moon, stars, and planets gave no light. Since there was no obvious sunlight the demarcation between night and day was not distinct; yet people were able to attend to their business by means of the Buddha's rays.

This great luminescence of Maṅgala Buddha was due to a wish he made in a previous life, the details of which are as follows: Once, when he was a bodhisatta, he was a man renowned for his great generosity. Hearing about his generosity, an ogre (*yakkha*) disguised himself as a Brahmin, approached the bodhisatta, and asked for the bodhisatta's two children. The bodhisatta gladly handed them over, whereupon the entire earth trembled all the way down to the water on which it floats. Then the ogre devoured the two children in the presence of the bodhisatta, and bright red blood flowed from his mouth as he ate. However, there arose not one iota of distress in the bodhisatta's mind—instead he was greatly delighted, thinking, "This is my excellent act of charity." He then expressed his wish: "As a result of this generous act of mine, may my body emanate rays in future bright like the blood (flowing from the ogre's mouth)."

On one occasion Maṅgala Buddha delivered a series of discourses to the Universal Monarch (i.e. King of the Entire World) Sunanda and his retinue numbering ninety *koṭis* (900 million), at which time all of them became fully enlightened arahants. Then the Buddha stretched forth his right arm and said, "*Etha Bhikkhavo*" (Come, monks), causing the entire multitude instantaneously to become ordained bhikkhus, complete with bowls, robes, and cropped hair.

During the time of Maṅgala Buddha the bodhisatta destined to become Gotama Buddha was a Brahmin named Suruci. On a certain occasion the Brahmin Suruci offered alms food for a week plus a set of robes to the Buddha and to each of his retinue of bhikkhus, numbering altogether one hundred thousand *koṭis* (one trillion) of monks. The set of robes offered to the most junior bhikkhu was worth 100,000 pieces of money. The god Sakka himself produced a huge jeweled pavilion for the occasion.

After Maṅgala Buddha's death and *parinibbāna* his relics were enshrined in a pagoda thirty *yojanas* (approximately 300 miles) in height made of powdered "red orpiment" (arsenic sulfide), oil, and butter, and encrusted with seven kinds of precious gems.

* * *

I hope you don't think I'm trying to mock Dhamma by mentioning this. It is right there in the texts, so we might as well admit it.

Burmese Buddhists may blandly accept these kinds of stories without raising an eyebrow; if it's in Theravada Buddhist texts, especially if it's in the scriptures and commentaries, then it's true, and that's all there is to it. It is not far-fetched at all. It's historical, gospel truth.

Devout Western Buddhists tend not to be so openminded when it comes to accepting such tales (and this certainly isn't the only apparent howler in the texts); they tend to prefer to pretend that they don't exist. Even to mention such stories as the biography of Maṅgala Buddha is considered to be crass bad taste.

But to ignore or reject facts is not so good. In fact that would seem to be a characteristic of delusion.

We needn't take such stories very seriously, but there is something important to consider with regard to them. The men who included this information in the Tipiṭaka and its commentaries were not particularly foolish, nor were they stupid. In all likelihood they were at least as wise and intelligent as modern Western Buddhists are, possibly more so. They simply belonged to a very different culture, and worked with a very different set of assumptions. It may be that 500 years from now people will look back on some of the assumptions of modern scientific materialist culture and see them as just as ridiculous as we consider the assumptions of ancient Indian mythologizers to have been.

One important point to bear in mind, one that many Western Buddhists ignore, is that, since the men who compiled and edited the Pali texts were well educated monastic scholars, and were certainly not stupid, *most* of the absurdities and misinformation to be found in the texts are not likely to be *obvious*. There is plenty of stuff that modern Westerners might consider to be absurd even in the so-called core texts (for example the mass of legends found in the Maṅgala-esque Acchariyabbhutadhamma Sutta of the Majjhima Nikāya (M123), or the strange Sela Sutta in which the Buddha reportedly shows his genitalia to a Brahmin and then licks his own ears and eyebrows, found in both the Majjhima and the Sutta Nipāta); but still, it stands to reason that most of what is unreliable is not *obviously* unreliable. Consequently it is a careless mistake to assume that whatever is not obviously ridiculous is therefore trustworthy.

Which leads us to one of the great dilemmas for intelligent Western Buddhists: We must sail a middle course between the Scylla and Charybdis of unquestioning Asian-style dogmatism on the one hand, and on the other the typical Western method of following "common sense" and casually dismissing whatever parts we don't like—which in some cases may be really essential parts.

This has been a dilemma since ancient times; we Westerners didn't invent it. Consider the following passage from the Sandaka Sutta, reportedly the venerable Ānanda's discourse to the non-Buddhist philosopher Sandaka (M76):

> *Here, Sandaka, some teacher is a traditionalist, finding truth in traditions. He teaches a dharma by tradition, from somebody else's words handed down, according to a collection of texts (piṭaka). But for a traditionalist, Sandaka, for a teacher who finds truth in traditions, some of it is well learned, and some of it is not well learned; and so [in some ways] he is right, and [in some ways] he is otherwise....*

> *And furthermore, Sandaka, here some teacher is a reasoner, one who investigates. He teaches a dharma hammered out by reason, following his investigations, based on his own intelligence. But for a reasoner, Sandaka, for a teacher who investigates, some of it is well reasoned and some of it is not well reasoned; and so [in some ways] he is right, and [in some ways] he is otherwise.*

From this it would seem that the alternative, the Middle Way between these two, would involve simply falling between two stools. However, what is required is not to accept or reject tradition or "common sense" too hastily, but to move forward carefully, with our eyes and ears open, as though walking on thin ice.

# FOUR WESTERN THERAVADAS

Several years ago a German monk sent me an article, "American Buddhists: Who Are They?" by Jan Nattier (which at the time of writing this can be accessed at ccbs.ntu.edu.tw/FULLTEXT/JR-EPT/jan.htm) describing, from a sociological point of view, the main types of Buddhism in America. According to this article, Buddhism in the US can be conveniently divided into three categories: Ethnic Buddhism, Evangelical Buddhism, and Elite Buddhism.

Ethnic Buddhism is practiced almost exclusively by Asian immigrants, and to some degree by their descendants; it tends to be based on Asian cultural traditions, and there is negligible interaction with Westerners not born into those traditions.

Evangelical Buddhism, according to the author of the article, is essentially the sect, tradition, or organization of Soka Gakkai, an originally Japanese lay Buddhist society which I think is an offshoot of Nichiren, a Pure Land sect of Mahayana Buddhism. It actively recruits followers and seems to have a very secular orientation, but I personally know little about it, so I'll leave it at that.

Elite Buddhism refers mainly to Buddhist meditation traditions found in the West, such as IMS-style Vipassana, Zen, and some Tibetan Vajrayana traditions. It is called "Elite" by the author because its followers tend to have university educations and to be relatively affluent financially. In fact many meditation centers in the "Elite" tradition are prohibitively expensive for those who are not wealthy. This form of Western Buddhism, according to the author, tends to have few people from ethnic minorities participating, and mainly involve people of European descent. Also, the participants tend to be middle-aged "baby boomers," and recruit relatively few younger people to their ranks.

My observations of American Buddhism, however, cause me to think that there are at least four distinct categories of Theravada alone. I don't know nearly as much about other systems and their various forms in the West, so I'll restrict my analysis to American Theravada, which is probably similar to what is found in most other Western countries. The four varieties I will call Ethnic Theravada, Western Monastic Theravada, Elite Theravada, and the Goenka System. There is overlap between these four categories, so their edges are a bit blurry.

Ethnic Theravada is essentially the Theravadin fraction of the Ethnic Buddhism described in the aforementioned article. Most Asian temples in the West seem to serve more as cultural centers for a local immigrant population than as a place for serious monastic practice or even for missionary work. What missionary work is attempted usually is not particularly successful, as traditional Asian assumptions about Buddhism as a religion, heavily based on culturally conditioned unquestioning faith, are offered to Westerners, most of whom cannot assimilate much of it. So, these Asian Buddhist temples often have relatively little English spoken on the premises, and the supporters of such places often go there to speak their own native language, eat their own native food, and perform their own native ceremonies. Westerners who come often feel out of place, even though they are often warmly welcomed. So this form of Dhamma is unlikely to have much of an impact on Western culture, except for the effects of a few charismatic Asian monks and nuns who become popular with Westerners. If Theravada is to take root and thrive in the West, it is unlikely to occur from this direction—unless some *extremely* charismatic Asian monk or nun comes along and inspires it.

Western Monastic Theravada is an offshoot of Asian Monastic Theravada more than of Western Ethnic Theravada. Most senior Western monks, as far as I know, have spent years in a Theravada

Buddhist country before living as monks in the West. Possibly the most obvious difference with Ethnic Theravada is that the monks at the temples are more Caucasian than Asian, and thus speak lots more English. The monks also tend to be much more strict in their monastic practices, for example following Vinaya more strictly and meditating more. And of course, the starting assumptions are somewhat different. However, there is overlap with Ethnic Theravada, as Western monastics tend to be strongly supported by immigrant Asian communities, possibly more so than by fellow Westerners of European descent. This is largely because earning merit by supporting the "Sangha" (in the traditional Eastern sense of the word) is fundamental to traditional Asian Buddhist culture, but not so in the West. Sometimes the monks of these two varieties of Theravada will meet together and interact, for example by performing formal ecclesiastical acts together; they may even mix together in the same monastery or temple. This form of Western Theravada does not consist entirely of monastics; it also includes lay participants in the system, including some rather conservative Westerners who can appreciate the fact that Dhamma has always been primarily based on a Sangha of renunciants, with the Buddha himself having been one of them.

One might naturally assume that this form of Theravada is the most viable form in the West, as Western monks and nuns are ordaining new Western monks and nuns. But its heavy reliance on Asian communities for support, and its general lack of regard from perhaps most Western people professing Theravada, cause this form also to seem rather limited in its potential to inspire Western culture with Dhamma. Also, of course, there is the question of how well a system designed for ancient India can be assimilated by the modern West. Charismatic Western monks and nuns may be less successful in facilitating this than charismatic Asian ones, largely because they're less exotic, and seen more as eccentrics: at least the Asian monastics are wrapped comfortably and respectably in their own cultural traditions.

Elite Theravada corresponds to the more or less Theravadin portion of the Elite Buddhism described above. It seems to be rather more popular with Westerners than the two previously mentioned forms of Dhamma practice. As far as I can tell, the two great capitals of this Buddhist genre in America, its Mecca and Medina, so to speak, are the Insight Meditation Society in Barre, Massachusetts, and Spirit Rock in Marin County, California. These two organizations are looked to as role models by countless Vipassana meditation societies in the US. Many places of this genre are rather luxurious, expensive, and markedly politically correct. The followers tend to be older, and leaning more toward Western materialistic hardheadedness than toward "woo woo." I know of one society that has candles and incense forbidden at the altars, because so many are worried about breathing toxic fumes, and at their main altar they have placed next to the Buddha image a statue of a female Mahayana Buddhist deity, for the politically correct sake of gender equality. This form of Theravada has sometimes been called "*Dharma Lite.*" This is in large part because in order to be popular it must appeal to many; and in order to appeal to many it must be easy, convenient, comfortable, and non-threatening.

Although it is apparently more popular in the West than the other two mentioned thus far, I feel that it is not an ideal conduit of Dhamma to the West. The majority of the teachings in the Theravadin tradition are either ignored or studied intellectually, leaving a pale shadow of a dismembered fragment of a great tradition; and furthermore Theravadin Dhamma is mixed up in a very eclectic manner with various other traditions, including rather non-spiritual secular traditions. I don't consider eclecticism to be a bad thing in itself, but mixing to the extent that genuine Theravada cannot be actually identified anymore is rather much. It should be borne in mind that Theravada Buddhism began as a systematic method for becoming enlightened in this very life, and renunciation (*nekkhamma*) is a fundamental aspect of it; so any version of Theravada that disdains radical renunciation and making Liberation one's very top priority in life is bound to represent only a partial and elementary aspect of it.

The fourth variety of Western Theravada is the Vipassana system founded by S. N. Goenka. It may be that the article mentioned above tacitly included this system with Elite Buddhism, but it is so divergent in many respects that I figure it deserves a class all to itself. It is the vehicle for a kind of *satipaṭṭhāna*, or mindfulness meditation, similar to the Mahasi tradition on which other Vipassana schools in the West have been based, plus its origins also are Burmese, but the similarities practically stop there. Goenka meditation retreats are free of charge, place great emphasis on determination and moral restraint, and involve some rather spartan self-discipline. I have never practiced the Goenka method, although I've read some of their publications and know several people who are or were followers of the system; and to a trained Theravadin it may seem overly simplistic in its approach to Dhamma. Yet it obviously appeals to many—so much so that retreat centers which charge no money have been established all over the world, and many followers of the method follow it with a kind of starry-eyed zeal which is relatively rare in Western lay Theravada. Long ago, when I was more sarcastic (and possibly more cynical) than nowadays, I used to call the Goenka people "the Jehovah's Witnesses of Buddhism."

I think a big reason for this is that the Goenka method is more difficult to practice than easygoing "Dharma Lite": for example there are no chairs, and two or three one-hour sits per day, in addition to other sits, in which the meditator is advised not to move, even if in a fair amount of discomfort. (The Mahasi method on which most Vipassana methods in the West are at least partly based used to emphasize this kind of "heroic effort" also, using slogans like "Pain is the friend of the meditator," and "Pain is the key that unlocks the door to Nibbana," and exhorting practitioners to remain motionless for the full hour even though the pain might be so intense that they fear they may die; but as comfort-requiring Westerners adopted the method more and more, this kind of teaching was heard less and less, even in Burma.) Anyway, because it is more difficult, completing a ten-day retreat or "course" is a real accomplishment, giving the practitioner not only the benefits of more strenuous practice, but a feeling of deep satisfaction from successfully doing something difficult. And doing what is difficult makes us stronger.

And so, although I'm a follower of the "second Theravada" (pretty much!), and personally don't follow the Goenka method, it strikes me as probably the most viable and successful form of Theravadin Dhamma that I've seen in the West so far—it seems to be getting more of the spirit of Dhamma to more people. It involves considerable practice, self-restraint, and even a moderate amount of renunciation. It's rather simplistic perhaps, but easily understood and relatively undiluted by other systems (although some feel that Goenka's own views on Dhamma are somewhat unorthodox and misleading). Plus it apparently changes people's lives profoundly, and for the better.

What I've been doing since my return to America is looking for some way for Dhamma to thrive, or at least survive without fatal mutations, in the West in such a way that it can have the most positive effect on an increasingly dysfunctional secular culture. Or maybe it would be fairer to say that I'm looking for a way for *me* to thrive while practicing it here. I'm still looking.

# TECHNICAL MATTERS: HOW TO BAKE AN ALMS BOWL

*(This is another essay/article that I thought would be of interest only to a few Buddhist monks with strict ways and obscure interests, but which was well liked by lots of laypeople too. In fact probably more laypeople than monks have expressed a liking for it. Sometimes things like this really surprise me. The essay is a description of a very premodern way of essentially coating iron with a kind of enamel...in this case an iron alms bowl coated with burnt sesame oil. Monks really should know this stuff, and plenty of other people just like to learn weird ancient technologies. Enjoy.)*

The ancient rules of monastic discipline specify that a Buddhist monk is required to own an alms bowl made of earth or iron, and that this bowl is to be baked in a fire from time to time. The commentaries state that an earthen or clay bowl should be baked at least twice, and an iron one at least five times. One of the skills that any junior monk should learn before becoming free of dependence on a teacher, along with sewing and dyeing robes, memorizing (and following) the Pātimokkha, and of course meditating, is the art of bowl baking.

However, most alms bowls aren't baked any more, and the art seems to be dying out. When I first came to Burma more than twenty years ago, clay bowls were already rare, and the "regulation" monk's bowl sold at Sangha supply stores was pounded, so I was told, out of the bottoms of 55 gallon oil drums and then coated with black lacquer. Over the years fancier bowls became more and more common, a typical model being made of iron or steel and somehow processed with a matte black finish very like that found on military hardware. Expensive stainless steel bowls imported from Thailand are becoming almost the standard; and some Burmese monks, and apparently most Thai ones, leave the shiny stainless steel unbaked and unblack.

Some years ago a book on Buddhist monastic discipline in the English language was published, which seemed to imply that to bake a bowl one simply sticks it into a fire. However, this would certainly not prevent an iron bowl from rusting, nor would it turn it any blacker than it already was. Bowl-baking involves coating the bowl with an enamel-like black finish that prevents iron bowls from rusting, and presumably would prevent clay bowls from being porous enough to absorb liquids from the monk's food, and thus would prevent them from becoming stinky and gross.

Even though most Western monks nowadays seem to use stainless steel bowls that are immune to rust, still it may be useful to monks who wish to follow the ancient ways, to see a method much used in Burmese forests for baking an enamel coating onto a bowl. It also may be useful to a few artsy-craftsy type laypeople who would simply like to know how to cover implements with a glossy black finish that was favored in ancient India before the invention of spray paint. Anyway, here is the method. The entire process, not including the cooking of the oil, takes about two hours or a little less.

**You will need:**

~at least one alms bowl
~about half a cup of sesame oil
~an old can to cook it in
~some steel wool, emery cloth, or similar abrasive
~water
~three big rocks or about nine bricks
~three small flat rocks or three smallish potsherds

~a piece of sheet metal about two or three times as wide as the bowl to be baked, and wider than the next item

~a metal bucket, pot, or other receptacle large enough to invert over the inverted bowl without touching the sides

~at least two potholders or thick, folded or wadded cotton cloths (not synthetic, silk, or wool) for handling very hot bowls

~enough firewood to keep a medium-sized fire going for a few hours

~fire

~a clock or watch

**Step 0: Preparing the oil.**

The sesame oil should be cooked over a fire until it is blackish sludge. When still hot it should have the consistency of chocolate syrup, and after it has cooled it should be about as thick as sweetened condensed milk. If it's too runny it will run down the sides of the bowl before it sets, and if it's too thick it is hard to spread it thinly.

The trick for cooking the oil quickly is to let it catch fire – consequently, it is best to do this outdoors over a fire, like the rest of the process. If the oil catches fire it may be ready in half an hour or so (depending on how much of it one is cooking); but if it doesn't catch fire the cooking process may take about *two days*. It was many years before I learned this important trick. One should start with about twice as much oil as one intends to wind up with, as some of it burns away. After preparing the oily sludge it can be kept for years, so it's good to prepare extra for future use.

*The fast way of cooking oil*

*Enough cooked oil for baking three bowls*

**Step 1: Simply stick the bowl into the fire.**

This step may be skipped if the bowl to be baked is plain, unfinished pottery or metal. But if there is old enamel, spray paint, or some other coating on it, it should be burned off in the fire. Dead leaves or other combustible debris may be put inside the bowl to help the inside burn also. Then it should be allowed to cool.

*Burning off the old coating*

**Step 2: Clean the bowl well.**

If the bowl was burned in the fire and has rust or burnt crust on it, it should be rubbed smooth with some abrasive. Steel wool works well. If a little of a previous baking's coating still remains, or if an iron bowl has a reddish tint from rust, so long as it's smooth there's no problem. At this point even a new bowl should be washed and rinsed carefully, so that it is clean, bare pottery or iron.

Incidentally, I once asked a monk friend of mine how the rust was removed in ancient India, before the invention of steel wool and sandpaper, and he said they used a kind of strong vinegar to dissolve the rust. This supposedly had been used in Burma in the old days also. But I'm not sure if vinegar really dissolves rust, and guess as an alternative that they simply rubbed the bowl with sand, or pumice, or something.

**Step 3: Smearing the oil onto the bowl.**

The trick with smearing the burnt sesame oil onto the bowl is to smear it as thinly as possible. If the black coating on the bowl has little cracks after the bowl is baked, and/or if the rim of the bowl has a crust of semisolid oil that flowed down the inverted bowl while baking, then this is a sign that one has spread the oil on too thick. (Such a bowl is still usable, however.) A good method is to dip one's finger(s) into the oil, and then make little dabs of the oil all over the bowl, and then spread it out in a uniform layer. Again, spread it as thinly as possible, using the oil sparingly, yet of course leaving no spot unsmeared. Smear the inside first; it's easier that way.

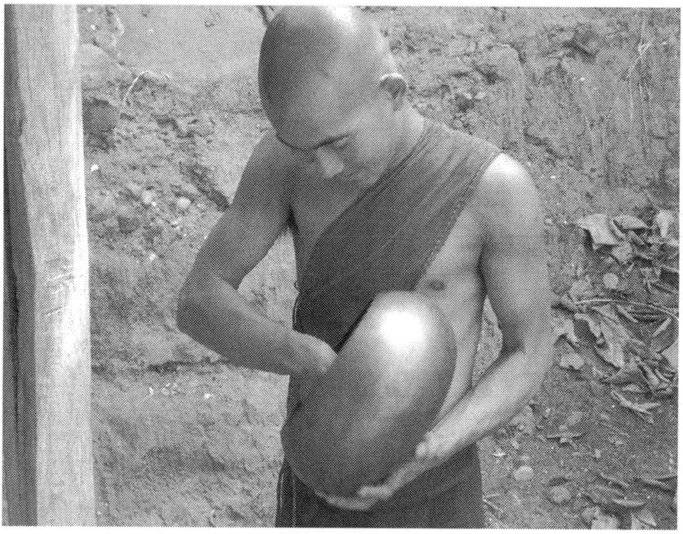

*Smearing the Bowl*

**Step 4: The actual process of baking.**

The piece of sheet metal is set on the rocks or bricks with maybe a foot of clearance with the ground, and the fire is maintained underneath. The flat stones or potsherds are set in a triangle of adequate size to place the inverted bowl onto them so that it doesn't come in contact with very hot metal. The bowl is placed upside-down onto the stones or potsherds, and then the cover is placed over the bowl. At this point one should note the time.

If the fire is small, one round of baking may take ten minutes or more. If the fire is medium-sized, it may take as little as five or six minutes. If the fire is a roaring big one, the coating will bake on and then promptly burn off again, requiring one to start over. This can be very frustrating when one has already done three or four rounds, with three or four layers baked on, so it is best not to have a big fire.

One should watch the smoke coming out from under the receptacle covering the bowl. After a few minutes smoke will be emitted, and then after a while it will stop. When the smoke stops, the bowl is done, and should be removed from the fire to cool. If the smoke stops and then starts again, that means that the baked oil is now burning off – that is not a good sign. Because it is difficult sometimes to gauge the smoke emissions, a clock is handy. The bowl should be checked after five minutes or so; if it is smoking a lot, or if it is still sticky, it's not done yet. To leave it just a little smoky or sticky is allowable, and much preferable to overbaking.

Some monasteries in Burma have a bowl-baking cover with a hole in it, to facilitate observing the smoke coming off the bowl. If the emitted smoke can be clearly watched, then a clock is unnecessary.

Different bowls will have different optimal baking times, depending largely upon their thickness and mass and what material they are made of. A thick iron bowl will take longer to bake, and much longer to cool, than a thin stainless steel one.

After removing the bowl from the fire it must be allowed to cool enough to be handled before applying the next coat. Consequently, it is just about as easy to bake two or three bowls as it is to bake one: while one is baking, another is cooling, while a third may be receiving its next coat of oil. Although a bowl may be baked by one person, two monks have an easier task than one, with one tending the fire and removing the cover and the hot bowl from the fire, and the other smearing the oil (with oil all over his hands). Whoever tends the fire should try to maintain it at a uniform size, and not too big.

**Step 5: Baking it again and again.**

As mentioned previously, the commentarial tradition advises at least two bakings for a clay bowl, and at least five for an iron one. Repeating Steps 3 and 4 above results in a layering of enamel, which causes the finish to be sturdier and to last longer. After the fifth baking, an iron bowl should be a beautiful glossy black. It should be washed before food is eaten from it.

~ ~ ~

Some monks with steel bowls bake only the outside for looks. (Recently I was informed that some wiseguy monks in Thailand smear their $200 stainless steel bowls with eucalyptus oil instead of sesame, to give them a luminous, iridescent finish.) The enamel tends not to adhere as well to stainless as to pure iron. Metal bowl lids may be baked this way too.

The sesame oil enamel is rather sturdy, but still one should be careful about scraping the bowl with sharp implements like forks while eating from it, and should not use strong abrasives when washing it. The coating on a well-baked alms bowl should last for two years at least. A mediocre job will last a year. A bad job, as with a bad life, is to be done again.

The method described above, or so I've been told, is a standard method imported into Burma from Sri Lanka long ago, but there are other methods. I visited one monastery in Mon State in Burma where they didn't cover the inverted bowl while baking it; they used a cauldron, so the heat surrounded the baking bowl on three sides at least. But even uncovered like that would probably be more sophisticated than the way it was done in ancient India by wandering ascetics. I've been told that it is possible to bake a bowl by carefully placing it very near a fire and occasionally rotating it so it bakes one part at a time. I assume this was the original way. It probably would be pretty rough, and not so pretty to look at, but at least it wouldn't rust.

# ONE OF MANY MIDDLE PATHS

*"We can never tell how patient or humble a person is when everything is going well with him. But when those who should cooperate with him do the exact opposite, then we can tell. A man has as much patience and humility as he has then, and no more."—attributed to St. Francis of Assisi*

The Middle Path, or Middle Way, in Pali *majjhima paṭipadā,* is a fundamental teaching of Buddhism; and according to tradition it was discovered by the Buddha on the night of his enlightenment, and was the main point made in his first formal discourse after his enlightenment, the Dhammacakkappavattana Sutta ("The Discourse on Rolling Forth the Wheel of Dhamma"), given to the five ascetics who became his first Buddhist monk disciples.

As it turns out, though, there are many Middle Paths. The Purābheda Sutta of the Sutta Nipāta, for example, sets up a number of pairs of opposites which a good monk wisely passes between. He is not attracted to gain, and has no aversion to loss; he is not opposed to craving, yet he is not in favor of it either; he is not impassioned, nor is he impassive; and so on. In the Aṭṭhakavagga, of which the *Purābheda Sutta* is a part, it is said repeatedly that a monk should have nothing received (*atta*) and nothing rejected (*niratta*), which also obviously is a pun: he should have no self (*attā*) and no not-self either.

Another good example of this multiplicity of Middle Paths is the *Lokāyātika Sutta* of the Samyutta Nikāya (S.12.48): In it, a non-Buddhist philosopher called a *lokāyātika* comes to the Buddha and asks him some questions about the nature of the world. *Lokāyātikas*, incidentally, were the ancient Indian predecessors of modern scientists; they were not so much interested in enlightenment, or the difference between right and wrong, as in determining natural law and understanding the world in general. In Bhikkhu Bodhi's translation of the Samyutta Nikāya the Buddha's questioner is called a cosmologist. Anyway, this worldly philosopher comes to the Buddha and asks, "How is it, Mr. Gotama, does everything exist?"

"'Everything exists':" the Buddha replies, "That is the oldest philosophy of the world."

Then the philosopher asks, "Well then how is it, Mr. Gotama, does everything *not* exist?"

Whereupon the Buddha replies that this is the second oldest philosophy of the world.

The worldly philosopher follows up by asking if everything is One—which turns out to be the third philosophy of the world; and then he asks if everything is a multiplicity—which of course is the fourth philosophy of the world.

Then the Buddha says that he avoids such extremes by adopting the Middle Way, or the Dhamma by the middle (in Pali, *majjhena dhammo*), which he identifies with dependent co-arising. Thus in this case dependent co-arising is a Middle Way which passes between the extremes of existence and non-existence, which is rather a mind-bender, and between the extremes of one and more than one, which is also a mind-bender. (Nāgārjuna's Madhyamaka school, one of the most important and mind-bendy philosophical systems of Mahayana Buddhism, is based upon this kind of thinking.)

However, all of this is some rather dizzying philosophy; and although I'm certainly not opposed to dizzying philosophy, I'd like to discuss a simpler, more practical version of the Middle Path, which is a version of the one taught in the Buddha's traditional first discourse: the Middle Path between self-indulgence and self-torture. The Sutta itself has the Buddha saying this:

> *There are these two extremes, bhikkhus, which he who has renounced the world should avoid. What are these two? A life following pleasures, devoted to pleasures and luxury: this is degrading, sensual, vulgar, ignoble, and without benefit; and [the other is] a life following self-mortification: this is painful, ignoble, and without benefit.*

> *By not approaching these two extremes, bhikkhus, the Tathāgata has realized the knowledge of the Middle Way which leads to vision, which leads to knowledge, resulting in calm, in higher knowledge, in full Enlightenment, in Nibbāna.*

After this the Buddha identifies the Middle Way with the Noble Eightfold Path, then teaches the Four Noble Truths, and then declares his own Enlightenment.

This Middle Path/Way between self-indulgence and self-torture is often conveniently interpreted to mean no gold Rolls Royce on the one hand, and no sleeping on a bed of nails and broken glass on the other. These kinds of extreme extremes actually have precedents in the Pali texts themselves; in fact, according to tradition, the Buddha before his Enlightenment indulged in extreme extremities on both sides. It is written that in his youth he was provided with three palaces, one for the cold season, one for the hot season, and one for the rainy season; that he was also provided with a harem of beautiful dancing girls and female musicians; and furthermore that his entire household staff was composed of young, beautiful females. On the other hand, shortly after he renounced the world he began the traditional ancient Indian regimen of extreme austerity and continued it for six years. According to one strange text, the *Mahāsīhanāda Sutta* of the Majjhima Nikāya (M.12), he followed such ascetic practices as going around naked, not bathing, eating only once every two weeks, and feeding on cow dung; and he eventually became so malnourished that if he rubbed his arms the hairs on his arms would simply break off, and if he grasped his belly with his hand he could feel his own backbone. So, people nowadays often equate the Middle Path with avoiding such extremities and give the whole concept of the Middle Path little thought. They don't want to sleep on nails anyway, and can't afford the gold Rolls Royce. Plus harems are politically incorrect nowadays.

It should perhaps be borne in mind, however, that the Middle Path between luxury and self-torture taught by Gotama Buddha involved wandering around homeless, wearing rags, sleeping under trees, having no family and no money, and silently begging for one's food in the street. This was the *Middle Way*, even though nowadays most people, including perhaps most monks and nuns, would consider it way beyond the range of acceptable austerity. As ancient Buddhism became more of a popular religious movement a new Middle Path developed, which was the Middle Path between self-indulgence and...the original Middle Path. This may be called the *traditional* Middle Path. And then when Buddhism came to the modern West, yet another Middle Path developed, which is the Way between self-indulgence and the *traditional* Middle Way. And although the Middle Path is now hugging up close to self-indulgence, still most people are veering off even closer to the pleasant extreme.

It may be that what is called for is an interpretation with a more psychological emphasis. After all, Buddhist ethics are primarily psychological. Whether what we do is right or wrong (or rather, skillful or unskillful) depends upon our mental states. Karma is volition. For example, if we prevent a snake from eating a frog, whether we do a good deed or a bad one depends on our intentions: if we do it out of compassion for the frog, we have done well; but if we do it out of aversion toward the snake, we have done not nearly so well.

Bearing all this in mind, I'll try to describe a variant of the Middle Way that may be easier for Westerners to relate to, and may have some real practical application in everyday life. Of course there are many Middle Paths, or interpretations of it (including the Eightfold Path), and the following is only one of them.

Many of us, (maybe most of us in the West, where we have more opportunity for such things), try to arrange our life so that it runs smoothly, so that nothing uncomfortable happens. We may settle our life into a standardized routine which is relatively predictable and "safe." It may involve something like, get up, have breakfast, go to work, come home, eat dinner, watch TV, go to bed. We may go out and have some fun sometimes, go on a vacation sometimes, go for a walk, and so on, but for the most part it's all set up to make sure nothing unpredictable and unpleasant happens. The lifestyle may not be all that pleasant or fun, but at least it's more or less predictable, familiar, and non-scary. It seems like especially in America we worry about what *might* go wrong, and then try to fix it before anything has even happened—and much of the time the worrying about what *might* go wrong causes more suffering than if whatever it is really went wrong.

We tend to avoid people who push our buttons, if we can. We generally tend to avoid reading books or watching documentaries that we know in advance we'll disagree with, in order not to feel uncomfortable; and if we find out partway through one that we disagree, we may not stay with it till the end. In other words, we avoid being "triggered."

"Triggered" is rather a new concept for me, largely because it is discussed very little in the Buddhist texts. One might try to study triggers in the Abhidhamma literature, for instance, and not find very much on the subject. It's not an outstanding issue in a Buddhist country like Burma. But it's mentioned often in American conversation nowadays, and strikes me as an interesting and important thing to mention.

It could be said that each of us has at least two personalities: the nice one when everything is running smoothly, and the triggered one, when everything isn't. The triggered personality may be angry, or bitterly complaining, or full of guilt and self-loathing, or even humbly obsequious and eager, even desperate, to please; there are many different ways of being triggered, and each of us has our own favorite version of it. The "smooth" personality is generally pretty nice: we may seem like we've got it all together when everything is calm. Most of us are pretty good people when we're not triggered. In fact most of us want to identify with the untriggered us, and consider the triggered version to be a kind of insignificant anomaly. Some of us even fear the triggered version. So we try to keep things unfluttered, unruffled, and "safe."

But the berserk version is just as much "us" as the smooth version. For example, a notoriously vicious dog is probably not vicious most of the time. Most of the time even a really mean dog may be quietly, calmly lying there on the ground scratching himself, licking himself, peacefully sniffing something, or whatever it is that a peaceful, friendly dog would be doing under the same circumstances. But that minority of the time, maybe less than 5%, is sufficient to qualify that dog as "vicious." Humans are not so different. Stanley Kowalski in *A Streetcar Named Desire* was pretty calm and even rational most of the time, although his bouts of hitting people, ripping things off walls, and smashing windows were still key features of his personality.

Consequently it has been said, for example by Saint Francis of Assisi, that we really don't know someone until we've seen them when things go wrong. People may seem good, wise, and "together" so long as everything's fine, but they may appear very different when the fecal matter hits the fan, so to speak.

The thing is, though, that triggering experiences are a valuable spiritual resource, and should not always be avoided. Triggers point out to us what our attachments are. Suffering in general shows us, or at least has the potential to show us, where we are still stuck. In a way the entire Universe is designed to bring up our "stuff," to show us again and again where we're stuck until we finally work it through and clear it up. Our existence is a matter of karma untangling itself, or at least trying to, like water seeking its own level.

If stuff doesn't come up and ruffle our feathers, so to speak, we often lack the opportunity to clear it, or even to become aware of it. Ram Dass used to tell the story of a swami who meditated alone in a forest for years, until spiritual light shone from his face. He figured it was time to go back into the world to share what he had learned, so he walked to a nearby town. Almost as soon as he got there somebody jostled against him on the sidewalk, and he flared up with indignation and—poof—his equanimity and seeming enlightenment were gone. Practicing in a sheltered, peaceful environment definitely has its advantages, but largely it prepares us for dealing with chaos, and the chaos also is necessary to help us to develop. This is one reason why in Buddhism it is said that a human birth is the best for spiritual development: beings in the lower realms lack the wisdom and opportunity, but beings in the higher realms have it so good, with so little trouble to trouble them, that their latent "stuff" doesn't come up, and they are little motivated toward improving their situation.

The reason why suffering shows us where we are still attached, and is thus an invaluable spiritual resource, is because, in accordance with the Second Noble Truth, *all suffering is caused by desire and attachment*. Whenever we are unhappy, it is because we want something. So it is a useful spiritual practice, whenever we are unhappy, to ask ourselves "What do I want?" Sometimes, like if one is slightly depressed, the answer may not be obvious, although usually it is. And sometimes the answer may be completely ridiculous, and our desire totally silly or futile. For example, let's say we want to go on a hike, or a picnic, or some other outdoor activity, and it starts raining. Well, we may be upset and disgusted, maybe even swearing and being rude to someone; and why? Because we want it not to be raining, which is an utterly futile desire causing an utterly futile unhappiness. All the wanting in the world may not cause a single raindrop less to fall. It's good to be aware of these things.

But being aware won't necessarily make the feelings of unhappiness go away. I remember once I was living at a monastery in Burma where my friend the abbot assured me the electricity stayed on 24 hours a day. Of course I didn't believe him, because there may be no place in all of Burma where the power is on all the time. Sure enough, it was on only 22 or 23 hours a day (certainly nothing to complain about, considering), with the one or two hours of blackout occurring at random, in a very unpredictable way. Also, this monastery was in the hills, and the well water was so cold that one gallon of boiling water added to ten gallons of well water got it up to just lukewarm enough to make bathing bearable. So sometimes I'd start boiling my bathwater on a little electric stove I had access to...and the power would cut off. Immediately I would observe frustration and disgust arising. I could easily remind myself that the desire wasn't going to make the electricity go back on, but still sometimes I'd be sarcastically criticizing the incompetent so and so's in charge of...and then suddenly the electricity would come back on, and my frustration and disgust would disappear almost as quickly as the power came on. It would be a sudden feeling of relief—ahhh.......

Still, observing such feelings is very useful and valuable, even if they don't just disappear as a result. By observing them we detach from them to some degree, which decreases our reinforcement of them, and which also decreases our identification with them. By observing anger, it's no longer "I'm *so* pissed off" but simply "Anger is arising." By observing mental states, it's no longer *we* who are disgusted, or scared, or guilty, or hateful, or whatever. We withdraw support to some degree, which helps the karma fueling its arising to run its course and expend itself. But it doesn't necessarily disappear all at once.

Paraphrasing venerable Ajahn Chah, a negative habit (like anger or disgust) is like a stray dog: If you feed it, it won't go away; but even if you stop feeding it, it may take awhile before it finally gives up and clears out.

Anyway, a psychological interpretation of the Middle Path is one in which we don't deliberately trigger ourselves by making icky things happen to us, but we don't run from triggers either, we don't necessarily avoid them. To some degree, actively making unpleasantness for ourselves, like by actively seeking out the company of people who bother us, is just making new karma, and not necessarily clearing out the old. But even this may be more spiritually effective than hiding or running away or building a wall around ourselves to keep the world off our back. It isn't necessary to make bad things happen to us anyway, as they will happen when the conditions are ripe, without us having deliberately to accelerate the process. Things we don't like will keep happening, naturally, until we eventually learn how to be OK with them. That's the way the Universe works.

Many spiritual teachers have recognized the value of being triggered. For example, George Gurdjieff, an Armenian sage of the early twentieth century, had a kind of ashram in France which also housed some Russian refugees, including one extremely difficult one. He was very fussy and foul-tempered and hard to get along with, and Gurdjieff's disciples disliked him and plotted to drive him away. Eventually they succeeded by playing some cruel practical joke like stealing his false teeth, rolling them in cow dung, and then putting them back. The Russian man left in a passion; and then Gurdjieff actually went after him, hunted him down in another country, and begged and bribed him to come back to the ashram. It wasn't because he missed him, but because he perceived that the fellow was excellent practice for his students in learning to handle life's difficulties wisely.

The practical applications of this practical Middle Path are rather more useful than avoiding beds of nails that we don't want and avoiding gold Rolls Royces that we can't afford even if we do want them. One bit of spiritual advice that arises from this approach is: Don't Cling to What Is Worn Out. Many of us cling to relationships that really ended years ago, or jobs we've grown bored with, or circles of friends we've outgrown, or habits that no longer bring us satisfaction, or even a physical environment that doesn't suit us anymore, mainly out of fear of change, fear that the unknown consequences of letting these things go may be more unpleasant than just staying in the rut. But even if there will really be a fair amount of unpleasantness, it may still be preferable. Being vulnerable to risks is spiritually conducive to waking up, or at least to learning about ourselves. So don't be afraid to take risks if you feel a change would be good for you. Dare the unknown. In a way, the Universe looks after those who live this way.

(Incidentally, I consider this lack of risk to be an important weakness of traditional monasticism. The wanderers of "primitive Buddhism" had plenty of opportunities to be severely triggered, while monks and nuns living in sheltered, comfortable monasteries nowadays may be like the swami described above, living in a kind of artificial wisdom through hiding from chaos.)

Another useful bit of advice is not to consider feeling uncomfortable to be necessarily a bad thing, regardless of what Consumerism tells us. Discomfort and emotional triggers help us, if we let them.

And when a trigger does happen, observe it. (This takes practice, and it may be helpful to start with little pet peeves, like the yapping dog next door, before making oneself vulnerable to monsters. Mindfulness practice is invaluable for this.) Observing it may not make it disappear, but it helps us to detach from our attachments, including our identification with feelings and other mental states.

Mental states are not us. Ultimately, we're neither the calm, polite personality nor the triggered, upset one. But that's No Self, and getting into the Buddha's second sermon, so I'll stop here.

# POINTLESS POTTHILA

*"...This is why most people who have studied a lot and become monks never get anywhere. Their knowledge is of a different kind, on a different path....The knowledge of the Buddha is not worldly knowledge, it is supramundane knowledge, a different way altogether."—Venerable Ajahn Chah*

Now for a refreshing (or boring?) change of pace: An article about mainstream, relatively uncontroversial Theravada Buddhist doctrine.

There is a well-known story in the commentary to the Dhammapada, the legend of Tuccha Poṭṭhila, explaining the origin of verse 282 of that text. It is well-known to Burmese Buddhists anyway; many Western Buddhists may be unfamiliar with it. So I present a translation of it here, based on the Burmese Sixth Council version of the commentary:

*"Indeed, by spiritual practice..." This Dhamma instruction was spoken by the Teacher while residing at Jetavana, with regard to an Elder named Poṭṭhila.*

*It is said that he was a master of the Tipiṭaka in the dispensations of the seven* [most recent] *Buddhas, and taught Dhamma to five hundred monks. The Teacher considered, "For this monk there is no thought of 'I will make an escape from suffering.' I will stir him up." So from then on whenever the Elder came to attend on him, he would say, "Come, pointless Poṭṭhila. Bow, pointless Poṭṭhila. Sit down, pointless*

*Poṭṭhila. You may leave, pointless Poṭṭhila." And when he had gotten up and left, he would say, "Pointless Poṭṭhila has gone."*

*He considered, "I have memorized the Commentaries and the three Piṭakas; I teach Dhamma to five hundred monks in eighteen great assemblies; and still the Teacher continually says to me 'Pointless Poṭṭhila.' The teacher must be saying it on account of my non-development in meditation." With a sense of urgency stirred in him he thought, "Now, I'll enter a forest and will carry out the Way of a* [true] *philosopher." So secretly having gotten his bowl and robes together, in the early morning he set out with the monk who was last of all to learn his Dhamma studies. Those sitting in the monastery enclosure repeating their lessons did not notice that he was their master.*

*Having traveled a journey of 120 yojanas* [roughly a thousand miles], *he arrived at a forest residence where thirty monks were residing; and having approached them, and having bowed to the Elder monk of the Community there, he said, "Venerable Sir, please be my refuge."*

*"Friend, you are a teacher of Dhamma. It is we who could learn something by being in dependence on you. Why do you talk like this?"*

*"Don't make it out like that, Venerable Sir. Please be my refuge."*

*Really, all of them were with encumbering influences exhausted* [*khīṇāsavā*, i.e., liberated, enlightened]. *Then that great Elder considered, "There is pride* [*māno*] *in this one on account of his learning," and sent him to a less senior Elder. That one spoke to him in the same way. In this same manner every one of them passed him on, till he was sent at last to the most junior of them all, a seven-year-old novice sitting in a well-lighted workplace doing some sewing.*

*With his pride humbled, he respectfully held up his joined hands to the novice and said, "Good man, please be my refuge."*

*"Oh Master, why are you saying this? You are a very learned senior monk. It is I who should learn something in* your *presence."*

*"Don't do like this, good man. Please be my refuge!"*

*"Venerable Sir, if you will be willing to accept admonishment, then I will be your refuge."*

*"I am, good man. If I am told, 'Go into a fire,' then I will even go into a fire."*

*Then he pointed out to him a pond not far away: "Venerable Sir, fully dressed as you are, go into that pond." Although knowing that he was dressed up in a very valuable double-thickness robe, he said this checking to see if he was indeed willing to accept admonishment. The Elder, immediately upon the novice saying this, waded into the water. Then when the edges of his robes were wet, immediately upon being told, "Come, Venerable Sir," he came and stood before him.*

*"Venerable Sir, say there is a termite mound with six openings. Now, by one of these openings a monitor lizard has gotten inside. Someone wanting to catch it would close off five of the openings and leave the sixth one open, and would catch it right at this opening that it had entered. Even so, you, with regard to the six sense doors, having closed five of the doors, tend to your work at the door of the mind."*

*To the learned monk, just this much was like the blazing up of a lamp. He said, "Let that be enough, good man," and, knowledge having descended into his karma-born body, he undertook the Way of a philosopher.*

*The Teacher, even sitting at a distance of 120 yojanas, observed that monk and having considered, "This monk, in order to be of broad understanding, ought to have something by which to apply himself," emitted a beam of light which spoke to him this verse:*

yogā ve jāyati bhūri / ayogā bhūrisaṅkhayo
etaṁ dvedhpathaṁ ñatvā / bhavāya vibhavāya ca
tathāttānaṁ niveseyya / yathā bhūri pavaḍḍhati

*Indeed, from spiritual practice broadmindedness arises;*
*From non-practice broadmindedness diminishes.*
*Having understood this twofold way*
*Of development and non-development*
*One should thereby establish oneself*
*So that broadmindedness will advance.*

*...At the conclusion of this teaching Poṭṭhila the Elder became established in the state of an Arahant.*

~ ~ ~

A few comments:

This story is very anachronistic, and is hardly likely to represent actual history. For example, there is mention of *seven* Buddhas; and, more obviously, mention of a Tipitaka existing even during the lifetime of Gotama Buddha himself, and even commentaries. Also, it seems unlikely that the venerable Elder would walk a thousand miles to meditate in a forest. Forests were pretty easy to find in India in those days. Furthermore, the Dhammapada itself is considered by Western scholars to be a relatively late addition to the Pali Canon. But even so, the subject matter of the tale is of interest; and a story doesn't have to be objective history in order to be potentially useful.

The word "pointless" is a makeshift translation of the Pali word *tuccha,* which literally means empty, like an empty pot or an empty hand. But emptiness has rather positive connotations in Buddhist philosophy, and I certainly wouldn't want to denigrate someone for being empty. "Vain" also might be appropriate, but it might sound like ven. Poṭṭhila was stuck on himself or overly concerned with his appearance. "Pointless" seems to come pretty close to the intended meaning of "lacking what is essential." "Futile" might come close to the mark also.

One may see that the word for "spiritual practice" in the Dhammapada verse is *yoga.* Here it means mainly meditation, not sun salutations and other physical practices associated with that word in the West.

The main interest of the story, aside from the messages that scholarship is not the Way, and that humility is a beneficial virtue, is the meditation instruction given by the enlightened little novice. One of the main purposes of sitting in meditation in a quiet place is to reduce stimulation of the five grosser senses so that one may more easily observe the movements of the mind. If practiced skillfully, directing one's attention to the mind may be deeper and more subtle than, say, observing bodily sensations like the touch of air at the nostrils. In Pali this kind of meditation is generally called *cittānupassanā,* reflecting upon the mind. Sometimes I call it "third gear," with first and second being variations on ānāpāna, or mindfulness of breathing.

There is a fourth gear, however, that is deeper and more subtle yet—observing the mind is still a deliberate process of observing; it is volitional, and therefore still karmic. The next step is to relax the mind completely while remaining very alert, without deliberately focusing on anything in particular. By not excluding anything, but keeping everything in the field of consciousness equally in focus, one reaches a profound state that the Catholic Christians have called "high contemplation." Different Buddhists call it different things. If one can practice it well it is an indescribable blessing.

However, no technique *in particular* is really necessary. If it works for you, then do it; and if not, then try something else. The important thing is to tend toward clearer consciousness, and the rest tends to take care of itself.

# TECHNICAL MATTERS: BUDDHIST FEEDING BEHAVIOR

Sometimes I am asked about whether Buddhists, or Buddhist monks, have many dietary restrictions. For laypeople keeping the basic five precepts there are almost none—no killing one's own meat, no stealing one's food, and no consumption of alcohol or other substances which cloud the mind—but Theravada Buddhist monks have plenty of restrictions.

Vegetarianism, however, is not one of them. In the Buddha's time the principle of *ahimsa*, or nonviolence to living beings, was not yet well established in the mainstream of Indian society, and the eating of meat, as is the case in the West today, was common, and socially acceptable. Monks being essentially beggars, and beggars not being choosers, they accepted meat put into their bowl, and ate it if they wanted to. It wasn't until Buddhist ethics became more integrated into Indian culture that Buddhists put more emphasis on vegetarianism; and some schools retroactively converted the Buddha himself into a vegetarian, although according to the evidence in the Pali texts (the oldest Buddhist texts we have) this appears unlikely.

When the Buddha's cousin Devadatta tried to take over the Buddhist Sangha he allegedly insisted on reform of monastic discipline, and one reform that he desired was to make vegetarianism mandatory for monks. The Buddha refused to change the rules in this case. There are numerous rules regarding the eating of meat found in the Buddhist monastic code, some of them remaining in ignored, vestigial form even in the canonical monastic codes of vegetarian Mahayana schools. And according to the Mahāparinibbāna Sutta, describing the death of the Buddha, the evidence suggests that the Buddha himself died after eating some bad pork.

According to the text, what the Buddha ate at his last meal was *sūkaramaddava*, *sūkara* meaning "pig," and *maddava* meaning "tender" or "soft." Most scholars who do not have a Mahayanist bias or a vegetarian axe to grind agree that in all likelihood the correct translation is "tender pork"; however, Mahayana Buddhists, possibly following the lead of an ancient school like the Sarvastivadins who favored vegetarianism, have interpreted the word to mean "something tender that pigs like," i.e. truffles, a kind of mushroom-like fungus. Hence the legend that the Buddha died after eating a mushroom.

It is interesting that the Sarvastivadin version of the Majjhima Nikāya is very similar to the Theravadin version, but nevertheless lacks an equivalent of the Jīvaka Sutta (M55). In this text Jīvaka, the Buddha's personal physician, informs the Buddha that non-Buddhists are saying that the Buddhists favor killing, since they eat meat killed for their sake. The Buddha denies this, asserting that a Buddhist monk is not allowed to eat any meat that he sees, hears, or suspects has been killed for his sake. In the monastic code to eat such meat would be a *dukkata* offense. Meat not killed for a monk is allowable though. (Whether meat killed for a *different* monk would be allowable is not so clear, although I would assume that it is not.)

In the modern West this rule seldom comes up, except for fertile eggs, which count as living baby chickens. Infertile eggs, like those usually obtained at a grocery store, are not fertile, and thus are OK to crack and cook for monks.

Other relatively well known dietary restrictions for Theravadin monks are: that they are allowed to eat substantial food only at the "right time," i.e. between dawn and midday; that they are allowed to eat only what was offered to them by someone who is not a monk; that they are not allowed to eat food that they have stored overnight, and thus must eat food they have received that same morning; that they are not allowed to cook their own meals (although reheating it is allowable); and that they are not allowed to ask for particularly good food containing ghee, butter, oil, honey, sugar, fish, meat, milk, and/or curd, unless they are sick or have received special permission from the person to ask for such things. Some of these rules are designed to prevent monks from being hermits, by requiring them to interact with laypeople. Others are to prevent them from being a burden on those laypeople.

Some less well known rules involve the eating of meat. For example, there are ten kinds of flesh which are forbidden to monks: 1) human, 2) lion, 3) tiger, 4) leopard, 5) bear, 6) hyena, 7)elephant, 8) horse, 9) dog, and 10) snake. Largely because of this, a monk is required to ascertain what kind of meat is being given to him. There is also a strange rule saying that a monk is not allowed to eat raw meat or drink raw blood unless he is possessed by a demon. I actually read of a case like this, in a book attributed to the great Zen master Dogen. He said that a monk had a strange craving for raw meat, yet when Dogen watched him eating he saw that the monk was not eating the raw meat, but rather a small demon perched on the monk's head was eating it. Anyway, that's what the book said. (To this day necromancers in Burma get ghosts and demons to do their bidding by feeding them raw meat and blood until they become dependent on their supply.)

Although the eating of meat is not forbidden to monks, ahimsa is taken to the extreme that monks in ancient times were not supposed to eat living, viable seeds. This has apparently been corrupted somewhat into a rule stating that only five kinds of fruit are allowable: 1) fruit that has been damaged by a knife; 2) fruit that has been damaged by a fingernail; 3) fruit that has been damaged by fire; 4) fruit that is naturally without seeds; and 5) fruit from which the seeds have been "expelled." I assume this originally meant that fruit with seeds should have the seeds cut out, dug out, or cooked so that the monk would not be killing living beings by eating it; but it has been corrupted into a formality by allowing monks to eat fruit with viable seeds so long as a non-monk has poked the peel with a knife or nicked it with a fingernail. Even a whole tray of fruit supposedly becomes allowable so long as one of the fruits is poked while it is touching the others on the tray.

Consumable substances are divided into four categories: 1) ordinary food, which can be kept only until noon of the day it is received; 2) the juices of fruits and vegetables, which may be kept till the following dawn, and thus may be drunk in the afternoon and at night; 3) five designated medicinal "tonics"—ghee, butter, oil, honey, and sugar—which may be kept for a week and used for medicinal purposes; and 4) medicinal substances not included in the other categories, including herbal medicines like garlic, ginger, and ginseng, plus modern pharmaceuticals, which may be kept indefinitely. The rule for mixing these four kinds of substance is somewhat complicated, and even many conscientious monks break the rule without realizing it; also some people have been mystified by certain aspects of my behavior that are conditioned by this rule; so I will attempt some explanation.

Whenever any of the four kinds of consumables are mixed together, they automatically come under the rule of the substance with the shortest time limit. For example, let's say a monk has some salt for medicinal purposes, and has had it in his possession for several months. Then one day he puts some on his food to flavor it. The salt automatically becomes ordinary food which can be kept only until noon of the day it is received; and since he has already had it for several months, his meal becomes food that has been stored overnight, the eating of which is a *pācittiya* offense. This also applies to sugar and milk in one's coffee: the coffee itself, arguably, could be considered an herbal tonic which can be kept indefinitely (it doesn't obviously fall under any of the other categories, especially if it's stored in the form of dry powder), the sugar can be kept for only a week, and the milk for only half a day, being considered regular food. (What category non-dairy creamer falls under is debatable, and somewhat controversial.) So I keep a jar of instant coffee, and always drink it plain; but if someone offers me a cup in the morning, I take milk with it.

With regard to the medicinal oil that can be kept for one week, there is a section in the ancient texts listing the kinds of animal fat that may be rendered and used in this regard; and one of the animals whose grease is allowable is the *susu* or *susukā*, which is often declared to be a shark or alligator, but which is probably the gangetic dolphin, which, I'm pretty sure, is still called *susu* in India. (And as far as I know, there are no sharks or alligators in the Ganges valley.) So although possibly illegal and extremely politically incorrect, consuming dolphin fat is ecclesiastically pure.

There are certain controversies regarding monks and food, especially with regard to the eating of cheese and chocolate in the afternoon. This is common for monks ordained in Thai traditions, but is practically nonexistent among monks in Burmese traditions —a Burmese monk who would eat cheese or chocolate in the afternoon would also eat rice in the afternoon (and, admittedly, there are some of those). One Western monastic scholar who wrote a book on monastic discipline actually implied that eating cheese in the afternoon is allowable because cheese is technically a kind of butter. He pointed out that butter in ancient India was made from curd, not cream like it is nowadays. Cheese can't be called curd, though, because curd is specifically designated as ordinary, substantial food. But how is cheese made? It is curd with most of the remaining whey pressed out of it, often with a small amount of culture or other flavoring added. So cheese is actually a kind of purified curd; with more non-curd ingredients removed than put in, it contains more curd than curds do. (In fact the Burmese word for cheese literally translates as "hardened curd," which is exactly what it is.) Furthermore it is obviously a substantial food, being a meat substitute for vegetarians. Probably the main reason why cheese is considered allowable in the afternoon by monks in Thai traditions is that famous monks like Ajahn Mun ate cheese in the afternoon, and implying that these saints did something wrong is just too much like troublemaking. Plus, of course, they want to eat cheese in the afternoon. Hard chocolate is considered allowable at the "wrong time" so long as it is dark, without milk added (because it is considered to be a kind of very thick juice); so many monks feast on the highest quality, most expensive dark chocolate in the afternoon.

In Burma, the strictest monks won't even drink tea in the

afternoon, largely because of an obscure rule stating that the juice of all leaves is allowable to be drunk at the "wrong time" except for the water left over from cooking greens. Tea leaves are commonly eaten as a salad in Burma, so tea would qualify as the juice from cooked greens. This is getting pretty extreme on the strictness meter, however.

There is also an obscure rule stating that the juice of all fruits is allowable except for the juice of grain (*dhañña*), presumably because beverages made from grain are usually fermented. The word for grain, though, is strangely interpreted in the sub-commentarial tradition to mean any fruit larger than two fists put together. So strict Burmese monks won't drink coconut milk in the afternoon, even though it seems quite kosher to me. Some Burmese monks won't drink Sprite either, because they think it's made out of some kind of large melon.

There are many more rules concerning food. Some are matters of etiquette; for example it is an offense to carelessly make slurping noises, scatter rice around, lick one's fingers, or talk with one's mouth full. But going into fine detail on all this stuff is too much, so I'll stop here.

# SOME (ALLEGED) PECULIARITIES OF THE BUDDHA'S PHYSICAL BODY

*(What follows is another essay which may* seem *to be disrespectful of Buddhism, but which is simply pointing out the difficulties of a modern western person capable of critical thought reading ancient eastern texts full of mythological elements. We have our own mythologies though, which later generations may find just as strange as you may find the following.)*

Theravada Buddhism maintains that the historical Buddha was not a god, but a human being—and not a deity manifested as a human being, like Christ or Krishna, but really a human being.

However...he is portrayed as being superior to any mere deity, and the gods from the heaven realms often descend to earth humbly to pay him homage. There is no omniscient, omnipotent Creator in the Buddhist cosmology, so the founder of Buddhism did not have to compete with Him, Her, or It.

Nevertheless, as Buddha-worship developed in ancient India, the Buddha was glorified into more than just an ordinary-looking human being, into more even than a tall, strong, handsome human being. Many strange physical peculiarities came to be attributed to him, one of the most obvious of which being that he was considered to be 4½ times the height of an average man, or about 26 feet (almost 8 meters) tall.

Many Burmese Buddhists accept without question this alleged great height of the Buddha, but we Westerners are much less likely to follow along. First of all, we're less likely to believe in mysterious metaphysical forces that would cause an exceptionally great person to diverge from the normality imposed upon us by our own DNA. And there are other biological complications to consider—for example, as height is doubled, area is squared and volume and mass are cubed, so a 26-foot-tall human would have insufficient lung capacity and bone thickness to support his great mass. Also, of course, the testimony of the ancient texts is compatible with the Buddha being tall, but not with his being taller than a giraffe. People who would meet him often mistook him for an ordinary monk, and on one famous occasion he exchanged robes with the monk Mahā Kassapa. His half-brother Nanda was only a few finger-widths shorter than him. Plus he lived in ordinary buildings, had a wife, and somehow managed to father a baby with her.

But his height is only the beginning. The Pali texts themselves, for example the Lakkhana Sutta of the Dīgha Nikāya, also maintain that the Buddha had 32 marks of a Great Man (*mahāpurisa*)—in fact any fully enlightened Buddha must have all 32 of them. The same is true for anyone who becomes a righteous king of the entire world. If any boy is born with all 32 of these marks, he is destined to become one or the other.

Without any further ado, the marks of a great man are as follows.

**1.** He has "well planted feet" (*suppatiṭṭhitapādo hoti*)—This has been interpreted by some to mean that he has perfectly flat feet, which would be borne out by the earliest representations of the Buddha's footprints; but it seems more likely that it means he steps with the entire foot coming down evenly, not coming down heel first or toes first.

**2.** On the soles of his feet he has the marks of wheels with a thousand spokes, complete with rims and hubs (*heṭṭhāpādatalesu cakkāni jātāni honti sahassārāni sanemikāni sanābhikāni sabbākāraparipūrāni*)—This also would support the flat feet hypothesis, considering that representations of the Buddha's footprints show these wheels quite clearly.

**3.** He has elongate heels (*āyatapaṇhi hoti*)—Some have interpreted this such that his heels stick out behind as far as the rest of his feet stick out in front, causing his feet to look like an inverted T.

**4.** He has long fingers and toes (*dīghaṅguli hoti*).

**5.** He has soft, tender hands and feet (*mudutalunahatthapādo hoti*).

**6.** He has webbed hands and feet (*jālahatthapādo hoti*)—The most obvious explanation of this one is that his fingers and toes have webbing between them; but possibly because this is considered more a birth defect than a sign of excellence the mark has also been interpreted as a kind of reticulated pattern of fine lines like netting on the hands and feet.

**7.** He has arched (or raised) feet (*ussaṅkhapādo hoti*)—This mark also has been interpreted to mean that his ankles are located at the middle of the length of his feet, making them T-shaped, which would be redundant if number 3 meant the same. Some have interpreted this to mean, alternatively, that his ankles are midway up his shins. The literal translation of the Pali, however, seems to support the arched instep interpretation, which would thus be in conflict with the flat feet interpretation of number 1.

**8.** He has legs like a goat-antelope (*eṇijaṅgho hoti*)—They are long, slender, and graceful.

**9.** Standing, without bending over at all, he touches and rubs his knees with the palms of both hands (*thitakova anonamanto ubhohi pāṇitalehi jaṇṇukāni parimasati parimajjati*).

**10.** He has his pudendum enclosed in a sheath (*kosohitavatthaguyho hoti*)—Some Mahayana Buddhists have this interpreted to mean that his entire genitalia are internal when not in use.

**11.** He has a golden complexion, his skin shining like gold (*suvaṇṇavaṇṇo hoti kañcanasannibhattaco*).

**12.** He has very smooth skin, and from the smoothness of his skin dust and dirt do not adhere to his body (*sukhumacchavi hoti, sukhumattā chaviyā rajojallaṁ kāye na upalimpati*).

**13.** He has single body hairs, his hairs growing one to each follicle (*ekekalomo hoti, ekekāni lomāni lomakūpesu jātāni*).
**14.** He has body hairs with upward-pointing tips, his upwards-tipped hairs being blue-black in color like collyrium and curling in rings spiraling to the right (*uddhaggalomo hoti, uddhaggāni lomāni jātāni nīlāni añjanavaṇṇāni kuṇḍalāvaṭṭāni dakkhiṇāvaṭṭakajātāni*).
**15.** He has a straight, upright body like a Brahma deity (*brahmujugatto hoti*).
**16.** He has seven eminences (*sattussado hoti*)—These seven eminences are traditionally considered to be the inner sides of his knees and elbows, his shoulders, and his chest; they are well rounded, without hollows.
**17.** The front part of his body is like a lion's (*sīhapubbaddhakāyo hoti*).
**18.** He is well filled in between his shoulders (*citandaraṁso hoti*).
**19.** He has the balanced dimensions of a banyan tree; the span of his outstretched arms is as long as his body, and his body is as long as the span of his outstretched arms (*nigrodhaparimaṇḍalo hoti, yāvatakvassa kāyo tāvatakvassa byāmo, yāvatakvassa byāmo tāvatakvassa kāyo*).
**20.** He has an evenly rounded torso (*samavaṭṭakkhandho hoti*)—This would seem to mean that his body is cylindrical in cross section.
**21.** He has an extremely refined sense of taste (*rasaggasaggī hoti*)—He allegedly tastes food with the entire lining of his mouth and throat, not just with his tongue. As ven. Bhikkhu Bodhi points out in note 856 of his translation of the Majjhima Nikāya, it is difficult to understand how others could note this trait in the Buddha or in anyone else through mere observation.
**22.** He has jaws like a lion's (*sīhahana hoti*).
**23.** He has forty teeth (*cattālīsadanto hoti*).
**24.** He has even teeth (*samadanto hoti*).
**25.** He has teeth without gaps between them (*aviraḷadanto hoti*).
**26.** He has very white canine teeth (*susukkadāṭho hoti*).
**27.** He has an extensive tongue (*pahūtajivho hoti*)—The Buddha reportedly could lick his own eyebrows as well as his own ears, and

could cover his face with his tongue.

**28.** He has a voice like a Brahma deity, sounding like an Indian cuckoo bird (*brahmassaro hoti, karavīkabhāṇī*)—Traditionally, the karavika bird has a call so strikingly beautiful that if a lion is chasing a deer through the forest and this bird begins to sing, it is said that both the lion and the deer will stop to listen, as if spellbound.

**29.** He has eyes that are deep blue, or blue-black (*abhinīlanetto hoti*).

**30.** He has eyelashes like an ox (*gopakhumo hoti*).

**31.** He has hair growing between his eyebrows that is white like a soft tuft of cotton (*uṇṇā bhamukantare jātā hoti odātā mudutūlasannibhā*)—This trait is presumably the origin of the "third eye" marking most Buddha images have between their eyebrows.

**32.** He has a head like a turban (*uṇhīsasīso hoti*)—This trait is often considered to be the reason why Buddha images tend to have a strange lump on top of their head, if not an even stranger knob or point, but it may simply mean that his head is well rounded. Apparently in ancient India to be circular in cross section was considered to be a sign of superior form. Many scholars consider the lump on top of the Buddha's head to be a vestigial topknot of hair, despite the probability that the Buddha, being a monk, had his head shaved.

Most of these marks are self-explanatory, and those that are not...well, they don't seem very important anyway. One thing about this assemblage of qualities that I find interesting is that whoever came up with them apparently was not very good at geometry or engineering, as some of them seem like they are mutually exclusive and could not be found on the same individual. Consider marks 4, 9, and 19. Now, many people have the dimensions of a banyan tree, with their height being nearly equivalent to the width of their outstretched arms. This is not so uncommon. But very few people have their palms resting on their knees when standing upright. This, combined with the Buddha's alleged long fingers (reaching down well below his kneecaps), would indicate that the distance from his shins to his neck would constitute much less than half his height. The entire length of one arm, plus the width of his shoulders, would be equal to his lower shins and feet plus his neck and head. So if we grant that his neck and head extend upwards as far as his shoulders extend from side to side, his shins would be about as long as his arms. The only way this would be possible is if his knees were located very high up his legs, about where the average human being's palms would rest. Thus he would have extremely short thighs and extremely long shins, and when sitting cross-legged his feet would be sticking way, way out to the sides, unlike the more normal-looking representations on Buddha statues.

Anyhow, if anyone did actually have all 32 of these marks, he would not be a handsome man, as the Buddha was said to be, but would be rather a grotesque monstrosity, even if he weren't 26 feet tall. As a further mild embarrassment, this list is found in the so-called *core texts*, the nucleus of the most ancient Buddhist scriptures common to most or even all of the most ancient schools of Indian Buddhism, which even many conservative Western Buddhists consider to represent the Canon as determined by the First Great Council, held shortly after the great blowing out of the Buddha's existence in this world.

Another list of physical marks, although heard of from time to time, is seldom seen; and that is the list of 80 minor marks (*anubyañjana*) of a great man, which the Buddha also allegedly had, in their entirety. There are at least two versions of the list which are not completely in agreement; the following is from a sub-commentarial text called the Jinalankara Tika.

**1.** "Closely knitted fingers and toes with no intervening gaps" (*cit'aṅgulitā*)
**2.** Fingers and toes tapering gradually (*anupubb'aṅgulitā*)
**3.** Rounded (in cross section) fingers and toes (*vaṭṭ'aṅgulitā*)
**4.** Copper-colored fingernails and toenails (*tamba nakhatā*)
**5.** Pointed and prominent fingernails and toenails (*tuṅga nakhatā*)
**6.** Smooth, glossy fingernails and toenails (*siniddha nakhatā*)
**7.** Ankles without bulges (*niguḷa gopphakatā*)
**8.** Evenness of the tips of all ten toes (*sama padatā*)

**9.** Manner of walking majestically like an elephant (*gajasamān'akkamatā*)
**10.** Manner of walking majestically like a lion (*sīhasamān'akkamatā*)
**11.** Manner of walking majestically like a wild gander or sheldrake (*haṁsasamān'akkamatā*)
**12.** Manner of walking majestically like a bull (*usabhasamān'akkamatā*)
**13.** Manner of turning to the right when walking (*dakkhiṇāvaṭṭa gatitā*)
**14.** Knees that are beautifully rounded on all sides (*samantato cārujaṇṇu maṇḍalatā*)
**15.** Well developed male organ (*paripuṇṇa purisavyañjanatā*)
**16.** Navel with unbroken lines (*acchidda nābhitā*)
**17.** Deep navel (*gambhīra nābhitā*)
**18.** Navel with rightward-spiraling whorl (*dakkhiṇāvaṭṭa nābhitā*)
**19.** Thighs and arms like the trunk of an elephant (*dviradakara sadisa-uru-bhujatā*)
**20.** Well proportioned body/limbs (*suvibhatta gattatā*)
**21.** Gradually tapering body/limbs (*anupubba gattatā*)
**22.** Fine body/limbs (*maṭṭha gattatā*)
**23.** Neither lean nor plump body/limbs (*anussann'ānanussanna sabbagattatā*)
**24.** Wrinkle-free body/limbs (*alīna gattatā*)
**25.** Body/limbs devoid of moles, freckles, etc. (*tilakādivirahita gattatā*)
**26.** "Regularly lustrous" body/limbs (*anupubba rucira gattatā*)
**27.** Particularly clean body (*suvisuddha gattatā*)
**28.** Physical strength of ten billion (10,000,000,000) powerful elephants (*koṭisahassa hatthībala dhāraṇatā*)
**29.** Prominent nose like a goad (*tuṅga nāsatā*)
**30.** Very red gums (*suratta dvijamaṁsatā*)
**31.** Clean teeth (*suddha dantatā*)
**32.** Neat, smooth, glossy teeth (*siniddha dantatā*)
**33.** Very pure sense faculties (*visuddh'indriyatā*)
**34.** Cylindrical (rounded in cross section) canine teeth (*vaṭṭa dāṭhatā*)

**35.** Red lips (*ratt'oṭṭhatā*)
**36.** Elongate oral cavity (*āyata vadanatā*)
**37.** Deep lines on the palms of the hands (*gambhīra pāṇilekhatā*)
**38.** Long lines (*āyata lekhatā*)
**39.** Straight lines (*uju lekhatā*)
**40.** Beautifully formed lines (*surucira saṇṭhāna lekhatā*)
**41.** Circular nimbus around the body (*parimaṇḍala kāyappabhāvantatā*)
**42.** Full cheeks (*paripuṇṇa kapolatā*)
**43.** Long and broad eyes (*āyatavisāla nettatā*)
**44.** Very clear eyes endowed with five hues (*pañca pasādavanta nettatā*)
**45.** Eyelashes with upward-curling tips (*kuñjitagga bhamukatā*)
**46.** Soft, slender, red tongue (*mudu tanuka ratta jīvhatā*)
**47.** Long, beautiful ears (*āyata rucira kaṇṇatā*)
**48.** Veins free of varicosity (*nigganṭhi siratā*)
**49.** Veins without bulges (*niggūḷa siratā*)
**50.** Rounded, elegant head like a parasol (*vaṭṭa chatta nibha cāru sīsatā*)
**51.** Long, broad, graceful forehead (*āyata-puthu nalāṭa sobhatā*)
**52.** Naturally well-groomed eyebrows (*susaṇṭhāna bhamukatā*)
**53.** Soft eyebrows (*saṇha bhamukatā*)
**54.** "Regular" eyebrows (*anuloma bhamukatā*)
**55.** Large eyebrows (*mahanta bhamukatā*)
**56.** Long eyebrows (*āyata bhamukatā*)
**57.** Supple body (*sukumāla gattatā*)
**58.** Very relaxed body (*ativiya somma gattatā*)
**59.** Very shiny body (*ativiya ujjalita gattatā*)
**60.** Secretion-free body (*vimala gattatā*)
**61.** "Fresh-looking" body (*komala gattatā*)
**62.** Glossy, smooth body (*siniddha gattatā*)
**63.** Fragrant body (*sugandha tanutā*)
**64.** Body hairs of equal length (*sama lomatā*)
**65.** Soft body hairs (*komala lomatā*)
**66.** Body hairs spiraling to the right (*dakkhīṇavaṭṭa lomatā*)
**67.** Blue-black body hairs of the color of broken collyrium (*bhinn'añjana sadisa nīla lomatā*)

**68.** Cylindrical body hairs (*vaṭṭa lomatā*)
**69.** Glossy, smooth body hairs (*siniddha lomatā*)
**70.** Very subtle inhalation and exhalation (*atisukhuma assāsa-passāsa dharaṇatā*)
**71.** Fragrant mouth (*sugandha mukhatā*)
**72.** Fragrant top of the head (*sugandha muddhanatā*)
**73.** Jet black hair (*sunīla kesatā*)
**74.** Head hair curling to the right (*dakkhīṇavaṭṭa kesatā*)
**75.** Naturally well-groomed hair (*susaṇṭhāna kesatā*)
**76.** Glossy hair and soft hair (*siniddha kesatā saṇha kesatā*)
**77.** Untangled hair (*aluḷita kesatā*)
**78.** Head hairs of equal length (*sama kesatā*)
**79.** Soft head hair (*komala kesatā*)
**80.** A luminous halo like a garland of beams of light emanating from the top of the head (*ketumālāratana vicittatā*)

There is not much to comment upon with regard to this list; although it is interesting how roundness and turning to the right (dexter) instead of to the left (sinister) have been considered signs of "rightness" or perfection throughout the world. I am reminded of Aristotle's belief that celestial motions had to be circular in order to be divine.

There is one of these "lesser marks" that I dearly love, though, and can't resist the urge to comment upon it. Nestled between mark 27, "particularly clean body," and mark 29, "prominent nose like a goad," is "*physical strength of ten billion powerful elephants.*" And they're not just ordinary elephants, mind you, but particularly powerful ones; the subcommentary states that the elephants in question are of the *Kalavaka* breed, which are presumably the strongest kind. Can you imagine how strong someone as strong as *10,000,000,000* powerful elephants would be? Of course not. He could mop the floor with Superman. He could wave his hand through solid rock or steel like it was air. Standing on (very) solid ground, he could throw a Volkswagen to Pluto, assuming that his aim were good enough and that the Volkswagen could withstand the prodigious forces unleashed upon it. It boggles the mind. And intelligent men, serious scholar monks dedicated to the cultivation of wisdom, came up with this stuff—assuming, of course, that they did not simply record empirical facts. We are all conditioned by our culture.

The main reason I've taken the time to write about all this is just for the sake of playing with ideas. I am a little reluctant to publish this, though, as it might reinforce a tendency in Western Buddhism, and in Western attempts at spirituality in general, of people casually dismissing any parts they don't like, or have much use for, when they adopt a spiritual system as a hobby—parts like the metaphysical workings of karma, the fundamental importance of renunciation in Dhamma, or the real possibility of full enlightenment in this very life for those willing to make the commitment, for example. This really is a dilemma in spirituality: how to balance faith with reason. Skepticism is a good thing, especially skepticism in the classical sense of *suspending judgement,* either for or against. This applies not only to ancient mythology, but to modern materialistic common sense also. Not only should we be skeptical with regard to legendary accounts of the Buddha, we should be skeptical with regard to whether this world is even real or not, maybe even with regard to whether one plus one equals two. For myself, I seriously doubt that one plus one really does equal two.

As Ajahn Chah used to say, even right view becomes wrong view if we cling to it. That applies to "Matter exists" and "1+1=2" just as much as it does to "The Buddha was 26 feet tall with long heels and the strength of ten billion elephants," or even "Desire is the cause of all suffering." I feel that it is best to regard ALL information as hypothetical.

# THE SPIKE (OR: TO BE RECITED IN THE EVENT OF MY DEATH)

In Asia I think about death more than I do in the West. This is partly because the possibility of death is much more readily obvious in someplace like SE Asia: heat stroke, icky tropical diseases, snakebite, political/social upheaval, or whatever might suddenly leap from the sheer unknown. Also, especially during times of miserably hot weather, the feeling occasionally arises that death would be preferable to many more years of drenching sweat and heat prostration. In the West it seems more the established thing not to think much about death, but just to worry about getting old. But in traditional Theravada, thinking about death is very much encouraged.

So during my years-long exile in Burma I came up with the idea that, in the event of my death, I would like the Salla Sutta of the Sutta Nipāta recited at my cremation—in Pali of course, plus in the native languages of whoever happened to be attending. So I translated it into English, just in case any speakers of that language attend. The English translation is as follows.

**Discourse on the Spike (*Salla Sutta*)**
—Sutta Nipāta III.8

The life of mortals here is signless and uncertain;

It is troublesome and brief, and it is bound to unease.

Indeed, there is no means by which those born do not die.
Even for one who has reached a great old age there is death, for such is the way of living beings.

Just as for ripe fruit there is always danger of falling,
Even so for mortals who are born there is constantly danger of death.

And just as clay bowls made by a potter
All end in breaking, even so is this life of mortals.

Young and old, those who are foolish and those who are wise,
All go under the power of death; all are destined for death.

When they are overcome by death, going on to the other world,
The father does not give support to the son, nor do any relatives to any other relatives.

See, even as the relatives are looking on and each of them crying out,
Every mortal is led away, one by one, like a cow to be slaughtered.

Thus is the world stricken by death and old age.
Therefore the wise do not grieve, having realized the way of the world.

Whose path you do not know, either whence he has come or where he has gone,
Not seeing either end, you lament him pointlessly.

If, lamenting, a stupid person who is harming himself
Would derive some benefit, then a discerning person would do it also.

But not by weeping and grief does one attain to peace of mind.
One's unease simply increases, and one's body is harmed.

One becomes thin and unhealthy-looking, harming oneself by oneself.
Those who have passed away are not benefitted by this. Lamenting is pointless.

A fellow not abandoning grief increasingly suffers unease;
Bewailing the deceased he falls under the power of grief.

See others also going along, men going in accordance with their actions,
Living beings floundering about here in the world, having come under the power of death.

For in whatever way they imagine, it happens other than that.
The state of separation is such as this. See the way of the world.

Even if a man would live a hundred years or more
He comes to be separated from the community of his relatives; he leaves behind life in this world.

Therefore having heard the Worthy One, one should dismiss lamentation.
Seeing the one who has passed away, one should think, "I can't have him any more."

Just as a burning shelter would be put out with water,
Even so a wise man endowed with understanding, an intelligent, skillful man,
Would quickly blow away any grief that has arisen, as the wind would do to a wisp of cotton.

Lamentation and longing, and one's own unhappiness—
One seeking ease for oneself should pull out the spike in oneself.

With the spike pulled out, unattached, having attained peace of mind,
Gone beyond all sorrow, the sorrowless one is completely gone out.

The Discourse is pretty much self-explanatory, so a detailed commentary would be superfluous. The title and the final verses, though, contain an ancient Buddhist metaphor that is noteworthy —the *salla*, i.e. the spike.

*Salla* has no direct equivalent in the English language. It apparently can mean any sharp, piercing object. A spike is a *salla.* A thorn can be a *salla.* Apparently a dart-like weapon used in ancient India was called a *salla.* A surgeon's probe is called a *salla.* So also is the quill of a porcupine. K. R. Norman, in his translation of the Sutta Nipāta, rendered it as "the barb." The main thing is that it stabs into the flesh. It pierces us, resulting in our suffering.

The spike is a common metaphor in very early Buddhist literature, but seems to have fallen out of fashion in later times. It is mentioned several times in the Sutta Nipāta, a collection which contains some very ancient texts. The Aṭṭhakavagga, very possibly the largest existing fragment of "primitive" Buddhist literature, begins and ends with discourses mentioning "the spike." One text within the Aṭṭhakavagga, the aptly-named "Discourse on the Uptaken Stick" (Attadaṇḍa Sutta), gives in its first few stanzas a poetic description of this affliction of the human heart:

Fear is born by a stick one has acquired;
Look at people in conflict.
I shall relate to you a feeling of urgency,
How it was felt by me.

Having seen mankind thrashing about
Like fishes in little water,
Obstructed by one another—
Having seen, fear took hold of me.

The world was entirely without substance;
All the quarters were shaken.
Wanting a settled abiding for myself
I saw nothing that had not succumbed.

But even in succumbing people are obstructed—
Having seen this, disaffection arose in me.
Then I saw a spike [*salla*] here,
Hard to see, stuck in the heart.

Subjected to this spike
Through all the quarters one runs about:
Having pulled out just this spike
One does not run, one does not sink.

Thus it appears that the spike is not simply death, as might be inferred from the discourse which takes its name. The spike is grief—chronic anxiety, or angst, arising from our friction and resistance against a world that we ourselves create. It is like someone having a dream at night and struggling to be free of the dream that they themself are creating. It is the spike of dissatisfaction with the way things are, as a result of our own doing; wanting them to change, or, just as unskillful, wanting them not to change.

(As an aside, the metaphor of not running and not sinking, found in the last quoted verse, is also a very ancient one, being found in other texts as well as this one—possibly the most well-known example of it would be the very first Sutta of the Saṁyutta Nikāya. I interpret it to mean that a wise person doesn't continue chasing his or her tail through Samsara, yet also doesn't simply fade out into stillness, unconsciousness, or oblivion. It is, like many metaphors for enlightenment, the razor's edge between the two horns of a paradox.)

I conclude this exposé of the spike in our hearts with one more early Sutta from the Sutta Nipāta.

**Discourse on Arousal (*Uṭṭhāna Sutta*)**

—Sutta Nipāta II.10

Get up! Sit up!
What use to you is sleep?
What rest is there for the afflicted,
Pierced with a spike and in distress?

Get up! Sit up!
Train steadfastly for peace.
Let not the king of death, knowing you to be clouded in mind,
Confuse you so you are come under his power.

Cross over this attachment
By which gods and men stay clinging and longing.
Let not the moment pass you by,
For those whose moment is passed sorrow indeed
When consigned to hell.

Cloudedness of mind, pollution, cloudedness of mind—
Following upon cloudedness of mind is pollution.
With uncloudedness of mind and with wisdom
One should pull out one's own spike.

# ABHIDHAMMA STUDIES I: "ERADICATING ABHIDHAMMA FROM THE FACE OF THE EARTH"

*"This book will be the guiding star of your life! Buddha's teachings will enlighten you to understand real knowledge and ultimate truths!" (—Dr. Mehm Tin Mon, PhD., Saddhamma Jotikadhaja, on the cover of his book The Essence of Buddha Abhidhamma, which a Western monk in Burma can hardly avoid, being offered a new copy almost as soon as he gets rid of the old one)*

The third receptacle, or "basket," of canonical texts in the Pali Tipitaka is Abhidhamma, which represents an attempt to systematize the teachings of the Suttas into one coherent, comprehensive system. In Burma it is generally considered to be the most profound and most important portion of the teachings of Gotama Buddha; and no monk is considered well educated if he has not studied it extensively. The Burmese government holds yearly national Abhidhamma examinations, and those who score highest receive public honors and titles.

Anyone who has spent much time in Burma will be familiar with the *Patthan pweh,* or Paṭṭhāna festival—an event in which monks recite Paṭṭhāna, the last portion of the Abhidhamma Piṭaka, over loudspeakers, in relay, sometimes around the clock for several days in succession. To a Westerner who appreciates peace and quiet they are little more than an affliction, but the Burmese love and esteem them. I have often considered that it would be more to the people's benefit to recite something they would actually understand, like a Burmese translation of the Dhammapada; as even most of the monks who chant Paṭṭhāna in Pali don't really understand it. It is considered to be "unreadable" as a literary document, even to those who know Pali.

The reason for these very loud chanting festivals is that, according to the commentarial tradition, the last book of the last section of the Canon (i.e., Paṭṭhāna), will be the first portion of the Tipitaka to disappear from this world, in accordance with the inexorable effects of impermanence. So by repeating these practically incomprehensible texts the monks are doing their best to keep Buddhism from disappearing from the earth. However—while Burmese monks revere and preserve Abhidhamma, the other two sections, Vinaya and the Suttas, are studied but not practiced all that much, allowing the disappearance to occur from first to last. For example, some monks specialize in chanting Paṭṭhāna at these festivals, charge for their services, and make quite a lot of money by doing it.

Whether Thai and Sinhalese monks share this reverence for Abhidhamma I don't know—I've never seen much sign of it in them if they do—but Western monks certainly have a different attitude toward it. More than half of Western monks, possibly more than three-fourths, consider Abhidhamma to be apocrypha, not taught by the Buddha at all, or for that matter by any enlightened being.

It is true that there are some non-Burmese people, including monks, who do believe and revere Abhidhamma; and rather amazingly, venerable Pah Auk Sayadaw, whose system is heavily based on it as well as on the commentarial tradition, has quite a few followers in the West and has even conducted 3-month retreats at the Insight Meditation Society in Massachusetts. Some of these people are even a bit fanatical about it: Once I heard of a woman who came to Burma to study Abhidhamma, and as the Sayadaw she went to didn't speak English very well, he suggested to her another Abhidhamma scholar who had studied English; the woman replied that if he had studied English she wasn't interested in being his student, as she wanted a master who had studied *only* Abhidhamma! Anyone whose attention had deviated from the Buddha's highest teachings was not master enough for her.

Still, most of us Westerners, myself included, pay little heed to Abhidhamma. I once was in correspondence with a British monk who called Abhidhamma scholars "abhidummies," who compiled a long list of faults in the abhidhammic approach to Dhamma, and who was of the opinion that the Abhidhamma Piṭaka should be "burnt at the stake." An American monk friend and I used to semi-joke about how our mission in life was to eradicate Abhidhamma from the face of the earth; and I even formulated a few oaths using the "*A* word," such as, "Your mother was an Abhidhamma scholar and your father smelled of elderberries."

Back around 1997, as an appendix to the first Dhamma essay I ever wrote, I listed evidence suggesting the less than authentic nature of Abhidhamma. It is included, in very slightly modified form, as an appendix to this post. I intend to discuss problematic Abhidhamma issues in another post also; but here I'll add the suspicious origin story accounting for the third Piṭaka. According to the commentarial tradition, one monsoon season the Buddha ascended into a heaven world, leaving behind a kind of holographic projection of himself so that those on earth would not notice his absence. He taught Abhidhamma to the gods and goddesses up there, and eventually a condensed version of it was released to human beings. The day the Buddha returned to earth, on the last day of the rains retreat (the full moon of October), is a national holiday in Burma, called Abhidhamma Day. Yet this legend seems suspiciously like a story made up after the fact to explain why a new system had suddenly appeared that was attributed to the Buddha—that is, explaining why, if the Buddha really taught it, nobody had ever heard of it before. It strikes me as very similar to the legend that the Buddha himself taught Mahayana, but since so few people in his day were wise enough to appreciate it (!) he caused the Mahayana scriptures to be hidden in the ocean and guarded by dragons for five hundred years. It is also somewhat similar to Tibetan monks "finding" previously unknown teachings of the Buddha in Himalayan caves even in modern times. Well, maybe a few of them are authentic. Maybe.

I am going to the trouble of debunking Abhidhamma philosophy here, although there are a few salient considerations. First is that even though Abhidhamma can hardly be considered Ultimate Truth by most critically-thinking Westerners, it may qualify as *conventional truth* so long as people believe it; and if it helps them to practice, or otherwise to approach nearer to enlightenment, then there is nothing wrong with that.

Also, all of this may be barking up the wrong tree in the West, as few Westerners, including Dhamma teachers, have more than a very superficial acquaintance with it. Besides, Westerners have their own equivalent of Abhidhamma, which they call *Science.* I prophesy that two hundred years from now, assuming that civilization hasn't collapsed by then, scientific materialism as a world view will be seen as just as unrealistic in its attempts to describe and explain reality as scientists nowadays would consider to be true of Abhidhamma. For a critique of the religion of the modern West, i.e., *Scientism,* which even Western Christians and Buddhists believe more than they believe Christianity and Buddhism, I refer the reader to the article "Buddhism and Scientism" on the website nippapanca.org. Here I will simply conclude the matter with a relevant quotation.

> *"To adopt scientific realism consciously, we must accept a number of underlying premises: (1) there is a physical world that*

*exists independently of human experience; (2) it can be grasped by human concepts (mathematical or otherwise); (3) among a potentially infinite number of conceptual systems that can account for observed phenomena, only one is true of reality; (4) science is now approaching that one true theory; and (5) scientists will know when they have found it. It seems a safe guess that most people who adopt the view of scientific realism are not aware of the many articles of faith that this view entails." —B. Alan Wallace, in Choosing Reality: A Contemplative View of Physics and the Mind (Shambhala, 1989)*

# ABHIDHAMMA STUDIES II: ARISING AND PASSING AWAY

A tenet of fundamental importance in Buddhist philosophy is *anicca,* usually translated into English as "impermanence." A spontaneous, direct realization of anicca is considered to be a main ingredient of liberating insight; and the ancient Pali texts have standardized the "spotless, immaculate vision of Dhamma" which is the first glimpse of enlightenment as "All that is subject to arising is subject to cessation." Clearly, this is an important truth to realize.

The Abhidhamma philosophy of Theravada Buddhism has interpreted this impermanence to mean that every conditioned entity in the universe exists for only about a trillionth of an eyeblink, i.e. less than a thousandth of a nanosecond. Thus whatever seems to last longer than this is really a series of individual entities flashing into and out of existence at unimaginably rapid speed. This idea has diffused out of Abhidhamma, and has come to be considered a mainstream tenet of Theravadin philosophy as a whole; and it has been cited as authoritative Buddhism by very reputable Western Dharma teachers, including Ram Dass.

However, this doctrine, if examined carefully, proves to be problematic.

One relatively obvious difficulty is that if everything blinks out of existence and then back into it again, we have something essentially arising from nothing. Let's say a particle A arises, then passes away, followed at the next moment by a corresponding particle B. Well, what is the *cause* for the arising of this particle B? Really, it can't be A, because A simply no longer exists. So B is arising from a nonexistent cause, which is the same as no cause at all. It arises literally from nothing. Theravada Buddhist philosophy does not endorse an Einsteinian interpretation of time, accepting that the past still exists somehow; the past is dead and gone. Because of this interpretation of impermanence, all cause and effect becomes inexplicable. If the arising and passing away were interpreted as a pulsation, with particle A not entirely disappearing, or perhaps undergoing a kind of phase through this version of space and into another, or whatever, then the theory might be saved, but Abhidhamma doesn't interpret reality this way, and I have no idea how the Abhidhamma scholars explain this seemingly glaring glitch in the system. They may have some way of explaining it, but I've never heard what it is.

Another apparent difficulty in this idea of extremely rapid arising, passing away, arising, and passing away involves the fact that meditators are actually required to *see* this happening in order to fully realize impermanence, and thus to get that first taste of enlightenment. Once after spending several months practicing in a forest I met with a Burmese monk friend of mine, who asked me about my meditation. He listened with great interest to what I had been experiencing, and then asked, eagerly, "Did you see *phyit-pyet*?" (i.e. did I see the momentary arising and passing away of phenomena). When I told him I didn't even particularly want to see it, his reaction was something like "pffft," and he immediately lost interest. According to many Burmese, if you don't see *phyit-pyet* you can't amount to much of anything as a meditator. Sayadaw U Pandita of the Mahasi tradition has declared many times that one should not accept a Dhamma teacher who has not at least experienced *udayabbaya ñāṇa,* the insight into arising and passing away, interpreted as seeing this trillion-times-per-second process.

The trouble lies in how seeing this could even be possible. It is not only matter, but also one's own mind which arises and passes away in this manner, and consciousness cannot be aware of its own nonexistence. So when phenomena, both mind and matter, are in their nonexistent phase, the meditator, no matter how advanced, could not be aware of it. The nonexistent sub-moments would not be experienced at all, and the existent ones would blend together like the frames in a movie film projected on a screen.

I once spent a rains retreat at the same place as a Western monk who was a disciple of venerable Pah Auk Sayadaw, and who thus naturally took the Pah Auk method and Abhidhamma much more seriously than most; and we occasionally debated this issue of whether or not the mind's own nonexistence could be experienced. He stressed that the meditator does not experience it as it is happening, but "reviews" it afterwards. However, this would seem to require one of two things—either the meditator is remembering the past, or else he/she is seeing into the past clairvoyantly. But neither alternative seems to work, since one can't remember what one never experienced, and looking into the past, according to Abhidhamma, is impossible since the past is absolutely no longer existing, and one cannot *see* what is nonexistent. Again, I have no idea how the Abhidhamma scholars, let alone successful Pah Auk meditators, could explain their way through this apparent impasse, despite the odd fact that many meditators sincerely believe they have seen everything, including their own mind, arising and passing away. (Incidentally, we also occasionally debated whether or not it is possible to really experience physical matter; but that is material for a different essay than this one.)

According to Abhidhamma, the mind arises and passes away at a rate seventeen times faster than does physical matter. For each moment of matter, a seventeen-stage mental process called *citta-vīthi* is claimed to occur. This process is also supposed to be observed by very advanced meditators; although this implies some more convoluted complications.

Orthodox dogma asserts that when nothing worth our while is occurring internally or externally, our mind is occupied by a kind of subconscious "test pattern" called *bhavaṅga.* This mental state remains exactly the same throughout a person's lifetime, and represents a single image, usually the last conscious perception that passed through one's mind in the previous life before the present "incarnation." *Bhavaṅga,* despite its seeming importance, is not discussed in the Suttas, but is mentioned only in the commentarial literature.

Anyway, a typical *citta-vīthi* would be something like the following: (1) Something, like a sensory object, arises to disturb the stream of *bhavaṅga*; (2) the *bhavaṅga* is then displaced, or "vibrates," although, of course, it would not have time really to vibrate within a single moment; (3) the stream of *bhavaṅga* is then cut off, leaving only the sensory object behind; (4) sensory consciousness is then directed toward the object; (5) sensory consciousness experiences the object, thereby initiating a "sense impression"; (6) consciousness "receives" the sensory object along with the sense impression in preparation for the next stage; (7) consciousness then investigates the object and the sense impression; (8) it then determines whether the object is *good* or *bad*; (9-15) this is followed by seven mind-moments of "conscious impulsion" (*javana*) which savor the sense impression; (16-17) which is then followed by two moments of "registering consciousness" in which the impression is fully registered in the mind. With the end of the second moment of registering consciousness the mind lapses back into the stream of *bhavaṅga* until another stimulus interrupts it. This would be a typical example of the process, although there are variations. Again, all of this should be observed by the meditator wishing to see ultimate reality.

However, it would seem that this would be impossible, even for a fully enlightened Buddha. For starters, one could not observe the seventeen-step process because it requires a complete seventeen-step process to perceive anything, including one of the seventeen steps. So by the time the very first step had been perceived, the other sixteen would no longer be existing to be observed.

Also, if one were observing one's own mental processes, the only step that could be an object of perception would presumably be the very last one, the second "registering consciousness." If one were telepathically observing the mind of someone else one might have the chance of seeing some of the internal steps in the process; but one still couldn't see them happening in sequence—and thus making a seventeen-step process out of it, not including all the *bhavaṅgas*, would require a great deal of inference and deduction, not direct observation.

The very fact that so many meditators sincerely believe that they have experienced this momentary arising and passing away of phenomena, including their own mental processes, is some fairly good evidence that much of what passes for deep meditative states (*jhāna*) in Theravada Buddhism is actually hypnotic trance, and the resultant "insight" merely the result of hypnotic suggestion. Not all insight is bogus of course, and not all *jhāna* either, but much of it is; and I would guess that most people who consider themselves to be *ariyas*, or Buddhist "saints" who have had at least a glimpse of Nibbāna, are mistaken. Especially if their tradition insists that they are required to see what is impossible, yet they manage to see it anyway.

If anyone can explain to me how Abhidhamma makes sense of all this I would be grateful, and will be happy to publish the clarification of the apparent paradoxes. I'm especially curious to find out how causation can happen at all if everything necessarily arises from nothing. The problem of how rebirth can occur instantaneously over long distances is rendered rather trivial when one realizes that contiguous causation from one moment to the next is equally inexplicable.

Personally, I suppose it might be better just to bear impermanence in mind according to the stock formula in the Suttas: *All that is subject to arising is subject to cessation.* Well said, and good enough.

# THE OUTSIDER (THE BĀHIYA SUTTA)

*(This is another one of my all-time favorite Theravada Buddhist texts, with some commentary. I go for the strange ones, and I can sympathize with outsiders.)*

In retrospect, I suppose it would have been more appropriate to have named my first blog "The Bahiya Blog." I named it Nippapañca because it's my favorite synonym for Nirvana, and because my website and email address were already called that. But nippapañca means something like "non-differentiation," and what can one write about that? The more one writes, the more differentiated everything gets. Writing about non-differentiation can get rather complicated actually.

But *bāhiya* means "outsider"; and that description seems to fit the contents and the author of these essaysmuch better. Even though I was born and raised in America, I'm certainly an outsider to the modern American way of life, even to the modern American Buddhist way of life. But I don't think like a native-born Asian either, and probably wouldn't even if I could, so I'm an outsider in the East as well as in the West. I'm pretty much of an outsider in the Sangha also, and pretty much always have been. But being an outsider definitely has its advantages, and so I'm not complaining. For one thing, an outsider to any system can see it from unusual and interesting angles; and I especially like unusual and interesting angles with regard to Dharma.

Also, as it turns out, one of my favorite discourses in the Pali

Canon is the Bāhiya Sutta, a strange sutta about a non-Buddhist philosopher (hence the name "Outsider") who was so eager to learn, so sincere, and so in tune with what the Buddha told him that he became enlightened almost immediately, despite the fact that he wasn't ordained into the Buddha's dispensation. Anyway, here is a translation of the text. I'll follow up with some unofficial commentary afterwards.

~ ~ ~

**The Bāhiya Discourse (Udāna 1:10)**

Thus have I heard: One time the Blessed One was residing at Savatthi, in Jetavana, in Anathapindika's park. At that same time, Bahiya the tree-bark wearer was staying at Supparaka, near the seashore, being honored, respected, venerated, adored, and worshipped, receiving the requisites of robes, alms food, lodging places, and medicines for the sick. Then to Bahiya the tree-bark wearer, having gone off alone, while in seclusion, the thought arose to his mind: "Whoever there are in this world who are Worthy Ones (*arahanto*), or who have attained the path to the state of being Worthy Ones, I am one of them."

Then a deity who had formerly been a close relative of Bahiya the tree-bark wearer, compassionate and desiring Bahiya the tree-bark wearer's welfare, having understood in his mind the thought which arose to the mind of Bahiya the tree-bark wearer, approached him. Having approached Bahiya the tree-bark wearer, he said: "Bahiya, you are neither a Worthy One nor one who has attained the path to the state of being a Worthy One. That way is not yours, by which you might become a Worthy One or someone attained to the path to the state of being a Worthy One."

"Then who in the world with its deities is a Worthy One, or one attained to the path of being a Worthy One?"

"Bahiya, in the northern districts there is a city called Savatthi. Now the Blessed One resides there, a Worthy One, a truly, fully Awakened One. That Blessed One it is, Bahiya, who is Worthy, and who teaches the Way to the state of being a Worthy One."

Then Bahiya the tree-bark wearer, being stirred in spirit by that deity, immediately left Supparaka, sleeping only one night at every stopping place till he arrived at Savatthi, Jetavana, Anathapindika's park. At that time there were several monks doing walking meditation in the open air, so Bahiya the tree-bark wearer approached those monks. Approaching those monks, he said, "Venerable Sirs, where is the Blessed One who resides here now, the Worthy One, truly, fully Awakened? I want to see that Blessed One, that Worthy One, that truly, fully Awakened One."

"Bahiya, the Blessed One has entered among the houses for alms."

So then Bahiya the tree-bark wearer, in a great hurry, left Jetavana, and, having entered Savatthi, he saw the Blessed One walking for alms in Savatthi: serene, inspiring serenity, with peaceful faculties, with peaceful mind, having attained the ultimate restraint and tranquillity, a Great One (*nāga*) restrained, watchful, and with secured faculties. Having seen the Blessed One he approached him, and having approached him he bowed his head to the Blessed One's feet, and said this to the Blessed One: "Venerable Sir, Blessed One, teach me the Way. Let the Fortunate One teach the Way which will be for my benefit and happiness for a long time."

This being said, the Blessed One said to Bahiya the tree-bark wearer, "This is not a good time, Bahiya. I am entered among the houses for alms."

A second time Bahiya the tree-bark wearer said to the Blessed One, "It is difficult to know, Venerable Sir, when the life of the Blessed One will come to an end, or when my own life will come to an end. Venerable Sir, let the Blessed One teach me the Way. Let the Fortunate One teach the Way which will be for my benefit and happiness for a long time."

And a second time the Blessed One said to Bahiya the tree-bark wearer, "This is not a good time, Bahiya. I am entered among the houses for alms."

But a third time Bahiya the tree-bark wearer said to the Blessed One, "It is difficult to know, Venerable Sir, when the life of the Blessed One will come to an end, or when my own life will come to an end. Venerable Sir, let the Blessed One teach me the Way. Let the Fortunate One teach the Way which will be for my benefit and happiness for a long time."

"Well then, Bahiya, thus should you train yourself—In the seen there will be only the seen, in the heard there will be only the heard, in the felt there will be only the felt, in the mentally sensed there will be only the mentally sensed. Just so, Bahiya, should you train yourself. And since, Bahiya, in the seen there will be only the seen, in the heard there will be only the heard, in the felt there will be only the felt, and in the mentally sensed there will be only the mentally sensed, from that you, Bahiya, are not *thereby.* And since, Bahiya, you are not *thereby,* you, Bahiya, are not *therein.* And since, Bahiya, you are not *therein*, you, Bahiya, have no here, no hereafter, no between the two. Just this is the end of unease."

Then, when Bahiya the tree-bark wearer had heard from the Blessed One this concentrated teaching of the Way, right then and there his mind was liberated from the encumbering influences, without uptake.

Then the Blessed One, having exhorted Bahiya the tree-bark wearer with this concentrated exhortation, departed. And then, shortly after the Blessed One's departure, a cow, a yearling heifer, charged Bahiya the tree-bark wearer and deprived him of life.

Then the Blessed One, having walked for alms in Savatthi, after his meal and returning from alms round with many monks, upon leaving the town saw that Bahiya the tree-bark wearer was dead. And having seen, he said to the monks, "Take up the body of Bahiya the tree-bark wearer. Put him on a cot, carry him away, and cremate him. Monks, it is a fellow liver of the Holy Life who has died."

"Even so, venerable sir," those monks replied to the Blessed One; so having taken up the body of Bahiya the tree-bark wearer on a cot, having taken it away and cremating it, and also having erected a burial mound over it, they approached the Blessed One. Having approached the Blessed One, and having paid their respects, they sat down to one side. And sitting at one side, those monks said this to the Blessed One: "Venerable sir, the body of Bahiya the tree-bark wearer has been burned, and a burial mound has been erected. What is his fate? What has become of him after death?"

"A wise man, monks, was Bahiya the tree-bark wearer. He entered upon the Way in accordance with the Way, and he did no violence to my dispensation of the Way. Completely blown out, monks, is Bahiya the tree-bark wearer."

Then the Blessed One, having understood this matter deeply, on this occasion he uttered this inspired utterance:

*Where water and earth, fire and wind gain no foothold,*
*There the stars do not shine, the sun does not blaze,*
*And there the moon does not glow; yet darkness there is not to be found.*

*And when a sage, through sagacity, a Holy Man, has known this for himself,*
*Then from form and formlessness, from ease and unease, he is freed.*

And this inspired utterance was spoken by the Blessed One; and thus have I heard it.

~ ~ ~

Thus the discourse. The Udāna Pali, of which this sutta is a part, is considered by Western experts on such matters to be a relatively very ancient text, common to many ancient schools of Buddhism; although the prose and verse parts are not considered to be necessarily contemporaneous in origin. It appears that if a sutta contains both verse and prose, the verse is typically older, with the prose material being a sort of commentary which was later incorporated into it. But with the Udāna, some of the prose appears to be very old; and the narrative of the Bāhiya Sutta appears, if only because of the unusualness and freshness of the subject matter, to be possibly even older than the inspired utterance itself. At any rate some of it is arguably at least as profound as the inspired utterance. But enough of theorizing about how ancient things are.

I've read some comments by a person named Leigh Brasington saying that Bahiya (I leave out the macron over the first "a" for convenience's sake) was probably a Brahmin ascetic who followed the Brihadaranyaka Upanishad. Brasington's reasons for coming to this conclusion were that a garment made of tree bark was common to these Brahmins, and that the Buddha's statements were reminiscent of teachings of the Brihadaranyaka itself, for example:

> *"The unseen seer, the unheard hearer, the unthought thinker, the uncognized cognizer....There is no other seer but he, no other hearer, no other thinker, no other cognizer. This is thy self, the inner controller, the immortal...." (—Brihadaranyaka Upanishad 3.7.23),*

and

> *"...that imperishable is the unseen seer, the unheard hearer, the unthought thinker, the ununderstood understander. Other than it there is naught that sees. Other than it there is naught that hears. Other than it there is naught that thinks. Other than it there is naught that understands...." (—ibid. 3.8.11).*

So the Buddha apparently modified the message of the Upanishad to emphasize *anattā*, No Self, presumably because Bahiya's interpretation of the upanishadic view of Self was interfering with his spiritual development. Thus this discourse may present some of the strongest evidence in the Pali texts that the Buddha was familiar with Upanishadic literature. No evidence is conclusive though.

The garment of bark probably consisted of fibrous inner bark material woven into a rough fabric, like burlap.

Supparaka was a seaport very near to what is now Mumbai (Bombay); so it would have been roughly a thousand miles away from where the Buddha was residing. So Bahiya's march was a very long one.

I used "Worthy One" as a rendering of *arahant* because that is literally what the word means. Apparently it was used for dignitaries in general in ancient India, and was adopted by the Buddhists and turned into a technical term meaning "enlightened being." The ancient Buddhists did a lot of that kind of adopting and adjusting of terms. But *araha* meaning "worthy" was not even necessarily a positive word in ancient times. For instance, in the Pali texts someone worthy of punishment can be called *araha*, worthy, of that punishment.

Most of the story is self-explanatory, so I won't insult your intelligence by explaining it. The Buddha's cryptic, Zen-like admonishment to Bahiya at the climax of the tale, however, is unusually deep for a Pali text. It's not just hard to understand, it's downright mysterious. But the profundity of the statement lies in its utter simplicity. The meaning seems to be something like this: If we experience mindfulness in such a way that we are totally in the present moment, not relying upon memory and associations at all to interpret what we are experiencing (unless of course it happens spontaneously, in which case we don't elaborate on this natural process but leave it exactly as it is), then the relations which entangle us in this world (*thereby*) fall away, causing "us" (*therein*), without support, also to fall away. Nothing can exist without relations. And this dissolution of an illusory self through being wide awake in the present moment, not clinging to an autobiography and a metaphysical interpretation to hold our psychological world together, is enlightenment.

Interestingly, it seems like most meditation teachers, at least in Burma, use the Buddha's instruction to Bahiya as support for their own method...and in my opinion every one of them uses it incorrectly. For example, teachers of the Mahasi method cite "in the seen there will be only the seen..." in support of the Mahasi method, *despite the plain fact* that the Mahasi method certainly does *not* teach only the seen. The Mahasi method and every other such method I've come across teaches noting or some other mental action or reaction in addition to the seen, the heard, etc. And if you are noting the seen, then you no longer have only the seen, do you. You have the seen AND the noting of the seen. With the Buddha's instruction in this text, the mind is essentially in a state the Christian mystics would call high contemplation, and the mind would be like a mirror, clearly reflecting whatever is set before it, but not reacting at all, not even focusing on this instead of that. The mirror clearly reflects, but does absolutely nothing, effortlessly. (Since writing this a monk ordained into the Mahasi tradition has informed me that the late venerable Mahasi Sayadaw himself did in fact teach such "panoramic mindfulness" to his very advanced disciples, although some teachers of the Mahasi method assert that one never stops noting in the practice.)

At the part where Bahiya becomes enlightened, I rendered the word *āsava*, usually rendered as "taint" or "canker" or some such, as "encumbering influence." This is because the Pali word literally means something that flows inward, towards the subject, which is what *influence* literally means also. I have read that the early Buddhists borrowed this term from the Jains, who considered karma to be a kind of sticky substance that flows into or onto our soul (*jīva*) and weighs it down, keeping it in this world. Thus an *āsava* is an influence that holds us down, so to speak. It keeps us from being free.

Also, I rendered the term *upādāna*, which is usually translated as "clinging," quite literally as "uptake," since that's what it actually says, and because it seems to me slightly more descriptive of what really happens. We take something up, even if only in our desires, and make it "ours," which of course messes life all up. According to the classic formula, craving leads to uptake, and uptake leads to the motive force of existence (*bhava*). I have read that in ancient India *upādāna* could also mean fuel, firewood; and of course it is the blowing out of the fire which is *nibbāna,* Nirvana.

It may seem strange that almost immediately after Waking Up, Bahiya is killed by a cow. Not even by a bull, or even a *big* cow, but by a little, female cow. There are two themes involved in this. First there is the idea, found in the commentaries and ignored by most Western laypeople, that although it is possible for someone not ordained in the Sangha to become enlightened, they'd better find a bowl, robes, and an ordination hall immediately, because no enlightened being who isn't an officially ordained Buddhist monk or nun will survive for more than one day. It may be, though, that this rather strange notion arose *after* stories like the one about Bahiya. Bahiya may have helped to set the precedent, and to give birth to the idea.

Again according to the commentarial tradition, there is another reason why Bahiya was killed by a (female) cow. In a previous life Bahiya was one of a group of four friends. One day, in a fit of criminal rascality, these four friends hired a prostitute to accompany them to a pleasure garden. They gang-raped her there, or committed some similar atrocity anyhow, which resulted in the girl's death. Her spirit longed for vengeance as a result of this, causing her to be reborn in demonic forms which sought revenge on her erstwhile murderers. In the case of this sutta she had assumed the form of a cow to wreak her revenge on the man who was now Bahiya. All four of the former friends eventually were killed by the being who had formerly been the prostitute.

When the Buddha says that Bahiya is "completely blown out" (*parinibbuto*) he asserts that Bahiya died in an enlightened state; and the final verses are also a "description" of that which cannot be described, i.e., Nirvana. No elements there. No light, and no darkness. No form, no formlessness. No ease, no unease. In short, Nirvana is beyond duality, and also beyond differentiation. Which brings us back to *nippapañca*, and the impossibility of really describing it, so I'll stop here.

# REFLECTIONS ON AMERICAN "PROTESTANT THERAVADA"

*(This essay was written rather late in the history of my first blog, after I had become gradually more exposed to western social issues influencing Buddhism. It is still pretty mild compared with some of my later stuff, but still it represents one of my early attempts to address the modern western mind's not entirely positive effects on a very ancient eastern enlightenment tradition.)*

In a previously written essay ("Dilemmas of Spirit," to be published in the book Buddhist Ethics, Buddhist Practice) I discussed some dilemmas which are practically inevitable to spirituality and spiritual systems, and one of those that I discussed was this: We must choose between wise, spiritually advanced systems that are so advanced that very few people can successfully practice them, resulting in great benefit for only a very few; or on the other hand relatively elementary systems that are so easy to understand and follow that almost anyone can practice them, although with almost none of them coming anywhere near to liberation as a consequence. So either way, benefits are minimal—either big benefits for a tiny minority, or small benefits for the great majority. Furthermore, there is an additional sub-dilemma that, over time, the first type of system tends to degenerate into the second.

Gotama Buddha, needless to say, was an extremely wise person; and it appears that he set up his system, known to the West as "Buddhism," in such a way as to transcend the aforementioned dilemma, and to avoid the sub-dilemma. What he did was to establish a system with two levels: Those who were willing and able to strive for full Enlightenment in this very life entered the Sangha and renounced home life, renounced worldliness, and became wandering, vagrant, radical ascetic meditators; while those who were not willing and able, yet who were willing to support those who were, and who had the humbler intention of just attaining a better situation in Samsara (like heaven or a good human rebirth), remained in lay life and practiced morality and generosity. Thus Dharma encompassed both horns of the dilemma, allowing its followers to follow a Path to total Liberation or a lesser, yet still wholesome and praiseworthy, Path to Heaven.

This system, although set up carefully and wisely, has degenerated in Asia somewhat over the centuries, largely because the Sangha became more a kind of secular priesthood than a community of ardent spiritual seekers striving for Enlightenment. On the other hand, in the West, especially in America, this bilevel system has been largely rejected with indifference, or even with contempt. American Theravada seems to be aiming for a "middle way" between unworldly renunciation and just settling for a better rebirth—but it falls between two stools, or perhaps falls far to the left of the lay-life stool, considering that meditation is taken up at an elementary level, but the lay virtues of keeping precepts and practicing generosity, especially generosity to renunciants, are largely abandoned by the majority. The result is mediocrity, sometimes smug mediocrity, with, as before, transcendental or liberating benefit for almost nobody.

This rejection of the distinction between Sangha and the lay community, for some even a scornful rejection of an ordained Sangha at all, has many contributing causes, not the least of which are humanism (which encourages the idea that we are all equal and equally worthy of respect), materialism (which contributes to lack of faith and general lukewarmness, as well as to the idea that everyone should do some worldly work for a living) and consumerism (which results in addiction to comfort and convenience, and resentment of serious practices like renunciation); but I do not intend to catalog the whole slew of contributing factors. Instead I'd like to emphasize one factor that to most American Buddhists is probably invisible: and that is our Germanic, Protestant Christian cultural conditioning.

Our cultural conditioning tends to be invisible to us. When I moved to rural Burma it struck me that Burmese villagers have no idea that their beliefs and behavior are so very obviously culturally conditioned. Then I went back to America, and it struck me that American Buddhist meditators have no idea that their beliefs and behavior are so obviously culturally conditioned. Probably all but a relatively few humans are aware of how culturally conditioned they are—mostly some educated, open-minded cosmopolitans who have been immersed in multiple, very different cultures. But even they tend to be oblivious to most of their *human* conditioning. It is extremely difficult to see ourselves objectively.

Even so, English-speaking Americans, and many Europeans also, are practically soaking in Protestant Christian cultural conditioning, regardless of whether they profess Protestant Christianity. For example, the English language shapes how Americans think, and the language itself is shaped significantly by traditional Protestant attitudes and assumptions. It is probably easier to discuss Protestantism than, say, Buddhism in the English language. We tend to think like traditional Protestants regardless of whether we sit in yoga posture and practice mindfulness of breathing.

This conditioning is invisible partly because our thinking mind is shaped by it, and we were raised into it; and it is also invisible partly because its roots extend all the way back to ancient Germanic culture. American culture is based mainly on English culture, and English culture (as opposed to Celtic Brittonic) began with Germanic culture. Probably most people do not realize that the English language, linguistically speaking, is Germanic. Old English was a dialect of Old German.

The warlike nature of German and Germanic peoples has made them prime villains in the history of Western civilization. (For example, they were very influential in collapsing the decayed Roman Empire and ushering in the Dark Ages, and in much later times were instrumental in bringing about the two World Wars.) So it is intriguing that now the German people appear to be one of the most peace-loving of nations. Tiu, the Germanic god of war, must be rolling in his grave. But the Germans, including the ancient, spear-wielding ones, certainly were not all bad. In addition to violence, emphasis on heavily armored cavalry with lances, and the origins of feudalism, they also added to European culture ideas of freedom, equality, and the dignity of the individual that had formerly existed in the republics of Greece and Rome, but which had gradually given way to more Eastern-style despotism. They did much to restore these ideals, although at first mainly among the fighters.

These egalitarian principles influenced the Germanic approach to religion—and it is no coincidence that the Germanic nations of Europe (including England and the Scandinavian countries) are where the Protestant sects of the Reformation arose and thrived, while the nations which still spoke languages derived from Latin remained primarily Roman Catholic.

Protestantism did not arise simply from Germanic ideals. There were other factors too, including a decline in the prestige of Catholicism due to corruption, schism, and the fact that the Church was not of much help during the plagues of the 14th century. Another factor was the rise of a capitalistic middle class—although this also was largely a Germanic development. Even the great bankers and merchants of medieval Italy were descended from Lombards and Goths, both Germanic tribes who invaded Italy after the collapse of Rome. Even the invention of gunpowder had an indirect effect. Everything is interconnected.

Much like the newly developing urban business class in India supported Buddhism, so the new businessmen of Europe supported the new Protestant sects, which endorsed ideas and attitudes more compatible with city people engaged in making money. Also of course there were rulers ambitious to reinforce their power by weakening the influence of the Pope; but Protestantism began as a peculiarly middle-class and somewhat materialistic approach to Christianity. So it should be no surprise that in the course of history it became integrated with such other cultural events as the Industrial Revolution and the rise of Capitalism.

The new Christians, with pronounced Germanic tendencies, wanted less stratification of the classes of society, and in particular no spiritual elite who would act as middlemen between the common man and God. They wanted to reconcile spirituality with living a worldly life and making a buck, or a guilder, or whatever. Thus it is no coincidence that one of the first and most basic innovations of Protestantism was to abolish monasticism. Monks and nuns were sneered at as useless parasites on society, or as superstitious bunglers. John Milton, a good Puritan, relegated deceased monks and nuns to a limbo beyond the cometary halo of the solar system in his great religious poem *Paradise Lost.* At least he didn't consign them all to Pandemonium, in Hell.

In addition to little respect for monasticism or renunciation, other characteristics of Protestantism included less faith in saints and miracles, disapproval of elaborate rituals and spectacles, more pragmatic worldliness, and less emphasis on emotional faith. The new sects began as zealous reform movements and involved deep conviction, but gradually over time most of them (but not all) became more reason-oriented and thus, inevitably, more lukewarm.

One unintended result of the relative loss of stratification within the system is that everyone tended more toward spiritual mediocrity—especially after the aforementioned first glow of zeal wore off. And possibly the logical conclusion of this development was *the lack of emphasis on the highest goal.* Whereas Catholic monastics in places like Spain were still striving to purify themselves through ascetic practices and meditation, the lukewarm-tending urbanized Protestants figured their membership in the organization and the following of its rules were good enough—plus of course declaring Christ as their savior. The highest goal of "You must make yourselves perfect, just as your Father in Heaven is perfect" fell by the wayside, or got choked by worldly weeds; although there was in some groups still the possibility of "sanctification," or of being Born Again (like George W. Bush was, for instance). This all didn't happen immediately upon Martin Luther nailing his theses on the door of a church in Saxony, but it obviously was well established by the beginning of the twentieth century. Even before the twentieth century some writers had already commented upon the marked difference between Protestant church congregations and Catholic ones: the Protestant ones were much more likely to read their hymns as though reading from a laundry list, and the Catholics much more likely to be weeping tears of profound emotion. This difference in inspiration occasionally resulted in the controversial conversion of a high-profile Protestant, like John Henry Newman, to Catholicism.

The resemblance of American "Vipassana" lay Theravada and Protestantism near the bottom of its slide should be fairly obvious. In fact it seems clear that American Theravada more closely resembles American Protestantism than it does Asian Theravada. This is largely because both, American Theravada and Protestantism, conform to the same secular culture, but it's also true that the secular culture itself is conditioned by Protestantism. As pointed out above, American secular culture has roots extending back to ancient Germanic cultures, and Germanic culture and Protestant Christianity are inextricably mixed. It is difficult to say what is Protestant-influenced because it is Western, and what is Western because it is Protestant-influenced.

American Theravada seems not to have enjoyed the honor of beginning with a zealous, non-down-slid phase. It has, practically right off the bat, resembled Protestantism in its much less pristine forms. There is little danger of decline, since it has begun with an *already* declined, lukewarm Protestant mindset. Some American Buddhist insight societies, only a few decades after the origination of the system in the West, are hardly any more spiritually inclined than a Presbyterian coffee-and-doughnut club with a weekly movie night. No renunciation. No saints or miracles. No highest goal, other than occasional lip service. Even coming together and hashing out lapses from virtue, or marital problems, or other painful issues among its members, as many Protestant congregations still do, is probably alien to the average American Vipassana community. The main purpose seems to be stress reduction and higher self esteem; and though there's nothing necessarily wrong with stress reduction, *true Dharma* extends infinitely beyond it.

Add to all this the American emphasis on individualism, and its resultant "self view," egocentrism, and alienation; the effects of consumerism (its power over our minds strengthened by teams of psychologists working for advertising agencies, striving scientifically to persuade us that we need what we'd really be better off without); the true religion of the West now being scientific materialism, which degrades all spiritual systems to a watered down second-place subsystem at best; and we've got ourselves a spiritual situation that is pretty much comatose.

We really shouldn't blame human beings for being human. Is a tiger *wrong* for killing wild pigs? Is a dung beetle *wrong* for making its babies eat poop? Why blame Americans for thinking and acting like Americans? We all have our good points too, of course. As a Western humanist might point out as easily as an Eastern mystic, we're all miracles. There's no need for blame. But still...certain characteristics of American culture are resulting in Theravada being practically stillborn upon arrival. Asian Buddhism certainly has its fair share of corruption and laxness, but what is often called "Sangha" in America is generally lower in faith and morality, if not in meditation, than the Dharma of a Burmese lay villager. I've been told that Jack Kornfield sometimes says that when the laypeople of Spirit Rock assemble together, Spirit Rock is "the largest monastery in North America"—if so, the largest monastery in North America has almost totally rejected renunciation, austerity, and the true essence of monasticism, or Sangha.

There are many exceptions to this rather bleak depiction of decadent-upon-arrival Western Theravada. The Western monasteries, though quite posh by traditional Asian standards, are inhabited by sincere practitioners; and their Western supporters are just as worthy of praise in their own way. Also, some non-monastic meditation groups are much more dedicated and serious than others, with some even requiring the keeping of five precepts in addition to regular meditation and study. Plus there are lone individuals to be found everywhere who decline to follow along with the majority (the majority of Vipassana meditators even, not just the majority of people at large), and whose integrity and innate sanity inspire them to try as energetically as they can, making the cultivation of enlightenment their highest priority in life. These people may be saving the world.

But for Theravada in the West to thrive while still bearing some resemblance to what the Buddha actually, originally taught, and while still having the same highest goal, i.e. Nirvana in this very life, a radical paradigm shift will be required. Major, fundamental perceptions, culturally conditioned assumptions that we as modern Westerners were practically born with, will have to be outgrown, or at least changed somehow. Either "Protestant" Theravada will have to give way to a more viable form of Dharma, or else it will have to become more *puritanical*, closer to the early, more zealous and inspired forms of Protestantism, in which the followers of the system were not only willing to be inconvenienced, but even willing to die through refusal to compromise the exalted principles that they revered and followed. As it is now, the West's greatest hope for Dharma is for it to be adopted wholeheartedly (or at least three-fourths-heartedly) by some radical countercultural movement. And at present it looks like that would be most likely to happen in response to a massive, chaotic upheaval in Western society. Most folks need to be beaten over the head with something, preferably Truth, before they become willing to change their ways. Even so, let's get on with it. It's time to Wake Up.

# ABHIDHAMMA STUDIES III: BRADLEYAN LOGIC AND BULLETPROOF BABY VULTURES

*"Logic is little tweeting bird." (—Mr. Spock)*

At the time of writing this, I still haven't finished reading F. H. Bradley's *Appearance and Reality*. If you are ever stranded on a desert island, or maybe living alone in a cave or hut in tropical Asia somewhere, it would be an excellent book for you to have, because 1) it's crammed full of strange, interesting, and challenging ideas, and 2) it takes practically forever to wade through the thing.

A few nights ago I encountered a strangely intriguing idea: Bradley claims that the smaller and simpler something is, the fewer, relatively speaking, are the relations which condition its existence which are *internal* to it. In other words, the smaller and simpler something is, the more the causes of its continued existence lie outside of its own boundaries, and thus the less it is self-causing, self-conditioning, or self-sufficient. And thus, according to Bradley, the less self-consistency it has, and so the less reality as an entity. So going with this idea, he asserts that, all else being equal, the bigger something is, the closer to totally self-consistent reality it is—the more *real* it is. This strikes me as mighty peculiar, yet I don't see the flaw in his logic.

He elaborates by stating that *any* object of finite (non-infinite) size cannot be entirely real, since anything with boundaries necessarily has external relations which condition it, "infecting it with externality," and thus it is not entirely self-conditioning and self-contained. Only what is infinite could possibly be fully real, still relatively speaking, since all of the conditions of its existence would lie within itself. This is still just relative though, because F. H. Bradley, like the mystics, asserts that Ultimate Reality, "the Absolute," is unconditioned, with no qualifying relations whatsoever.

The reason why I mention this in my useful and profound course in Abhidhamma Studies is because of what happens if we move in the opposite direction from infinity, toward an object that is completely elemental, simple, and small. According to our friend Bradley, such an object would contain *none* of the conditions of its own existence, they would all be external to it, and thus the self-essence of such an object would be completely "dissipated" and non-existent. A completely simple elementary particle would have no intrinsic reality, even in terms of relative truth. It would be purely imaginary.

More or less ironically, the scholar-monks who developed the Abhidhamma philosophy held essentially the opposite point of view, and constructed an entire phenomenal universe out of completely simple elementary particles (mentioned nowhere in the suttas), plus the spaces between them, plus, sort of, the conditional relations between them. (Modern physicists may be in a similar situation with their never-ending search for the ultimately elementary particle.) The Abhidhamma philosophers were aware of some of the same logical paradoxes that F. H. Bradley perceived, such as the self-contradiction of an "individual" object or subject composed of a multiplicity of constituent parts, thereby constituting the seeming impossibility of mutually contradictory unity and plurality occupying the very same space and time. They tried to avoid this impossibility by claiming that what is ultimately real is that which is completely indivisible and elemental, and then postulated a minimum possible size in space and duration in time—then, letting alone those wiseguy Mahayanists, along came a 19th-century British logician, probably completely unaware of Abhidhamma, who declared what is ultimately elemental and simple, without being infinite, to be unreal and impossible, a mere appearance covering up an essential void. The question of how real something can be if all the conditions of its existence are completely external to itself, completely *other*, is worthy of consideration, even if we have no use for the likes of F. H. Bradley.

It may be valid to say that the entire phenomenal universe IS composed of ultimately simple elements, more or less as Abhidhamma asserts, but that they are without self-essence and thus ultimately unreal; so that each elemental "particle" is caused by something else and is causing something else in accordance with what in Buddhism is called Dependent Co-Arising—which the Madhyamaka Buddhists, at least, identify with Emptiness.

Before moving on to the vitally important subject of indestructible baby vultures, I will sum up the foregoing discussion with a moral: If what is big is more real and true than what is small, then you can't trust little people. (No doubt this is why elves, fairies, and leprechauns have acquired such a reputation for capriciousness and unreliability.) Also, generally speaking, all else being equal, men would be more real than women. Then again, elephants would be more real than humans of either gender. And I still fail to see the flaw in Bradley's logic here. I don't agree with everything he says, though.

> *This brief account, however incorrect to the eye of common sense, may perhaps, as part of our main thesis, be found defensible. (—F. H. Bradley)*

~ ~ ~

The final text in the Pali Tipitaka is the Patthāna, an Abhidhamma text consisting of five thick volumes in the Burmese Sixth Council edition. It is so complicated and abstruse that even some Abhidhamma scholars consider it to be unreadable. The Buddhistic scholar A. K. Warder declared it to be "one of the most amazing productions of the human mind." Patthāna, almost needless to say, is a towering monument of dogmatic intellectuality. (The whole thing, as far as I know, has never been translated into English.)

The purpose of Patthāna is to describe all the ways in which phenomena can interact and condition each other. Orthodox Theravadin tradition asserts that a thorough understanding of these conditional relations is essential for a thorough understanding of dependent co-arising, and thus of Dhamma, and of Reality.

According to this text, there are 24 possible ways (called *paccayo*) in which phenomena may condition each other's existence. Strangely, despite the extreme intellectuality of the system, some of these 24 *paccayos* are synonymous and redundant. For example, of the last four *paccayos* on the list, *atthi-paccayo* ("presence condition"), *natthi-paccayo* ("absence condition"), *vigata-paccayo* ("disappeared condition"), and *avigata-paccayo* ("non-disappeared condition"), the first and fourth are essentially identical, as are the second and third. I once asked a Burmese monastic scholar why some of Patthāna's *paccayos* have exactly the same meaning and function, and he explained, according to tradition, that the redundancies are for helping people of different temperaments to understand difficult concepts—if they don't understand it under one name, they may understand it under another. But it seems to me that presence and absence are fairly straightforward concepts (a tripod stands if its third leg is present, and falls if it is absent), while some of the most mysterious and inscrutable *paccayos* have no redundancies to help us. So I still don't know why some *paccayos* on the list have exactly the same meanings as others. Maybe the ancient formulators just liked the idea of a total number of 24.

Interestingly, the Abhidharma referred to by ven. Nāgārjuna, and by Mahayana philosophy in general, which I guess originally came from the Sarvastivada school of Buddhism (a school closely related to Theravada, which split away from it around the time of the third council, and which, I have read, still exists in vestigial form in southern Japan), in its analogous text to the Theravadin Patthāna, lists only *four* conditional relations to account for all phenomenal reality—"efficient condition," "percept-object condition," "dominant condition," and "immediate condition" (*hetu, ārammaṇa, adhipati,* and *anantara paccayos* in Pali). But my purpose here is not to describe or summarize all possible conditional relations, much less their convoluted combinations.

Mainly I want to discuss a particularly strange and interesting one: *pacchājāta paccayo,* "after-arisen condition" or "post-nascence condition." This refers to a condition which occurs *after* the phenomenon that it conditions—or in other words, a cause which happens *after* the effect that it causes. One might imagine, as a possible example of this, a precognitive dream or genuine premonition which modifies our present behavior. But Abhidhamma says that true precognition is impossible; not even an omniscient Buddha can really see the future, for the simple reason that the past and future do not really exist. According to Abhidhamma, only the present moment is real...then the next present moment is real...then the next one. So from this perspective it would seem like *pacchājāta paccayo* would be totally impossible. For that matter, even *purejāta paccayo*—*pre*-nascence condition—would appear to be an impossibility, since something that just doesn't exist cannot cause or condition anything in the present moment. But of the two impossibilities, a cause coming *after* its effect would seem to be even more impossible, if that means anything at all.

Venerable Nyanatiloka's *Buddhist Dictionary*, a very useful and valuable book (although tending toward some rather rigid dogmatism), defines the *paccayo* in question as follows:

> *Post-nascent-Condition (pacchā-jāta-paccaya) refers to consciousness and the phenomena therewith associated, because they are—just as is the feeling of hunger—a necessary condition for the preservation of this already arisen body.*

It seems that all the venerable author is saying here is that "after-arisen condition" implies a condition or cause which sustains, or helps to sustain, a continuing ("already arisen") chain, or momentum, of events. But this is certainly not the same as a condition coming after what it is actually conditioning. I fail to see how a feeling of hunger now could condition my pre-existent (and therefore non-existent) body of yesterday, or how a (non-existent) feeling of hunger tomorrow is conditioning my body today. It would seem, rather, that hunger now conditions my body (or rather the grouping of elemental particles cumulatively *called* "my body") now, and that hunger tomorrow will condition my body tomorrow. It may be that ven. Nyanatiloka was hard put to make sense of an idea that does not make much obvious sense. His interpretation of the condition relies upon a figurative manner of speaking, on conventional truth; but from the perspective of Abhidhammic "ultimate truth" there simply is no pre-existent body. All that is real, and all that is conditioned, is Now.

The medieval commentarial tradition of Theravada goes farther out onto the limb, yet closer to the apparent meaning of the term, with its standard example of *pacchājāta paccayo.* The example involves baby vultures. According to the commentary, mother vultures do not feed their chicks. Instead, the babies grow because they are *going* to eat *after* they reach maturity. Thus the cause of their growing now is the food they will consume in the future. If we interpret it to mean that the chicks' hunger, or the intuitive appreciation of the fact that they *will* eat someday, is what causes them to grow, then we are back to a present cause for a present effect, and a genuine post-nascence condition once again falls to the ground.

Of course, skeptical modern wiseacres with some knowledge of science could argue that the monks who concocted this example were laughably ignorant of principles of elementary biology, let alone ornithology. But devout traditionalists could argue back, and with some reason, "What! Do you wiseacres think you are wiser than venerable renunciants who dedicated their lives to the cultivation of wisdom? Have you seen a specimen of *every* species of vulture actually feeding her chicks? Maybe the venerable Theras who composed the commentaries knew something that you don't. Besides, some of the most central tenets of Abhidhamma philosophy are derived from these same commentaries." So let's give the medieval commentators the benefit of the doubt, and assume that they were right. (Let's assume that there's an obscure species of vulture inhabiting a remote area of the Himalayas...) It turns out that baby vultures are, potentially, an invaluable resource, and extremely great benefactors to the human race.

It seems to be simple logic that, if a baby vulture has grown at all, if its mass has increased by so much as one milligram, then it simply *must* reach maturity, in order to eat, in order to have grown. If a vulture chick has grown because it's going to eat after it reaches maturity, then by golly it's going to eat after it reaches maturity, and nothing can stop it from doing so. Thus it follows that any baby vulture that has grown at all must be *absolutely unkillable* before it reaches maturity. I assume there would be two main possible explanations for the unkillability of vulture chicks: 1) they are bulletproof, bombproof, fireproof, poisonproof, and, in short, completely indestructible; or 2) they are necessarily lucky. The form of their unkillability would determine their potential value to humankind.

It would be a simple matter to determine which of the two possibilities above is the actual fact. All it would require is for a qualified scientist (or, if he is prudent, one of his graduate students) to attempt to kill a baby vulture—say, by shooting it with a high-powered rifle. If the bullets all ricochet off the defiantly cheeping bird, then it may be presumed indestructible. (There is also a theoretical possibility that the bullets would pass through, and the flesh would simply close up again behind them, leaving the chick unharmed, but I consider this unlikely. For instance, the baby vulture could then be completely vaporized, and it would then have somehow to reconstitute itself, like the legendary Phoenix. But, maybe the Phoenix itself was a juvenile vulture, which would be interesting, but somewhat of an unwelcome complication.) On the other hand, if all attempts to shoot the bird fail—for example the shots always miss, or the gun misfires, or some disabling calamity suddenly befalls the shooter (hence the prudent use of disposable grad students)—then we may conclude that it is necessarily lucky.

If vulture chicks are physically indestructible, then they could be *extremely* useful. They could be used to cover the nose cones of reentry vehicles in the space program, for example. Or, more importantly, they could be grouped together and formed into containment vessels for nuclear fusion, thereby practically ending the world's energy problems, including our dependence on fossil fuels. But the following thought experiment causes me to doubt their superman-like indestructibility: If this were the case, then a baby vulture could be launched by rocket into the sun—where it would roast, without dying, for perhaps billions of years; and after the sun ceases to exist it would then have to float through space, probably for many, many more billions of years, until inevitably landing on an earth-like world where, after reaching maturity, if it had not reached it already, it could find some suitable carrion to eat. So it seems more plausible that they are just necessarily lucky. Even Jungian synchronicity could account for extreme luck, without necessitating any appeals to unknown laws of the Universe, as the indestructibility hypothesis requires.

Absolutely lucky vulture chicks could also be invaluable to the space program; one baby vulture brought along on each mission would ensure that the vessel it was on would not explode, or crash, or be lost in the depths of space. At least one vulture chick aboard every commercial airline flight would similarly prevent crashes and other fatal disasters. And if, through repeated bizarre coincidences, the bird simply could not be placed aboard the vessel, then that would be obvious, sufficient grounds for aborting the flight. Thousands of lives could be saved.

I have urged several scientists to study this potential goldmine of unkillable baby vultures; but despite the potential huge benefits for the human race, only one scientist so far, at a small institute in California, has shown any interest—yet nowadays he is more interested in acquiring funding for a space mission to land on the sun. Instead of relying on as-yet untested lucky vulture chicks to avoid incineration, he plans to go at night. Perversely, NASA has shown no interest at all in the potential effect of baby vultures on the exploration of space. I assume they've lost all enthusiasm for such things since funding that study which determined that American civilization has reached the stage of irreversible collapse anyway. (For more information, do a Google search on "NASA civilization irreversible collapse." It's not funny though. It's rather a buzz kill actually.)

~ ~ ~

During the writing of this article my Burmese friend ven. Iddhidaja has cautioned me that, if I were to study Abhidhamma more extensively, I might realize that it is true. I admit that sometimes what appears ridiculous on the surface may turn out to be profoundly true, or at least logically viable—the idea that big things (or people) are more real than small things (or people), for example. On the other hand, I seriously doubt that prolonged, intensive study of the Koran or the Book of Mormon would result in me acknowledging it as Divine Truth, and converting accordingly (although I will say that the Koran, at least, has some wisdom in it). Sometimes what appears absurd at first, stays absurd. I do like absurdity though. Nonsense is the beginning of wisdom.

# TECHNICAL MATTERS: ECCLESIASTICAL PRECINTS (SĪMĀ)

Recently I was recruited as Sangha technical advisor for a new Buddhist ashram to be constructed in the highlands of central Bali. Monasteries can be extremely simple; so with regard to the monastic area of the ashram, the only technical advice really required concerns the formal ecclesiastical precinct, or *sīmā*. So lately I've been brushing up on the subject of sīmās.

According to the Pali text Vinaya Mahāvagga, in the chapter on Uposatha, monks were uncertain as to how to know whether they were in the same congregation as other monks living nearby—that is, whether or not they should perform formal acts of the Sangha together. They brought this matter to the Buddha, who said, "Bhikkhus, I allow an ecclesiastical precinct (*sīmā*) to be authorized. And thus, bhikkhus, should it be authorized: First, boundary markers (*nimittā*) should be announced—*pabbatanimittaṁ* (a mountain or hill), *pāsāṇanimittaṁ* (a rock), *vananimittaṁ* (a forest or grove of trees), *rukkhanimittaṁ* (a single tree), *magganimittaṁ* (a path or road), *vammikanimittaṁ* (a termite mound), *nadīnimittaṁ* (a river or stream), *udakanimittaṁ* (any body of water)...." And after this a formal act of the Sangha is conducted to authorize the new precinct.

There are a few other kinds of *sīmā* that are more or less

"automatic," and do not require a formal act to authorize them. For example, monks living within the boundaries of a village or town may use those boundaries as a *gāmasīmā*, or "village *sīmā*." Monks living in a remote forest area may use an automatic *sīmā* with a radius of seven *abbhantaras*, an *abbhantara* allegedly being a unit of measurement about 14m in length. Also, monks completely surrounded by water may use a kind of water *sīmā* with a radius equivalent to the distance a man of average strength can fling water in all directions. (I once used this sort of *sīmā* in Yokohama Bay, in Japan; the sayadaw I was with had a boat rented so we could do uposatha inside a valid *sīmā*.)

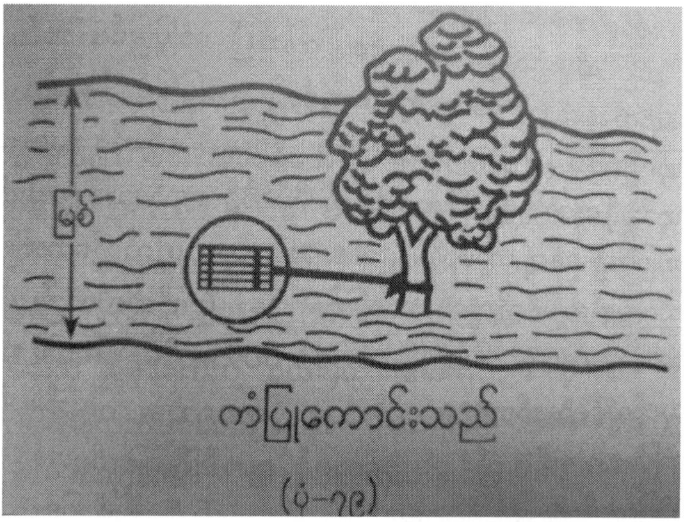


*an illustration from ven. U Silananda's book,*
*showing a kind of water sima*
*(the circle around the raft represents the sima boundary,*
*defined by the distance a man of average strength*
*can fling water in all directions)*

All the monks who live within the same agreed-upon boundaries are considered to be of one congregation, and are thus required to participate in the same formal acts, or at least to agree to them. (Interestingly, the main definition of a schism, or *saṅghabheda*, is a situation in which two separate communities of monks perform separate formal acts within the same *sīmā*.) Thus it is clear that a *sīmā* was a kind of parish—the size of some of the allowable boundary markers (a mountain, a forest) indicates this, as does the fact that the maximum allowable size for a *sīmā* is three *yojanas* on a side; so assuming purely for the sake of argument that a *yojana* equals 15km, the maximum allowable ecclesiastical precinct or parish would be about 2000 square kilometers, or 780 square miles. This maximum limit is to prevent monks from being unable to arrive easily at the congregation place within a single day. There is another rule which specifies that a *sīmā* may not be divided by a river unless there is a permanent means of crossing it, such as a bridge or ferry. This also is to ensure that monks living within the *sīmā* can reach the scene of a formal act without undergoing an ordeal.

At the other end of the scale, the minimum allowable size is just big enough to allow 21 monks to sit together. This is because the largest formal act of the Sangha (called *abbhāna*) requires a minimum of 21 monks to participate in it. But despite this relatively tiny minimum size, still it is clear that the original purpose of a *sīmā* was to be a territory or "home turf" determining which monks were members of the same community.

Ironically though, if one goes to a monastery in Myanmar one will find that a *sīmā*, or *thein*, usually refers not to any bounded territory within which a community of monks resides, but rather to a single building, the monastery's congregation hall—which, as often as not, has zero monks residing there. So the average ecclesiastical precinct has come to have a total population of zero. This situation is the inevitable result of corruption in Vinaya, which in this particular case is largely due to a peculiar glitch in the monastic rules themselves, unforeseen by the ancient formulators of the Theravadin monastic code.

This appears to be an opportune point at which to point out that this article is not intended to be a comprehensive exposition on *sīmās*. As far as I know, no such comprehensive exposition exists in the English language, unless maybe it is in volume III of the English translation of the *Vinayamukha*, authored by the Thai Sangharāja ven. Vajirañāṇavaroraso. The definitive work in

Burmese is considered to be a book entitled သိမ် သင်တန်း (*Thein Thin-tann*), by ven. Sayadaw U Sīlānanda. Otherwise, curious monks should consult the Vinaya itself and its commentaries, the latter especially with regard to how to do the boundary marker announcements. The main purpose of this article is to discuss how the concept of *sīmās* has been corrupted, and how the Sangha can cope with the corruption in order to keep things legal and "ritually pure." Consequently this article may be of little or no interest to laypeople.

All or almost all ecclesiastical acts in Burmese monasticism have become corrupt, and the situation appears to be only slightly better in Thailand; I'm not sure what it's like in Sri Lanka, but I would guess that it's not so good there either. But the fact that a Sangha's "home territory" has shrunk down to a single building which may be home to nobody is not entirely the fault of the Burmese, or the Thais. It's due in part to the likelihood that ancient Indian monks did not realize that Buddhism would exist for more than 2500 years, and that the boundary markers of *sīmās* could be forgotten or could even disappear altogether, with no way of knowing whether there is or is not a pre-existent *sīmā* in a given place, and no convenient way of eliminating one if there is one. A *sīmā* has no expiration date, even though its boundary markers may have been trees, roads, ponds, or termite mounds that ceased to exist centuries before.

The establishment of a new *sīmā*, as mentioned above, involves first naming all the boundary markers in all (eight) directions; but although there is a formal act for abolishing an old *sīmā*, it does not mention any boundary markers. The key words in the act of abolishment are simply, in Pali, "That *sīmā* agreed upon by the Sangha as the area of common communion, of one uposatha observance—that *sīmā* is abolished as the area of common communion, of one uposatha observance." The assumption is that the boundaries of the *sīmā* to be abolished are known, and that by performing this formal act within those known boundaries, the act is accomplished. There is no provision for invisible, forgotten, ancient *sīmās*.

The Vinaya explicitly specifies that no new *sīmā* may be authorized which overlaps with an old one. Such a *sīmā* is invalid. Consequently, especially in Asia, before a new *sīmā* is established, a very complicated ritual is performed to ensure that there are no invisible, pre-existing *sīmās* overlapping with the intended new one, which might invalidate it. This ritual is very labor intensive, and is by far the most difficult part of creating a new *sīmā*.

The way it is done in Burma is that the entire ground which will contain the new "precinct" is divided up into rectangles a few feet on a side, and a formal act of abolishment is performed inside each rectangle, just in case an ancient, invisible *sīmā* is there. Thus new *sīmās* tend to be scarcely bigger than the area of a single building; dividing up 2000 square kilometers into little rectangles and doing formal chanting in each one simply is not feasible.

*Ground divided up into little rectangles to allow the abolition of any old sima that might be there*

Of course, an obvious solution to this problem would be to change the words of the formal act, stating that any *sīmā* existing within such and such boundaries is officially abolished. There may be some Sanghas that have actually tried this. But the trouble is that conservative Asian theras may consider such a deviation from the actual words of the Vinaya to be invalid; and if a *sīmā* is suspected to be invalid, all formal acts conducted within that *sīmā*, including the ordinations of new monks, could also be suspected of invalidity. A *sīmā* must be like Caesar's wife—above suspicion. Thus a new ecclesiastical precinct must have two qualities: it must be valid according to Vinaya, and it must also be uncontroversial and acceptable to as many monks as possible, preferably all of them. If Burmese sayadaws consider Thai *sīmās* to be invalid, or if Thai ajahns consider Burmese ones to be invalid, or Western monks consider *both* types to be invalid, it simply breeds problems. So it's best to be as conservative as possible when making *sīmās*.

As it turns out, I am one of those aforementioned Western monks who considers most *sīmās* in Burma and Thailand to be pretty much invalid. The situation has to do not with abolishing old *sīmās*, or with the tininess of new ones, but with the boundary markers used, the *nimittā*.

For some bizarre reason that I can only begin to guess at, the standard method for establishing a new *sīmā* in Myanmar is as follows: After any old *sīmā* is abolished (which abolishment also may be invalid, although I'll get back to that), holes dug where the boundary markers are to be are filled with water, again and again, until the ground is saturated and the water doesn't immediately seep into the ground and disappear. Then the formal act is conducted after declaring these holes full of water as *udakanimittā*, or bodies of water used as boundary markers. A few hours later the water is gone, and the Burmese set up marble or concrete posts to show where the real boundary markers are *supposed* to be. But of course the boundary markers have evaporated, and are nonexistent. There used to be an ancient commentary which specified that any water boundary marker should have water in it all year round, like a pond or a well, in order for it to be a valid marker. The official Theravadin commentary, however, rejects this, claiming that a water boundary may be nothing more than a temporary mud puddle that animals have wallowed in. (It is interesting, and justifiable, that the venerable author of the *Vinayamukha* declared the orthodox commentator to be "shameless" for having said this.) Clearly, in order for something to be a boundary marker or *nimitta* it should not only not be easily movable, it should not be *in-*

*visible*! This is simply common sense. Consequently, at my own ordination at a Burmese monastery in California, I disregarded the nonexistent water *nimittā* and relied on one of those automatic *sīmās*, like maybe the seven-*abbhantara* one.

Based on what I have been told, the situation in Thailand is hardly better. I have been informed that boundary markers in Thailand are often *pāsāṇanimittā*, or rock markers. The thing is, though, that the rocks are the size of cannonballs, and are buried in the ground where no one can see them—with quasi-markers similar to the ones the Burmese used to show where the small, invisible rocks are *supposed* to be. Again, it is hardly to be expected that a boundary marker which nobody can see would be a valid marker. Also there is the issue of how small a rock can be and still be a valid *nimitta*. Obviously, it should be large enough not to be easily moved, unlike a pebble or a cannonball. The commentary suggests the size of an ox as reasonable, although the size of an elephant would make the rock a hill, not just a rock. Hills are allowable markers too, though. Better too big than too small.

I remember once a Western monk I knew mentioning that at one Western monastery in the Ajahn Chah tradition the Sangha used big concrete blocks as boundary markers for their *sīmā*. He considered this to be invalid, not considering concrete to be rock, or any of the other allowable kinds of markers. But it seems to me that concrete is pretty clearly a kind of artificial rock—man-made, but still rock. So if it's too big to be moved, I would consider it to be valid. But the fact that *some* monks would consider it invalid may be sufficient reason for seeking a different kind of marker. Again, a *sīmā* must be above suspicion.

All in all, the best, most uncontroversial *nimitta* to use would be a tree. It's clearly allowable in accordance with the ancient Indian texts, and nobody is going to argue with it. One just doesn't argue with trees. The only limitation is that it must be a kind of tree with its hardest wood, its heartwood, on the inside; in other words, bamboo and palm trees are not allowable *rukkhanimittā.* And banana trees, having no hard wood at all, are completly out of the question. (Incidentally, the new *sīmā* planned in Bali will be completely surrounded by a moat, and thus will have water *nimittā* all the way around. I've never seen a *sīmā* like that before; and considering that the congregation hall will be designed like a temple besides, if it ever materializes it will be very cool. My idea is to enter the hall by crossing a narrow bridge and passing between two fires—a symbolic purification thing. But I digress.)

It may be assumed that Theravada Buddhist monasteries being constructed in non-Buddhist Western countries need not bother with abolishing any ancient, invisible *sīmā* before establishing a new one, considering that it is extremely unlikely that there have ever been *sīmās* officially established there before modern times. If this is the case, then I don't see any good reason why new Western monasteries should not establish *sīmās* which encompass the entire monastery, in accordance with the original purpose of *sīmās*. On the other hand, there is still the issue of conservative Asian monks suspecting the validity of a new *sīmā* established without making sure there are no old ones already established there. For example, some monks consider *sīmās* established even in the dispensations of prehistoric Buddhas to be still potentially valid. If so, then no place on earth, including the continent of Antarctica, would be guaranteed of having no invisible ancient *sīmā* which could muck up (invalidate) the establishment of a new one. Also, it is known that monastic Buddhist missionaries came to western North America with a Chinese expedition well over a thousand years ago, long before Columbus ever discovered the place; so in North America at least there may actually be a few invisible ancient *sīmās*. But in my opinion most Sanghas in countries that have never been Buddhist needn't worry too much about ancient *sīmās*, and may as well establish new ones without going through the laborious abolishment rituals beforehand. But doing the abolishment may be the only way to create 100% confidence in the most conservative of Asian theras. As for myself though, I'm way too skeptical ever to arrive at 100% confidence in anything.

As mentioned above, Burmese Sanghas divide up the area intended for a new *sīmā* into little rectangles, and chant the formal acts of abolishment inside each rectangle. In ven. U Sīlānanda's definitive Burmese book, he points out that since the smallest possible *sīmā* is just large enough to accommodate 21 sitting monks, the rectangles for abolishment need be no smaller than this. This used to make good sense to me, and seemed to make the abolishment process easier...until I realized that there is one complication with it. What if the area of an intended new *sīmā* really does have an invisible, very small, ancient *sīmā* contained within it, and what if the rectangles drawn on the ground *bisect* this small *sīmā*? Then when the Sangha is doing the formal act of abolishment inside each rectangle, some of the monks may be inside the ancient *sīmā*, and others outside of it; and thus the formal act may be invalidated by having some of the monks outside the *sīmā* and an insufficient number within it. A minimum of four bhikkhus must be within the boundaries, and within arm's reach of each other, in order for the formal act of abolishment to be valid. So it seems that in order to avoid this possibility and to ensure that the abolishment of any tiny invisible *sīmās* is valid, the rectangles should be just big enough for four or five bhikkhus to squat within them and do the ritual ceremonies. Maybe in future if there is ever another Great Council, this glitch in the monastic rules could be straightened out somehow; and maybe that troublesome bhikkhuni issue could be officially settled also. Then again, the monks who participate in Great Councils tend to be too conservative to deal with controversial issues, and content themselves with little more than rearranging Pali punctuation marks.

There is one other way that I know of for creating a large *sīmā* without having first to divide up the entire area into little rectangles, and that is to establish a *gāmasīmā*, or village parish. This is done sometimes in Myanmar. The way it is done is to have the government officially declare the precints of the monastery to be its own village. This may work in a Buddhist country like Myanmar, but whether politicians in Western countries would give enough of a damn officially to declare a Buddhist monastery its own village is another matter. It may be worth a shot, though. One disadvantage of a *gāmasīmā*, however, like all "automatic" *sīmās*, is that the priviledge of *avippavāsa* does not apply, that is, the right of any bhikkhu inside the *sīmā* to be separated from any of his three robes at dawn without committing a *nissaggiya pācittiya* offense. But nowadays even strict and "exemplary" bhikkhus tend not to follow such rules about being with all three robes at dawn, etc. The Byzantine complications of Theravadin monastic discipline render corruption and laxness a virtual inevitability in the Sangha. But still, the validity of ordinations is a relatively important issue, so all this stuff about precincts and little rectangles may not be totally irrelevant.

*A pseudo sima marker,*
*showing where the real sima marker is supposed to be*

# THE MEANINGS OF THE WORD "SANGHA"

*(This is another slightly controversial and contentious one. Many western Buddhists who refer to themselves or to their meditation group as Sangha may not like it. But still this stuff needs to be said. The attitudes of most western Buddhists are very alien to traditional Buddhism, and to the attitudes of the overwhelming majority of Buddhists, who are of course Asian. To what extent the western mind can adopt Theravada as a philosophy or spiritual system without turning it into something radically other than Theravada is a fascinating question, with this essay barely touching upon that particular sticky issue.)*

Way back in ancient times, maybe ten years ago, a Western monk living here in Myanmar sent me some old copies of the Inquiring Mind magazine, a journal of the Western Vipassana community. I remember there was a regular section in the magazine that had me somewhat confused—it was called "Sangha Speaks." The confusing thing about it was that it was never a monk who was speaking, or a nun either. It was always a layperson, and sometimes even a relative beginner in Dhamma.

Before I was ordained as a monk, and for many years afterwards, I had almost no interaction with Western-style Buddhism. For that matter, I tried to keep at arm's length even Southeast Asian-style Buddhism, pursuing as much as I was able ancient Indian, *original*-style Buddhism. So it wasn't until after my return to America in 2011 that I learned, and very quickly, that lay meditators in the West refer to themselves as "Sangha." In fact many of them consider themselves to be members of THE Sangha, even to the extent of taking refuge in their own lay community, when and if they take refuge in the Tiratana, or Three Treasures—the "Triple Gem."

A few months after my return in 2011, while I was still struck by this still (to me) strange and exotic fact, I happened to explain to an American fellow who had volunteered to feed me that day that in Asia, and in the Pali texts, the word "sangha" refers almost exclusively to monks, with its adoption by lay meditators being, as far as I could tell, a modern Western innovation. He harrumphed once or twice while I was explaining this, and immediately after our brief conversation, and as a result of it, he informed a mutual friend of ours that, in his opinion, I was "opinionated."

But what I had said about "sangha" was not a matter of mere personal bias; really, I was stating a straightforward, empirical, and rather obvious fact. In a Buddhist country like Burma, "sangha" and "monks" are practically synonymous. If a visiting Western lay meditator were to walk through a door, or sit on a platform, with a sign on it saying "SANGHA ONLY," he or she would either be politely requested to go somewhere else, or would be stared at and regarded as an ignorant and/or arrogant barbarian. It is true that if a Burmese Buddhist person were asked, "Does the Sangha include nuns and novices?" they might consider it for awhile and say, "Well, it could…"; but in Buddhist Asia ordinary laypeople, even though they might keep five or eight precepts, meditate every day, and attend retreats regularly, just do not make the cut. Unless maybe they are Goenka meditators who have absorbed Western attitudes about Buddhism.

So anyway, to make a long story much longer, ever since 2011 I've been curious as to whether there is any precedent in the literature of Pali Buddhism for lay meditators in general being included under the designation of "Sangha." I have heard a rumor, or legend, that there is at least one Sutta which declares lay disciples (*upāsakā/upāsikāyo*) and/or lay supporters (*dāyakā/dāyikāyo*) to be members of the Buddhist Sangha. If I've ever read it I don't remember reading it, and I don't know which Sutta it might be. If any of you out there know the reference, please do us all a favor and post it in the Comments section, or send it to me in an email so I can post it, or something.

I have at hand two Pali-English dictionaries: the Pali Text Society dictionary edited by Rhys Davids and Stede, and the Buddhist Dictionary of venerable Nyanatiloka. These are arguably the two most important Pali-English dictionaries for a Western, English-speaking student of Dhamma to have. The PTS dictionary gives the following three definitions for "Sangha":

1. multitude, assemblage (some of the references given are to a sangha of birds in the Jātaka literature, the sangha of a person's relatives in the Salla Sutta of the Sutta Nipāta (Sn 584), and a sangha of devas in the Nālaka Sutta, also of the Sutta Nipāta (Sn 680).)
2. the Order, the priesthood, the clergy, the Buddhist church (Obviously monks and nuns.)
3. a larger assemblage, a community (This definition is rather obscure, and, judging from the references, appears to refer to a group of people more numerous than just a few (a *gaṇa*), and who are not necessarily Buddhist.)

Nyanatiloka's Buddhist Dictionary simply says this:

> *SANGHA (lit.: congregation), is the name for the Community of Buddhist Monks. As the third of the Three Gems or Jewels (ti-ratana, q.v.) and the Three Refuges (ti-saraṇa, q.v.), i.e. Buddha, Dhamma and Sangha, it applies to the ariya-saṅgha, the community of the saints, i.e. the 4 Noble Ones (ariya-puggala, q.v.), the Stream-winner, etc.*

So the two dictionaries I have had ready access to are evidently not very complete, and are not quite conclusive in resolving this issue.

But then this year I spent the rains retreat at a monastery possessing the huge, encyclopedic Tipiṭaka Pāḷi-Myanmar Dictionary (တိပိဋက ပါဠိ-မြန်မာ အဘိဓာန်). The compilation and publication of it was begun decades ago and is still not completed, although it is complete up through volume 21, which goes about halfway through the letter "s"; so I looked up "sangha" in it. The entry is three pages long and contains no fewer than 27 definitions, not including several more pages of definitions of compound words beginning with "sangha-," or rather "*saṁgha-*." A paraphrase of the various interpretations follows.

The etymological derivation is as a noun form related to the Pali verb *saṁhanati*, meaning to join together, to make complete. (On the other hand, the PTS dictionary relates it to *saṁharati*, to bring together, to collect—although in either case the resultant meaning is essentially the same: assembly, congregation.)

1. in general, for example in Jātaka stories, any group of living beings. (For some reason I do not fathom, following this statement, and before the first numbered subentry, there is the explanation, in parentheses, that "*saṁgha*" may be used as a Vinaya technical term referring to four or more fully ordained monks or nuns. One monk or nun alone is a *puggala*, an "individual"; and two or three constitute a *gaṇa*, or "gang." Thus a sangha is, in this technical sense, a congregation of ordained renunciants (all male or all female) numerous enough to conduct formal ecclesiastical acts.)

1(a). a herd of pigs. (This would be called a *sukarasaṁgha.* The only reference given is to the Jātaka literature.)

1(b). a herd of deer or other game animals.

1(c). a group of male or female inhabitants of a town. (The single reference given is to a story in the Majjhima Aṭṭhakatha, in which a crowd of townspeople gather at a park.)

1(d). a group of wealthy brahmins. (The primary reference is to the Caṅkī Sutta of the Majjhima Nikāya, in which some brahmin householders, upon hearing that the Buddha has arrived in their vicinity, form "in groups and bands" (*saṁghasaṁghī gaṇībhūtā*) to go pay their respects to him.)

1(e). any group of beings receptive to admonishment or spiritual instruction. (Thus in the stock formula describing the virtues of the Buddha, when he is called *satthā devamanussānaṁ*—"teacher of gods and humans"—the gods and humans instructed by him, in this sense, form a sangha.)

1(f). all beings who have attained to any of the eight classes of ariya-hood, that is, path and fruit of the four stages. (That is, all those who have "experienced" Nibbāna at least for one moment, and who are thus either fully enlightened or else firmly established on "the path of no return," so to speak. There are numerous references throughout the Tipitaka for this sense of the word. This sense is called the *ariyasaṁgha*, or "Sangha of the Noble Ones.")

1(g). all fully ordained Buddhist mendicant renunciants, especially Theravada ones. (This group is referred to as the *sammutisaṁgha*, or "conventional Sangha." There are of course lots of references for this sense too.)

1(h). all of the paths and fruits of the four stages of ariya-hood, taken in abstraction from the beings who have attained them. (This is called the *paramatthasaṁgha*, or "ultimate Sangha," and is, as far as I can tell, peculiar to the Abhidhamma literature.)

1(i). the mendicant renunciant disciples who form the following or entourage of a Buddha. (For example, in the Suttas when it says that the Buddha went to such and such place with a following of 500 bhikkhus, those 500 bhikkhus would constitute the Sangha in this sense. It is referred to as the *buddhapamukhasaṁgha*, or the "Sangha with Buddha at the front.")

1(j). If I understand this one correctly, and if the old Burmese monk who explained it to me understands it correctly, then it would be essentially, although in a less technical sense, the same as the next one, i.e., the ordained Sangha taken very generally. (In Burmese this is called the အမှတ် မရှိသော သံဃာ, or "nondescript Sangha." The only references are to the Nidhikaṇḍa Sutta of the Khuddakapātha and the commentary to same, in which Sutta the Sangha is cited simply as an opportunity for merit, and a source of treasure that cannot be lost or stolen.)

1(k). the totality of all ordained Buddhist renunciants as a society, organization, or "corporate entity." (For example, if someone makes a donation to "the Sangha" in general, and not to an individual monk, to the resident sangha of a particular monastery, or to some other specified group, then this is the Sangha that it goes to, and all of the members of the Sangha share in the ownership, in communistic fashion. The Sangha in this sense is called the *cā-*

*tuddisasaṁgha*, or the "Sangha of the Four Quarters"—east, south, west, and north. This is primarily, but not exclusively, a Vinaya term.)

1(l). any and all bhikkhus, that is, all fully ordained Buddhist monks. (This is called the *bhikkhusaṁgha*, and it is probably the most common meaning of the word "*saṁgha*" found in the texts, both Vinaya and Suttanta.)

(Following the foregoing subentry is a paragraph in parentheses giving more technical Vinaya definitions: (i.) a group of (at least) four bhikkhus in good standing, and who are thereby qualified to conduct most formal ecclesiastical acts, such as sangha uposatha. (This sense goes by the designation of *catuvagga bhikkhusaṁgha.*) (ii.) a group of (at least) five bhikkhus in good standing, and who are thereby qualified to conduct formal acts requiring (at least) five bhikkhus, particularly the sangha invitation ceremony at the end of the rains retreat, and ordination ceremonies outside of the "Middle District" of the Ganges Valley. (This one is called *pañcavagga bhikkhusaṁgha.*) (iii.) a group of (at least) ten bhikkhus in good standing, considered in the sense of being qualified to conduct ordination ceremonies in the Middle District. (I.e., *dasavagga bhikkhusaṁgha.*) (iv.) a group of twenty bhikkhus in good standing, who are thereby qualified to conduct a reinstatement ceremony, or *abbhāna saṁghakamma*, for a monk who has undergone penance for committing a *saṁghādisesa* offence. (*Vīsativagga bhikkhusaṁgha.*) (v.) a group of more than twenty bhikkhus in good standing, considered in the sense of being qualified to carry out any and all formal acts of the Sangha. (Called *atirekavīsativagga bhikkhusaṁgha.*))

1(m). the Community of all fully ordained Buddhist nuns. (I.e., the *bhikkhunīsaṁgha.*)

1(n). the Community of all bhikkhus and bhikkhunīs combined (This is called the *ubhatosaṁgha*, or the "Sangha of Both.")

1(o). a congregation of fully ordained monks or nuns who live in the same general locality and who perform their formal ecclesiastical acts together. (This is one of the more common meanings of the word, and is presumably the sense implied at the beginning of a recitation of a formal act: *suṇātu me bhante saṁgho*—"Venerable sirs, may the sangha hear me." The Pali term for this sense is *samānasaṁvāsaka saṁgha*, or the "sangha living in the same community.")

1(p). a congregation of the renunciant disciples of a non-Buddhist philosopher, such as Pūraṇa Kassapa.

2. the qualities of the (ariya-)sangha, as found in the stock formula beginning "*suppaṭipanno bhagavato sāvakasaṁgho...*," and which is the traditional object for the meditation technique of reflection upon the Sangha (one of the forty traditional standard meditations in Theravada).

3. the very name "sangha." (I'm not exactly sure why the venerable authors of the dictionary bothered to include this one, unless maybe it was for the sake of being totally comprehensive. The only reference is to a passage in the Vinaya declaring that monks should not cling to the word/name "*saṁgha*."

4. Saṁghā is the name of an elder bhikkhunī whose verses are included in the Pali text Therīgāthā.

Oddly, there is a separate entry for "*saṁgha*," *saṁgha*$^2$, with an allegedly different etymological derivation, in that it is considered to be a contraction, or abbreviation, of *saṁgha*$^1$+*sannipāta*, referring to the act of the coming together, or the convocation, of a sangha. The only reference is to Vinaya commentarial literature.

It appears that the venerable scholar sayadaws who compiled the dictionary were not aware of any reference in the Pali texts to laypeople being included in a specifically Buddhist Sangha, let alone THE specifically Buddhist Sangha. It appears that they weren't aware even of semi-ordained novices being members of *the* Sangha, which is more surprising. Definition 1(e) seems to come closest to filling these two voids. Then again, it may be that the Burmese dictionary, huge and comprehensive-seeming as it is, is not really complete; for example, the sanghas of birds, relatives, and devas cited in the PTS dictionary are not explicitly mentioned here, although they would fall under the first general definition of "any group of living beings."

With regard to lay meditators calling their group a "sangha," I see no problem at all. Obviously, if a herd of deer, a herd of pigs, or an assembly of devas can be called "sangha," then so can a group of people who practice Buddhist meditation. They are, after all, a group of living beings.

With regard to lay meditators considering themselves to be members of THE Sangha, as in the trinity of Buddha, Dhamma, and Sangha, an issue does arise however, as it appears to receive no support from the Pali, especially if that aforementioned legendary Sutta doesn't exist. And even if it does exist, the reference in question would appear to be an obscure anomaly in the textual tradition. The concept of Refuge has undergone a modern mutation.

As a newcomer to the whole Sangha scene I was taught that, traditionally, laypeople take refuge in the bhikkhu-sangha, i.e., in monks, while monks take refuge in the ariya-sangha, which, maybe ironically, includes laypeople. It is fairly clear to me that when Burmese Buddhists take the third Refuge, what they mainly have in mind is monks; and throughout the Suttas, again and again, when a person converts to Buddhism he or she utters the same stock formula beginning with, "Wonderful, venerable Gotama! Wonderful, venerable Gotama! Just as, venerable Gotama, one might set upright what has been overturned...." and ending with, "I go to the venerable Gotama as a refuge, and to the Dhamma, and to the Sangha of bhikkhus." However, if Western lay Buddhists have some personal antipathy for taking refuge exclusively in monks, then there is presumably no major obstacle to their taking refuge in the ariya-sangha as monks are supposed to do, especially since there is support for it within the tradition anyway, going way, way back.

But for a group of lay meditators living worldly lives to consider monks, radical renunciation, and the so-called Holy Life to be unnecessary and/or irrelevant to Dhamma, and to consider their own group to be representative of THE Sangha, is arguably not just a variation within Theravada Buddhism, but a major deviation *from* Theravada Buddhism. This is all the more evident when one notices that many members of these lay sanghas do not even consider themselves to be Buddhists, and that many of those who do consider themselves as such nevertheless reject even basic fundamentals of the system, both theoretical and practical.

It is good to bear in mind, even if the thought is an unsavory one, that Theravada, and Buddhism in general, was founded *by* a bhikkhu, mainly *for* bhikkhus. As G. C. Pande wrote in his monumental *Studies in the Origins of Buddhism*, "There is little reason to suppose that Buddha addressed himself to Everyman and not to the monk. As a matter of fact, the Buddhists appear to have been from the beginning primarily a community of monks." (p. 401 of the 3rd edition) The Buddha was a renunciant ascetic sage who established Dhamma first and foremost as a system for maximizing one's chances for full Enlightenment in this very life; and that system practically *begins* with a formal renunciation of worldliness. People who were serious about waking up in this very life would be ordained into the Sangha and strive; those who were not so serious would humbly admit this fact, do the best they could within a worldly context, and support those who they felt were really giving it a serious shot. Thus Buddhism was designed as a kind of professional spectator sport, with laypeople being fans supporting their favorite team—and thereby supporting Enlightenment in this world, even though they themselves do not feel completely ready for it.

Yet this approach, designed by an enlightened being (who was probably a genius besides) is vehemently opposed by the current attitude of Western culture in general. It's too radical, demanding, and damned inconvenient at one end, and too humble at the other. So nowadays in America Theravada Buddhism is little more than a tiny fringe movement, with an ordained Western resident Sangha of possibly no more than a hundred people, supported mainly by Asian immigrants, very loosely affiliated with a rather larger, yet still small movement which has mutated so extensively as scarcely to merit the name "Doctrine of the Elders," yet which is disproportionately vocal with regard to what Theravada should and should not be like—and then there's the Goenka people. Among many lay communities, "sangha" has become an English word no longer bearing a Pali meaning. In view of all this, it seems to me that, in order for Theravadin Dhamma with some kind of renunciant Sangha maintaining it to prosper in the West, as something more than just a tiny fringe movement, it will probably have to be endorsed and supported by some relatively radical countercultural movement which, apparently, does not yet exist. On the other hand, Dhamma may survive and prosper, in a way, by mutation into some form of Dharma with an "r" which is very different from the design of Theravada—yet which still requires a radical counterculture of some sort, since any really inspired spiritual system automatically generates that. The mainstream simply does not lead to Enlightenment.

There is nothing *necessarily* wrong with a mutation of Theravada into something very different in the West, a kind of Doctrine of the Newcomers which is no longer Theravada. It is a plain fact that Theravada was designed for ancient India, which was in many ways *extremely* different from the modern Western world. However, any new form of authentic Dhamma or Dharma will still require a SANGHA dedicated to waking up in this very life, "in the present way of being." Those who give top priority to anything else—money, family, reputation, security, whatever—will still not make the cut.

# TECHNICAL MATTERS: CONFESSION (PAṬIDESANĀ)

In the Pali texts the practice of confessing one's transgressions, or unskillful acts, is declared to be a valuable resource for one endeavoring to live a spiritual life. From a Buddhist perspective one does not make confession in order to absolve oneself of "sin," but rather as an aid to restraint in future. At any rate, this is the ideal; in actuality the making of confession in Theravada Buddhism has become, for the most part, a formal ritual, a kind of esoteric formula recited in order to expiate ecclesiastical offenses, i.e. broken rules. The practice of confession, as far as I know, is most prevalent among the Sangha of monks; although Buddhist laypeople also, at least in Burma, may make a practice of confessing their lapses from morality, especially to a monastic who is their teacher. But usually if a layperson breaks a precept she or he simply takes the precepts all over again, thereby pushing RESET (so to speak).

It should be emphasized that making confession in no way absolves one of the karma one has generated through some ethical misstep or other—sacred incantations and other rituals do not erase karma, at least not in an orthodox Buddhist universe. We reap what we sow. So if someone has created some bad karma, the best thing for him or her to do is to dilute it down by adding to it plenty of good karmic actions, and/or to accept the consequences with mindful equanimity. One makes confession to a teacher or fellow traveler primarily for the sake of helping one to restrain oneself in future. Plus, of course, it's good to be honest. Then again, on second thought, open honesty is probably the most important reason for not concealing one's lapses from established virtue. Concealment of the truth may not only require occasional lying or chronic hypocrisy, but it also generates and reinforces deep interpersonal alienation.

At some monasteries in Burma the monks make confession every day; and some—especially younger, ultra-careful ones—may waste no time and seek out another monk for confession practically as soon as they are aware of having broken a rule of discipline. On the other hand, the technical minimum for deferring confession for a monk who is not living alone, without even another monk within easy walking distance, is half a lunar month, since it is against the rules for a monk to participate in a full-moon or new-moon uposatha ceremony with unconfessed offenses, if there is someone he can confess to. In the first part of the recitation for Sangha uposatha, before the rules of the Pātimokkha are recited, it is stated explicitly that any monk who listens to the recitation and remains silent when he knows he has unexpiated offenses, is guilty of lying, which is a serious obstacle for one living the Holy Life (not to mention the breaking of another rule). In this case at least, one may technically qualify as a liar without saying a word, by keeping one's mouth shut when the reciter asks repeatedly, "I ask the venerable ones, are you entirely pure?" This becomes somewhat of a quagmire for monks who habitually commit *nissaggiya pācittiya* offenses ("to be expiated with relinquishment") such as using money or keeping extra (more than three) robes, since the only way to expiate such an offense is to relinquish the forbidden commodities before making confession—which most monks are unwilling to do. So they make confession, which does not absolve them of these offenses, and then they participate in uposatha, thereby committing yet another offense. This may eventually inspire monks to avoid confession and uposatha observances altogether. There are quite a few like that, actually. If any of them are reading this, then shame on you—tsk, tsk (← I click my tongue at you). Then again, one is not supposed to make confession if one is not aware of having committed any offense. There are a few monks out there who can go for weeks without breaking any rules (and there are lots of rules, and some are very easy to break); and if any of those are reading this, then congratulations, venerable sir. Please be careful not to despise those who are not as conscientious as you are.

The standard Burmese method for making confession is as follows. Two monks, A and B, squat down within arm's reach of each other, barefoot, with right shoulders bared, and with their own palms pressed together before them. Then they say:

A: *ahaṁ bhante sabbā āpattiyo āvikaromi* ("Venerable sir, I make plain all offenses.")
B: *sādhu āvuso sādhu sādhu* ("Very good, friend, very good, very good.")
A: *ahaṁ bhante sambahulā nānāvatthukā sabbā āpattiyo āpajjiṁ, tā tumhamūle paṭidesemi* ("Venerable sir, I have committed altogether several offenses of various types; at your feet I confess them.")
B: *passasi āvuso tā āpattiyo* ("Do you see, friend, those offenses?")
A: *āma bhante passāmi* ("Yes, venerable sir, I see.")
B: *āyatiṁ āvuso saṁvareyyāsi* ("In future, friend, you should restrain yourself.")
A: *sādhu suṭṭhu bhante samvarissāmi* ("Very good, very well, venerable sir, I will restrain myself.")
B: *sādhu sādhu sādhu* ("Very good, very good, very good.")

Then they switch roles, with A reciting B's part and vice versa, except that the senior monk is always Bhante and the junior one is always Āvuso, and with a little bit of modified grammar to indicate greater respect of Āvuso for Bhante than the other way round. There are a few minor variations to this procedure, and I'll mention at least one of them before I'm finished.

I've mentioned elsewhere that most formal acts in Theravadin monasticism, at least in Burma, have become corrupted into virtually pointless formalities, and this one is no exception to the general rule—you may notice that practically nothing is actually confessed, other than the vague assertion that one broke numerous unspecified rules, which is exactly what everyone else confesses. The rote, blah-blah-blah nature of it is so ingrained that often one monk will begin his line before the other has finished his, in order to get it over with more quickly. Also, sometimes two monks will "confess" their offenses to a third monk in unison, since their confessions are invariably exactly the same.

A common Thai method, or so I have heard, is to make five separate confessions, one for each general category of offense expiable via confession: namely, *thullaccaya* ("gross offense"), *pācittiya* ("to be expiated"), *pāṭidesanīya* ("to be confessed"), *dukkaṭa* ("wrongly done"), and *dubbhāsita* ("wrongly spoken"). I do not have a commentary handy, so I'm not sure whether orthodox tradition endorses this; but the method is more or less in accordance with the formula for confession given in a medieval, non-canonical vinaya handbook called *Khuddasikkhā*. The *Khuddasikkhā*, however, does not endorse making confession for un-committed offenses, whereas it is my understanding that the aforementioned Thai tradition makes all five confessions regardless of whether the monk is aware of having broken them, just to be thorough. So it attempts to be stricter, but actually winds up being even more nonsensical than the Burmese "blanket" method, considering that Burmese monks do not *necessarily* confess offenses they didn't commit. (And it is unlikely that a confessing monk has broken rules in all five categories, since one especially, *pāṭidesanīya*, is very difficult to break nowadays. There are only four of them for monks, with two of them involving interactions with fully ordained nuns which, according to the overwhelming majority of the Theravadin Sangha, have been extinct for centuries; one involving begging from a family determined to be "in training," which is interpreted by tradition to mean that they are designated Ariyas; and one involving a monk living in a dangerous forest who allows lay supporters to endanger themselves by bringing alms to his place. Another category, *dubbhāsita*, applies to only a single rule, against making a derisive joke at another person's expense.)

Thus it is fairly obvious that the standard formal procedure for making confession involves the speaking of untruth. Even monks who consider themselves to be Ariyas (a danger sign in itself) do the same, saying "Yes, I see," when they see nothing, and "I will restrain myself," when they know full well they'll break the same rule again. Plus if they're Thai, they may confess categories of offense they've never committed. This kind of talk is not necessarily *lying*, however, since one is lying only if one is deliberately trying to deceive someone; and most monks are too cynical or too ignorant with regard to Vinaya matters for anyone really to be deceived. They know how it is, kind of. But even if it's not lying it's still wrong speech of a sort, as it is talking *nonsense*, also known as B.S. And talking B.S., even in formal Pali, or especially in formal Pali, is not so good. Sometimes I've considered that the Catholics have a much better system for going about all this confession business.

Very early in my monastic career I adopted a compromise method, intermediate between the Burmese method and common sense, taught to me by my first Vinaya teacher, ven. U Tejaniya (not the famous one). In this method I make a single confession, but divide up the offenses by category, and distinguish between one (*eka*), two (*dvi*), and several (*sambahulā*) offenses per category, and between a single broken rule in one category and more than one "of various types." So, for example, if I killed mosquitoes, used water having doubt whether or not it had living beings in it, looked at a girl's face while she was offering alms, and *tried* to kill a few mosquitoes but failed, I'd confess one *pācittiya* and several *dukkaṭas* of various types, and nothing else (*ahaṁ bhante ekaṁ pācittiyāpattiṁ ca sambahulā nānāvatthukā dukkaṭāpattiyo ca āpajjiṁ, tā tumhamūle paṭidesemi.*) In situations where there was another monk around who was game, I have even named which rules I broke (in Burmese or English), not just the categories, before making the Pali confession. Burmese monks have shown no objection to my making confession like this, although sometimes they have remarked that I do it like a Thai monk. Then again, there are some monks who feel uncomfortable around any monk who seems to want to follow Vinaya correctly. It's best to make confession to monks who are more comfortable with that.

If one becomes used to the traditional way(s) and then reads the original Pali Vinaya, one may be surprised. The formula for confession as given in the Vinaya Mahāvagga Pali itself (section 92 in the Burmese Sixth Council edition, uposathakkandhaka, āpattipaṭikammavidhi) is simply as follows:

A: *ahaṁ āvuso itthannāmaṁ āpattiṁ āpanno, taṁ paṭidesemi* (" Friend, I committed the offense of such and such name. I confess it.")
B: *passasi* ("Do you see?")
A: *āma passāmi* ("Yes, I see.")
B: *āyatiṁ saṁvareyyāsi* ("In future you should restrain yourself.")

That's all there is to it. The key phrase here is *iṭṭhannāmaṁ āpattiṁ*, the offense of such and such name—which certainly entails naming which rule one broke, and not just the general category. Otherwise, this canonical, officially sanctioned method is much simpler than the later variations, and at least relieves one of the burden of quasi-lying about restraining oneself in future. And since one is specifically naming one's offenses, one is much less likely to quasi-lie about "seeing" also.

There is a difficulty, however, in stating in the Pali language exactly which offense one has committed, and in understanding it when another monk states it. This works, of course, only if both monks involved in the process of confession are sufficiently fluent in Pali, which is relatively rare. So it is presumably quite good enough for two monks to tell each other exactly which rules they broke in their own vernacular language, and then to recite the Pali formula—and they might as well do the one in the Vinaya, and not one of the later versions. For that matter, it might be best if they do the whole thing in their own language.

More obvious evidence that monks are expected to say exactly which rules they've broken, and not just the general categories, is the rule forbidding monks with the same unconfessed offense to make confession together. Clearly, the only way they could be sure that they hadn't committed the same offense would be to compare their broken rules. Vinaya states that if all the monks in the same community have broken the same rule, one of them is required to set out on foot to find a monk who is innocent of that offense, to make confession to him, and then to come back so the other monks can make confession to him. Almost needless to say, this particular rule is almost universally flouted in Burma, even at relatively strict monasteries. Rather, the standard method for avoiding this rule in Burma is, when a monk makes confession to another monk who also has not yet made confession, he makes his confession twice—once for his "several offenses of various types" and once for making confession to a monk with the same unexpiated offense. This method entails a fair amount of B.S., especially to the extent that the confessing monk says the standardized "I will restrain myself," while knowing full well that he's certain to break the very same rule the next time he makes confession, and also in the sense that, when he makes confession the second time, he confesses "several offenses of various types" when the only offense to confess is one *dukkaṭa*, of one type. If I remember the commentary correctly it declares that the rule against confessing with an equally guilty monk is broken and confessed simultaneously, which is rather convenient. It's still quasi-dishonest though, if one says "I will restrain myself" when one intends to keep breaking the same rule in future, as a matter of tradition. My way of avoiding this particular messiness is simply to wait for two Burmese monks to make confession together, and after they have magically purified themselves of offenses I make confession to one of them. I may as well let them take the hit, since it is their preferred, traditional way of doing it anyway.

The Vinaya Pali (in the paragraph immediately following the standard formula cited above) also gives a formula for confessing doubt about an offense:

> *ahaṁ āvuso itthannāmāya āpattiyā vematiko; yadā nibbematiko bhavissāmi, tadā taṁ āpattiṁ paṭikarissāmi* ("Venerable sir, I am in doubt about the offense of such and such name; when I come to be without doubt, then I will rectify that offense.")

I have never actually seen or heard of this sort of confession being made by real live monks, but its existence in Vinaya further reinforces the rather obvious notion that one is not supposed to confess offenses of which one is oblivious, which one doesn't "see"—or even offenses of which one thinks one *maybe* committed. One should be sure before declaring that one has broken the rule.

It may be futile to criticize confession like this to traditional Asian monks, and to suggest that they adopt a practice that is a bit more meaningful than just mindlessly following tradition, but in the West there is really no good reason to import Asian corruptions—the West provides enough corruptions as it is.

Here is a debatable case of possible Western Vinaya corruption: Is it allowable to make confession by telephone? On the one hand, an act like confession should be carried out "face to face" (*sammukhāvinayo*), and, presumably, with the two monks involved squatting within arm's reach of each other. On the other hand, monks in the West are relatively scarce, and there may not be another monk within a hundred miles, and it may be better to make confession long-distance than not at all. In fact, even when there are other monks nearby, it may *still* be damned difficult to make confession. For example, once I was staying in an American city in which I was the only resident bhikkhu, and I had some broken rules to confess. It turned out that an American "ajahn" with several years since his ordination, along with a relatively senior Thai monk, came to town for the American one to deliver a Dhamma talk. When I met him I asked if I could make confession with him, whereupon he became clearly, acutely nervous, suggesting again and again that I should make confession to the Thai ajahn. I explained that the Thai monk understood little English, and I wouldn't be able to explain much to him. So finally the American monk admitted that he didn't know how to make confession; at his monastery they simply read the necessary blah-blah-blah off a card. (Can you imagine a Christian monk or priest who doesn't know how to do confession? And what kind of confession is reading something you don't understand off a card?) So, I went to the Thai monk, asked permission to make confession, and started my recitation, taking care to avoid the peculiar Burmese pronunciation of Pali. Before I got very far with it he interrupted me and instructed me to repeat after him; whereupon he proceeded to recite some Pali stuff that I had never heard before. I followed along once, but when he wanted me to repeat it a second time I just stood up in frustration and walked away. (What kind of confession is that, when someone who doesn't know you tells you what to confess?) So, shortly after that, I called a Burmese monk I know in California, squatting on the floor of the house where I was staying, with my hands together, right shoulder bared, and holding the phone to my ear with the other shoulder while reciting the ancient Pali words.

*Burmese monks making confession before a ceremony*

# THE AUTOPILOT

*(The matter of karma (in Pali, kamma) is one that I am asked about pretty often. Most people, including most Buddhists, don't understand it very well. Many westerners reject the notion of karma out of hand, largely due to the misunderstanding, and the incompatability of that misunderstanding of it with tenets of scientific realism. What follows is a very basic attempt to describe karma in a way that even a western materialist can accept. It doesn't describe karma in all its mysterious metaphysical aspects, but rather in a very common empirical one that applies to essentially everyone. If that can strike some traction, then maybe next one may move on to tackling some of the more mysterious metaphysical aspects. But this is a good start.)*

Long ago, before I ever became a Buddhist monk, I used to consider karma to be some kind of mechanical law of the Universe that science hadn't discovered yet, something like a psychic law of conservation of energy, or, "for every action there is an equal and opposite reaction." I had the notion that karma had the effect of some sort of cosmic accounting, with our goodness and badness recorded for future compensation.

But after studying Dharma a little I realized that, according to Buddhist philosophy, karma equals *cetanā*, with this *cetanā* being a purely psychological state, nothing outside of us at all. A famous sutta in the Anguttara Nikāya (sometimes known as A.VI.63) has the Buddha declaring *cetanāhaṁ bhikkhave kammaṁ vadāmi* —"Bhikkhus, it is *cetanā* that I call karma." And of the five *khandhas*, or "aggregates," which in relatively non-technical Buddhist philosophy constitute the entirety of a conscious being in this world, the fourth of the five, *saṅkhārakkhandha*, or the "aggregate of karma formations," is identified in the suttas with *cetanā*.

The most common rendering of *cetanā* into the English language is "volition," although this may be somewhat misleading. At the very least it may cause English-speaking students of Dharma to see karma in a very restricted way, which limits their appreciation of the fact that karma is of fundamental importance in conditioning our life in each moment; and an understanding of it is very helpful for gaining an understanding of ourselves.

*Cetanā* as volition should not be confused with mere decision-making, or identified with just making up our mind and intending to do something. It's not so much the shape of the pipes as what's flowing through the pipes, so to speak. It might be more useful to see it more as *urge* than as mere intention, something more like Schopenhauer's *will*—although it is not the ultimate Reality upon which everything is based, as Schopenhauer philosophized it to be. *Cetanā*, and thus karma, is the momentum of our mental energy, the mind's "habit energy." It is the habitual force of our perceiving mind, derived from the past and reinforced by it, which acts as a kind of automatic pilot for running us when we are not entirely awake...which is pretty much all the time, isn't it.

The more mindful we are, which is to say the more conscious we are, the less we identify with the automatic pilot, and the less it controls us and runs our life for us, based upon the past, which is when it acquired its habits. The more conscious we are, and the more in the present moment, the more possibilities and options we are able to see, and thus we can act accordingly, rather than mechanically following the one option that our habitual reaction has served up. If we eventually manage to wake all the way up, and thus are fully mindful, then the habitual mental energy from the past may still manifest itself, but it no longer has any power to control our lives.

We really have little if any control over what thoughts and feelings arise in us. We can maximize or minimize the chances of some sort of mental state arising, by various means, but we really don't know what is going to turn up until it turns up. It is the momentum of karma, based upon the past, which determines what arises in the mind. Only after it arises we may observe it and, if conscious enough to manage it, see whether or not it is appropriate to follow along with this thought or desire. So we may not be able to control what karma brings up, but at least we are able not to be enslaved to it. We can still be free from its rigid, limiting control. All this is one way of understanding the idea that an enlightened being creates no new karma, and thus has no "volition," thereby not adding to the habit energy/momentum already there from the past.

*Moha*, often translated into English as "delusion," goes hand in hand with karma. *Moha* is essentially a state of semiconscious stupor which allows our karmic momentum to control us like puppets. In other words, we're not awake enough to take full responsibility, so the automatic pilot, the "ego," does the best it can. So if one is fully mindful, moha as well as enslavement to karma disappears.

The idea of enlightenment in terms of Waking Up is easy to disregard; we may see it as just a kind of poetic metaphor, and let the significance of it slide off us like water off the proverbial duck's back. Yet if we really are wise and devoid of *moha*, then we really are in a state that is comparable to the ordinary state the way a person who is wide awake is compared to a sleepwalker, or someone who rolls over or scratches himself without completely waking up. A conscious person is *aware* of many things the ordinary person is unaware of—how often do we feel the cloth against our skin, or hear the sound of the refrigerator, or feel the breeze on our arm? How often do we blink or swallow with conscious awareness? How many of us can see that a feeling of desire or fear that arises (maybe strongly arises) is just a kind of habit that isn't us, but is just a kind of robotic program designed to get us through life somehow? Full mindfulness and full wisdom really are a matter of being fully awake.

Sometimes if I suddenly notice that I'm being unmindful and start being more aware, there is a subtle yet really obvious feeling of being more expanded and more conscious; it really is very similar to snapping out of a dozy, groggy state. Also there is a feeling of loss of limitations, as though invisible walls are falling away.

It is a feeling of spaciousness and freedom, with *complete* freedom being another synonym for Enlightenment. We tend to be much groggier, more limited, and more enslaved than we realize, controlled by semiconscious habits, lurching around like sophisticated robots.

Theoretically we could just "snap out of it" and Wake Up, just start being really alert and take full responsibility for our every choice and action; there's nothing necessarily stopping us from that; but it tends not to work out that way in "real life." Instead, we practice Dharma, which gradually clarifies what faculties we have, allowing us to make a little more progress (if we are sincere about making progress). Instead of relinquishing the ego once and for all, a Dharma practitioner systematically cleans it up and lightens it by replacing crude karmic habits with finer ones, or at least diluting the cruder ones down. It's difficult to go the whole way when we identify with the autopilot instead of with consciousness itself, though. Spiritual progress is a matter of letting go of what is familiar, of that to which we are "habituated"; it is a matter of becoming free, which is scary—at least the autopilot is scared. Waking Up is like death for the autopilot. So again, we wind up taking hesitant baby steps toward being able to "do" what is ultimately effortless.

Enlightenment ultimately is not a result of "doing," and is not the gain of anything. Rather, it is the dropping away of unnecessary limitations, including semiconscious stupor, karmic momentum, and identification with the ego, with "me."

And all this is setting aside the issues of transcendental knowledge, psychic powers, and the notion that karma creates our reality, with some of the habitual momentum of past karma coming from previous lives. That may be true also, but for the present moment it is practically irrelevant; the "law of Karma" applies anyway.

# ON THE FOUR STAGES OF MEDITATION: OR, ON THE UTTER FUTILITY OF THE WORD "JHĀNA"

I've been intending to write this article for several years. I have continually put it off, though, as the task of writing it has always seemed rather daunting. Some articles are fun to write; some even overflow and practically write themselves; but this one has always loomed before me like a school term paper that has to be written. Still, though, the subject—the nature of *jhāna*—is a fundamentally important one in Buddhist philosophy and ethics, as well as a controversial and troublesome one. So I feel it is time to stop procrastinating and sit down and write the damn thing.

The idea of jhāna is important because it holds such a central place in Buddhist practice, or at least did at one time, back in the old days. To give just one example of this, in the Mahā Satipaṭṭhāna Sutta (D22)—maybe a little ironically, as it is practically the Bible for Vipassana meditators who disregard jhāna—Right Concentration, *sammāsamādhi*, is *defined* as the four jhānas. The commentarial tradition has backed away from this idea, for reasons I may attempt to discuss, maybe, but the Sutta says it pretty clearly. So according to the Sutta, if we don't have jhāna we don't have Right Concentration, the eighth step of the Noble Eightfold Path. Some suttas seem to imply that the eighth step is even the most important step.

The idea of jhāna is controversial because, although the word "jhāna" is tossed around quite a lot in some circles, people, even ostensible authorities on the subject, often disagree on what jhāna actually *is.* And the trouble comes from the combination of the first two: important + controversial → trouble. So it's good to do a little investigating.

One bit of troublesomeness that steps in even before the controversy starts raging good and hard is the fact that, although jhāna is declared to be Right Concentration, also it is declared in the Pali texts to be *uttarimanussadhamma*—a "superhuman state." So if the suttas are to be taken at face value (which the commentarial tradition pretends to do, but really doesn't), then in order to have Right Concentration, a requisite for correct Dhamma practice, one must be essentially *superhuman*, at least with regard to one's meditation.

Another bit of trouble, which itself is a major cause for the controversy, is that jhāna is not clearly, precisely, unambiguously defined in the suttas. Literally, or so I've been told, the word means something like "blazing" or "illumination," which is not very helpful, except perhaps to imply that it is a more intense state of mind than ordinary consciousness and not some kind of semiconscious trance. Practically every time jhāna is described in the suttas, the description takes the form of essentially the same stock formula, which is as follows (this quoted from the Mahā Satipaṭṭhāna Sutta itself):

*(katamo ca bhikkhave sammāsamādhi?)*

*idha bhikkhave bhikkhu vivicceva kāmehi vivicca akusalehi dhammehi savitakkaṁ savicāraṁ vivekajaṁ pītisukhaṁ paṭhamaṁ jhānaṁ upasampajja viharati;*

*vitakkavicārānaṁ vūpasamā ajjhattaṁ sampasādanaṁ cetaso eko-*

*dibhāvaṁ avitakkaṁ avicāraṁ samādhijaṁ pītisukhaṁ dutiyaṁ jhānaṁ upasampajja viharati;*

*pītiyā ca virāgā upekkhako ca viharati, sato ca sampajāno, sukhañca kāyena paṭisaṁvedeti, yaṁ taṁ ariyā ācikkhanti "upekkhako satimā sukhavihārī"ti, tatiyaṁ jhānaṁ upasampajja viharati;*

*sukhassa ca pahānā dukkhassa ca pahānā pubbeva somanassadomanassānaṁ atthaṅgamā adukkhamasukhaṁ upekkhāsatipārisuddhiṁ catutthaṁ jhānaṁ upasampajja viharati;*

*(ayaṁ vuccati bhikkhave sammāsamādhi.)*

(And what, monks, is Right Concentration?)

Herein, monks, quite secluded from sensual pleasures (or "objects of desire"), secluded from unskillful states, a monk, with discriminative thought and reason, with exhilaration and pleasure born of seclusion, having attained first jhāna, abides in it.

Having allayed discriminative thought and reason, with inward serenity and unification of mind, without discriminative thought or reason, with exhilaration and pleasure born of concentration, having attained second jhāna, he abides in it.

With the fading away of exhilaration he abides in equanimity, attentive and aware, and he experiences pleasure through his body, so that the Noble Ones say of him, "Equanimous and attentive, he is one who abides in pleasure"; having attained third jhāna, he abides in it.

Having abandoned pleasure, having abandoned pain, along with the former cessation of happiness and unhappiness, without pain, without pleasure, with the equanimity of purity of attentiveness, having attained fourth jhāna, he abides in it.

(This, monks, is called Right Concentration.)

First of all I would observe that the very fact that jhāna is almost always described with a stock formula is peculiar. The Buddha himself, presumably an enlightened being, probably would not have used the same exact formula every time he described such an important part of his system. It would appear that the stock formula, easily plugged in to passages in suttas, was the result of dogmatization, possibly in the hands of people who never knew the Buddha, or deep meditative states.

With regard to the translation above, I would point out that "pleasure" and "pain" (*sukha* and *dukkha*) are apparently referring to physical sensations or feelings, the more mentally-oriented positive and negative being "happiness" and "unhappiness" (*somanassa* and *domanassa*). So in first jhāna there is still thinking as well as physical and emotional pleasure and pain, or at least pleasure; in second jhāna no more thinking, but still the possibility of both kinds of pleasure/pain; in third jhāna no thinking, no happiness or unhappiness, but still physical feelings; and finally in fourth jhāna not even that, but only affectively neutral mindfulness (or "attentiveness") and equanimity.

Also I would point out that *cetaso ekodibhāvaṁ*, often rendered as "one-pointedness of mind," is not necessarily the bringing of the conscious mind to a *point*, which would imply the narrowing of consciousness to such an extent that one could be oblivious to everything except only what is concentrated upon, as in a deep hypnotic trance. It can also mean that the mind is single or unified, whatever that means. I'll eventually get back to that point.

And thirdly I would point out that the above description of jhāna, which is essentially *the* description of jhāna in the Pali texts, can be, and certainly is, interpreted in different ways by different people, including different meditation instructors and other people who consider themselves to have attained jhāna.

My father, among many other things, was an amateur hypnotist, and so I am familiar with the basic principles and characteristics of hypnosis; and it seems to me that *most* of what passes for jhāna, at least in Burma, is really hypnotic trance. For example, not far from my monastery in northwestern Burma there is a meditation center which, I've been told, guarantees meditators that by the end of one retreat, even if they are beginners, they will be able to sit for several hours at a stretch without moving, and furthermore they will be able to ascend into the heaven realms and descend into the hell realms in some kind of psychic body, and meet the denizens of these places. And it is to be expected that the denizens will look and act in accordance with how traditional Burmese Buddhists believe they would. That sounds like hypnosis to me. But the results are so dramatic that people are reluctant to consider that it's not the real deal—whether or not they are sophisticated enough to have heard of hypnosis.

But this confusion evidently does not occur only in little-known, out of the way meditation centers. Probably the best-known meditation center in Burma which advocates and teaches some semblance of jhāna is Pah Auk Tawya in southern Burma; and some of what I have seen and heard of the place indicates that hypnotic trance is confounded with Right Concentration even there (assuming of course that hypnosis and jhāna are not really and originally the same thing, which is itself a debatable subject).

For example, I remember reading in a book written by ven. Pah Auk Sayadaw (I don't remember the title; it had a blue cover) a "success story" of a woman practicing samatha meditation under Sayadaw's guidance who remembered a past life as a royal white elephant who attained human birth in its subsequent life through the merit acquired by offering a flower to a pagoda. This sort of story is easily acceptable to Burmese Buddhists, falling in line with their cultural conditioning, yet it may appear rather suspicious, to say the least, to a critical Westerner.

Another example was told to me by a young Western meditator at Pah Auk many years ago. He had been assigned the practice of seeing, with the "samādhi eye," the internal organs of himself and others. (This is not supposed to be just an exercise of the imagination, but an actual seeing, through finely honed concentration, of those organs.) He told me that once he was in the meditation hall "seeing" the bones of the person sitting in front of him.

He was doing this with his eyes closed, since the physical eye is not what is supposed to do the seeing. So after looking at the other person's bones to his own satisfaction, he finally opened his eyes to discover that, without his knowledge, the other person whose bones he had been observing had gotten up and walked away—so he was "seeing" bones that weren't there. When he reported this to his meditation instructor, he was informed that it didn't matter.

These two cases (and I could give more) are not so much cases of doubtful jhāna as cases of doubtful psychic powers derived from a jhāna-oriented technique, and they illustrate the possibility that what is *called* jhāna and psychic powers may really be, in such cases, hypnosis and the power of suggestion influencing one's imagination. Hypnosis is not bad or wrong, and may really be useful in some situations, yet if that's what it is, then the person experiencing it should probably be aware of the fact, and not call it something that it is not. It would be interesting if some scientists from a hypnosis lab like the one at Stanford University were to bring a PET scanner or some such to a place like Pah Auk and test whether the practitioners of jhāna were hypnotized or not. The results might result in some heated indignation from the teachers and devout practitioners of the method, however, and a denunciation of the tests. Human nature being what it is, that could be expected with a fair amount of confidence, assuming that the tests came out positive.

This is not to say that *all* jhāna at a place like Pah Auk Tawya is hypnotic, but I would guess that most of it is. I've been told that even ven. Pah Auk Sayadaw has acknowledged that much of what people have experienced along the lines of past life regressions and so on have just been vivid figments of imagination. Yet hypnosis appears to be inherent in the system.

It would seem that this confusion of jhāna with hypnotic trance (again, assuming that they haven't been identical from the beginning) did not originate in Burma, but began even in ancient times. The traditional meditation technique of *kasiṇa*, for instance, described in detail in the great hypnosis—I mean, eh, meditation manual *Visuddhimagga*, is very similar to techniques employed to induce hypnotic trance. The aforementioned hypnosis lab at

Stanford uses, or has used, a method involving the subject gazing at a small circle on the wall before him or her, which, aside from the smaller size of the circle, is pretty much the same as a *kasiṇa* disc. I do not remember if it is mentioned in the suttas themselves, but tradition has it that while one is sitting in fourth jhāna one's breath and heartbeat slow to virtual nonexistence, and one becomes oblivious to one's environment, including even physical injury...which is also symptomatic of deep hypnotic trance. Yet I fail to see how going into a state of suspended animation like that of a hibernating squirrel could be called higher consciousness or "purity of mindfulness."

Bearing this in mind, I consider it possible that the alleged confusion could have occurred relatively early, even before Theravadin orthodoxy set in, during the first century or two while the system was undergoing its phase of explosive systematization. I know enough about early Christian history, and have seen enough of modern Asian Theravadin ecclesiasticism, to know that orthodox doctrine is usually decided by members of the system more interested in scholarship and Church politics than in actual practice of Dharma; and even with the best intentions the truth can become very distorted by fellows who are working not from personal experience, but from intellectual theory. And thus, somehow, what may have originally been a convenient, rather loose description of the progression of stages in Buddhist meditation ossified into a stock, formulaic description of superhuman mental states, in the same category as psychic powers and the four stages of sainthood or Ariya-hood, accessed only by a relatively tiny minority of monks. At this point I suppose I should explain my theoretical version of jhāna.

The very same formula found in the texts can, as has already been mentioned, be interpreted in different ways. One way is to see it as a progression in the development of meditation in general, not only the most advanced, "superhuman" stages. Thus first jhāna could be elementary meditation in which the meditator has a perceptual "primary object" of meditation, and in which he or she has not yet entered any particularly deep or refined mental states. It could still be a relatively "normal" state of mind, although clarified and pacified by the meditative practice. In Roman Catholic monastic traditions this level of meditative practice is simply called "meditation."

But with second jhāna one enters the realm of what the Christian mystics call "contemplation." At this stage one is not only no longer indulging in discursive thought; one is no longer focusing the attention on any perceptual primary object at all. The mind becomes clear, luminous, and relatively silent. Thoughts may begin to arise, yet they simply pass away under the dissolving light of mindfulness and do not reach the stage of linking together into a "train of thought." At this second stage of meditative practice one's more basic mental processes of feeling are still in the dualistic realm of positive pleasure and negative pain, however. One may still experience physical pleasure and pain, and one may still feel the exhilaration and joy from conscious expansion; and, although the stock formula doesn't explicitly assert it, one may still experience various feelings of happiness *or* unhappiness. Feelings of grief or anguish could theoretically arise at this level, although they would not lead to any elaborated dramatic story being cooked up, since one is not focusing on them specifically, and the linking together of perceptions into narratives or themes has already been abandoned along with first jhāna.

With third jhāna, in accordance with the hypothesis, not only thinking but also a dualistic experience of emotional states would be transcended. Physical pleasure and pain would still be discerned, however subtly, as dualistic "realities," though.

Finally, with fourth jhāna, the entire dualistic complex of perceptions and feelings, from top to bottom, would be transcended —not necessarily suppressed or eradicated, but no longer a focus of consciousness, no longer a variegated, dualistic "reality." The mind would be like a mirror, reflecting whatever naturally comes to mind (which would be relatively little, quantitatively), without discriminating it, without focusing on it, without attributing significance to it. The mind would, temporarily, be free from the self-generated limitations of the mundane mind. But even fourth jhāna, supreme meditative state that it is (setting aside further and presumably later elaborations of the system, like formless jhānas and the state of "the attainment of cessation") is conditioned, with a beginning and an end, and is not true enlightenment.

The evolution of jhāna into trance states, even superhuman ones, going with the hypothesis, has resulted in traditional Theravada splitting into "two sāsanas," two teachings. Sometimes in Burma one may be asked, "Which Sāsana do you belong to, the Vipassana Sāsana, or the Samatha Sāsana?" But I really don't think the Buddha originally taught two rival approaches to Nirvana. My experience as a long-term meditator, as well as a person who arguably thinks too much, leads me to feel that mindfulness is really the key to Dharma practice—not so much the *eradication* of unskillful mental states as the neutralization of them through the detachment and non-identification of mindful awareness. The thing is, though, that we cannot detach from what we are oblivious to. Deeper jhānas, which are "purifications of mindfulness," allow the meditator to be mindful of subtle states that the ordinary person walking around and making noise does not even suspect the existence of.

The more awake and attentive one is, the more subtle the phenomena one is able to observe, thereby "transmuting" it into awareness. The four jhānas are, according to this interpretation, the progression of meditation from the most obvious, crudest phenomena, which is all most people tend to be aware of, to the most refined, until the whole field of consciousness is no longer subconscious, or semiconscious, but conscious.

Even in fourth jhāna a meditator would be conscious; in fact he or she would be more conscious than an ordinary person in an ordinary waking state. One would not be *oblivious* to anything; it would simply become irrelevant, and remain undiscriminated. In this sense advanced jhāna may be said to be a kind of temporary, artificial enlightenment; in the texts jhāna is called "temporary liberation" (*samaya vimokkha*). Thus it would mean more than just temporary liberation from mental defilements by lapsing into a tranced pinpoint or laser beam of attentiveness.

But trance states have always been in vogue in India, as have their dramatic psychic effects, and scholar monks, church politicians, and even conscientious Dharma practitioners who were not strong in meditation, or maybe just not strong in discernment, could be misled into thinking that popularly revered trance states, and the seeming powers that they can evoke, were the real thing. And thus the four stages in which Buddhist meditation progresses, including the most elementary level, mutated into superhuman mental states, and became almost unapproachable to the majority, almost mythical.

It seems to me that, practically by definition, anything a human being attains would by that very fact *not* be "superhuman." If a human attains it, then it is human. So in this sense even enlightenment itself would not be a superhuman state. But if consciousness expands beyond what is characteristically human, transcending humanity somehow, for example by transcending *form*, then I suppose it could be called a superhuman state, although a *person* technically would not attain it; it would be attained by somehow leaving the *person* behind. In this case, transcendental states, say, from second jhāna on up, could reasonably be called superhuman; but elementary first jhāna, still bound to human thought, could hardly be above the human level.

So anyway, I consider the word "jhāna" to be futile, a useless word now, because the meaning of the word is so controversial, with different people meaning different things when they use it, that it simply results in more confusion than information. Better to describe a meditative state in one's own words, or just to remain silent, than to use a word as vague and non-descriptive as "jhāna."

I suspect that the state of being a "stream enterer," a *sotāpanna*, was not originally a superhuman or transcendental state either... but we needn't get into that here. That's a whole different kettle of wax.

Well, that wasn't so hard to write.

# ON DEPENDENT CO-ARISING

*yaḥ pratītyasamutpādaḥ śūnyataṁ tāṁ pracakṣmahe /*
*sa prajñaptir upādāya pratipat saiva madhyamā //*

"What is dependent co-arising, that we call emptiness;
It is making-known-with-regard-to, it is just the Middle Way."
—ven. Nāgārjuna *(Mūlamadhyamakakārikā XXIV:18)*

Buddhist philosophy, like any other major belief system, contains elements which are rather weird and difficult to understand. All of us believe things that we don't fully understand, which is odd, but that's just the way we are. Science teaches us that light can behave like a material particle or like an energy wave, and how it behaves depends upon how we observe it. Very few people, if any, really understand this, but we go ahead and believe it anyway. Even most people who think they understand it probably don't. Buddhist philosophy is like this.

It's not just a matter of some peripheral, unimportant parts being weird either—some of the most fundamental teachings of Buddhism belong to the Weird and Difficult to Understand category. *Anattā*, or no self, is one of these; although it seems to me that although no self may not be fully comprehended intellectually, it can be realized intuitively, without thinking, without much difficulty...because, of course, "self" depends upon thought for its existence, regardless of whether that "self" is a subjective person, an objectified person, or an objectified object or "thing."

No thinking, no self. But no self is something we can at least *sort of* understand intellectually to the extent that there's nobody really there. That much is straightforward.

There is another fundamental doctrine of Buddhist philosophy which is even weirder in its own way, and which almost *nobody* really understands, assuming for the sake of argument that anybody as a "self" exists to understand it anyway. This is the doctrine of *paṭicca-samuppāda*, or dependent co-arising. Unlike most Pali Buddhist philosophical and ethical terms, like *sati* ("mindfulness"), *samādhi* ("concentration"), *mettā* ("loving-kindness"), etc., *paṭicca-samuppāda* has no standardized, streamlined English equivalent. It goes by many names, including "conditioned genesis," "dependent origination," "causal genesis," etc. This, I assume, is partly because it is not well understood by scholars. They don't feel fully comfortable with this or that designation.

This points to one of the weirdest things about dependent co-arising: On the one hand it is considered to be essential to an understanding of phenomenal existence, and essential to an understanding of Dharma. On the other hand, hardly anyone really understands it. It's like a paradox.

It is considered to be *so* essential to Dharma that the Buddha's own enlightenment involved, radically, a realization of *paṭicca-samuppāda.* After his enlightenment, according to tradition, the Buddha sat for many more days in Bodh Gaya under various trees reviewing dependent co-arising in forwards order, then in backwards order, then forwards *and* backwards…reflecting upon the essence of Dharma itself. In the texts, like in the Great Discourse on the Simile of the Elephant's Footprint (M28), it is asserted that "He who sees dependent co-arising, sees Dhamma; he who sees Dhamma, sees dependent co-arising." Also, in the Great Discourse on Origins (Mahā Nidāna Sutta, D15), a text presumably intended to be a definitive statement on the subject, the Buddha says this: "Profound, Ānanda, is this dependent co-arising, and profound it shows itself. It is from not understanding, not penetrating this Dhamma, Ānanda, that the human race is like a tangled snarl of thread, become like a tangled thicket of tall grass or rushes, and one does not pass beyond the realms of woe, misfortune, calamity, Samsara." Thus dependent co-arising is considered to be Extremely Important.

But on the other hand, as was already mentioned, very few people, Buddhist or otherwise, really understand it. According to the legend, immediately after the Buddha's enlightenment he considered just keeping his mouth shut and being a *paccekabuddha*, fully enlightened yet silent, because he felt that nobody would understand *paṭicca-samuppāda*, and he didn't need the headache of trying to get the point across. It turns out that his initial feeling was not too far from the mark.

Most Westerners, as far as I have seen, are willing to admit that they don't understand it. Many of them seem to feel a bit uncomfortable around the idea of dependent co-arising, largely because people feel uncomfortable in the presence of the unknown. The Burmese, on the other hand, memorize a stock formula consisting of twelve links, the so-called "twelve *nidāna* theory," and then memorize a few definitions and brief explanations, and then believe that they understand it. What the Buddha himself allegedly felt that nobody would understand, now is supposedly understood by millions of Burmese Buddhists, with most of them, including most monks, not practicing or penetrating very deeply at all. They memorize a few dogmas and think they've got it. Nowadays I am reluctant to suggest that American Buddhism is superior in any way to the traditional Burmese version; but still it does appear that Westerners have the advantage over the Burmese in this case, to the extent that they freely admit they don't understand dependent co-arising, whereas the Burmese can be quite smug in their belief that they can understand Dhamma by memorizing stock formulas.

The stock formula in question, which is the *usual* form dependent co-arising takes on paper, is a kind of linear causative sequence beginning with *avijjā paccayā saṅkhārā*, "conditioned by ignorance are constructs," and ending with *jāti paccayā jarāmaraṇaṁ sokaparidevadukkhadomanassupāyāsa sambhavanti*, or "conditioned by birth there come to being aging and death, grief, lamentation, pain, distress, and despair." The formula in its full glory looks something like this:

> *Katamo ca, bhikkhave, paṭiccasamuppādo? Avijjāpaccayā, bhikkhave, saṅkhārā; saṅkhārapaccayā viññāṇaṃ; viññāṇapaccayā nāmarūpaṃ; nāmarūpapaccayā saḷāyatanaṃ; saḷāyatanapaccayā phasso; phassapaccayā vedanā; vedanāpaccayā taṇhā; taṇhāpaccayā upādānaṃ; upādānapaccayā bhavo; bhavapaccayā jāti; jātipaccayā jarāmaraṇaṃ sokaparidevadukkhadomanassupāyāsā sambhavanti. Evametassa kevalassa dukkhakkhandhassa samudayo hoti. Ayaṃ vuccati, bhikkhave, paṭiccasamuppādo.*

This is not the only form that the doctrine assumes. Another, less elaborate formula may be translated into English somewhat like this:

> *In the existence of this, that becomes; from the arising of this, that arises; in the nonexistence of this, that does not become; in the cessation of this, that ceases. (Imasmiṁ sati, idaṁ hoti; imass'uppādā, idaṁ uppajjati; imasmiṁ asati, idaṁ na hoti; imassa nirodhā, idaṁ nirujjhati.)*

This version of the doctrine is less common than the twelve-*nidāna* theory, but it is still a common stock formula, encountered repeatedly in the suttas. Yet even the standardized twelve-*nidāna* version has many variations in the texts, with more and less than twelve links. Even the aforementioned *Mahā Nidāna Sutta* itself, the Great Discourse on Origins, which is the most elaborate canonical explanation of dependent co-arising found in a single discourse, and which presumably was intended in ancient times to be definitive, endorses a formula similar to, but not the same as, the standardized stock form. And there are some suttas, such as the Sakkapañha Sutta of the Dīgha Nikāya and the Kalahavivāda Sutta of the Sutta Nipāta, which contain similar longish sequences of "this arises from that" without being officially acknowledged as being forms of dependent co-arising. Below is a comparison of four different versions of the sequential cause of all our suffering:

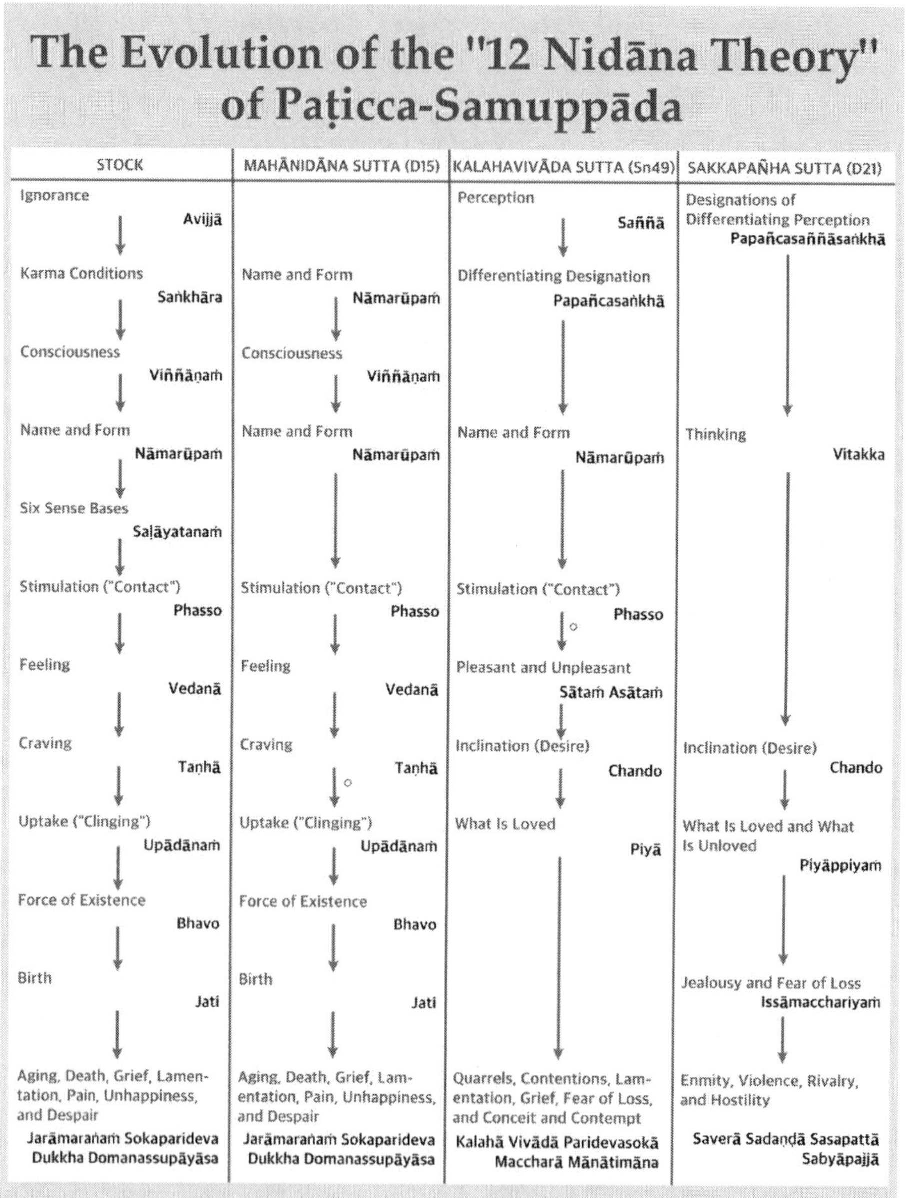


*showing four different versions from four suttas, with the first being the final, orthodox version, and the following three being early prototypes*

The facts that the sequence takes many forms, that some of them are not explicitly stated to represent dependent co-arising, and that even the largest, supposedly definitive text on the subject shows a somewhat deviant form of the standard, suggest that ancient monks were having difficulty grappling with the idea of *paṭicca-samuppāda*, and that while the Pali Canon was evolving over time the doctrine itself evolved, appearing in different forms in different suttas. It may even be that the longish sequential "this causes that" formulas were originally not intended to be formal explanations of dependent co-arising (although at the least they were probably intended to be examples of it).

Furthermore, even the standardized, finalized twelve *nidāna* theory is not without controversy. The official, commentarial party line for Theravada is that the twelve links occur over the span of three lifetimes: Ignorance and karma conditions conducive to rebirth occurred in a previous life, which resulted in rebirth-linking consciousness and the formation of a present, living mind and body, which in time experience stimuli which inspire craving, "uptake," and new karma conducive to continued existence…which then results in birth, old age, death, grief, and all the rest in a future life. But over the centuries some Buddhist philosophers, and I believe at least one major school, preferred to interpret the sequence as occurring within a single lifetime (which does, however, result in a kind of short circuit of the system if *saṅkhārā* and *bhavo* are both interpreted to mean karma). And some, including the famous and influential English monk Ñāṇavīra, have preferred to understand it all as totally simultaneous. As ven. Ñāṇavīra used to say, the text goes "This arising, that arises," not "This *ceasing*, that arises." Even the weak link where the chain is broken, thereby allowing one off the wheel of Samsara, is somewhat controversial. It is my understanding that the position of orthodox Theravada is that the sequence is broken between feeling and craving—feeling experienced with concentrated mindfulness and insight is neutralized and loses its power of inducing craving—yet I have been informed that other interpretations, including Ñāṇavīra's, place the weak link elsewhere.

Partly because of all this, and partly because I intuit that an enlightened being describing the nature of samsaric reality would probably not give complicated, elaborate explanations which assume as a given a pluralistic universe, I assume that the simpler, This Being, That Is version comes closer to what the Buddha originally had in mind, and that the twelve-*nidāna* stock theory is a later ecclesiastical artifact. And if that is the case, then dependent co-arising could be more a kind of logical, conditional if/then system than an empirical cause-and-effect sequence describing real causes producing real effects. Consequently I have been of the opinion for many years that as a general rule Theravada Buddhists, including venerables Buddhaghosa and Ñāṇavīra, do not understand dependent co-arising very well. And consequently, if we can accept the quote from M28, they don't understand Dhamma. Oh well. The Buddha allegedly thought nobody would understand it anyway.

One of the many reasons why Mahayana Buddhism came into existence was as a reaction to the trend toward dogmatic, formulaic, intellectual analysis found in the older "Hinayana" schools. The rigid, word-laden approach to "understanding" dependent co-arising was one of the targets of the new movement; and in my opinion the proto-Mahayanist philosopher Nāgārjuna comes about as close as anybody to really explaining *paṭicca-samuppāda*, or, as it is known in Buddhist Sanskrit, *pratītya-samutpāda*. The Madhyamaka philosophy associated with Nāgārjuna is directed primarily toward dependent co-arising as the essence of Dharma, and endeavors to interpret everything phenomenal in accordance with it. Nāgārjuna was a genius, revered by Mahayana Buddhists almost like a second Buddha; and it is my impression that he really did understand dependent co-arising better than did ven. Buddhaghosa ("the St. Paul of Theravada"). But this is not intended to be an essay on Nāgārjuna or Madhyamaka, so I won't dwell upon him much.

I will mention, however, that Nāgārjuna identified dependent co-arising with Emptiness, and thus also with No Self, as well as with the Middle Path itself. His most important work, the Mūlamadhyamakakārikā, is a radical account of dependent co-arising, but dedicates only one short chapter to the stock twelve-*nidāna* theory which was prevalent in probably all of the early schools and couldn't easily be rejected; his account in that chapter, number 26, the second-to-last chapter, is not so different from how a Theravadin would explain it. The main difference is that an orthodox Theravadin considers each of the twelve links to be *real*; whereas Nāgārjuna considers anything dependently co-arisen to be *empty*, lacking in any self-essence or authentic individuality—it is only *relatively* real. Each link exists, or seems to exist, only in relation to something else. The whole system is devoid of ultimate reality, and depends for its existence upon the system itself, in a kind of recursive, self-perpetuating illusion. But enough about Madhyamaka. If you are interested you can read the Mūlamadhyamakakārikā yourself. There are a number of translations of it.

What I would like to do now is give a very fundamental example of how this works. It involves possibly the most fundamental of all discernible qualities: sameness and difference.

First of all, sameness and difference are *relations*; they do not exist in and of themselves, but only in relation to something. That is, they are relative. There is no pure sameness or pure difference, since they exist only relatively with regard to something else, as attributed conditions, not as self-existent essences. Pure, abstract sameness or difference without any particular thing being the same or different would be practically meaningless.

Furthermore, sameness and difference cannot exist independently of *each other*; there can be no sameness without difference, or vice versa. One way of demonstrating this is by attempting to imagine one without the other. Try to picture a universe that is absolutely uniform throughout: We can imagine a space that is a uniform white, for example—but the only way to imagine it is by ourselves *not* being members of that universe, and being different from everything else. Like modern science tries to do also, we try to sneak an invisible observer in through the back door. On the other hand, if we try to imagine a universe that is absolutely *non*-uniform, things get much weirder. How could there be an entire universe in which everything was completely different from everything else? Each *point*, each pixel on the screen, would have to be different. In order to avoid two adjacent points/pixels being similar, the resolution would have to be infinitesimally fine...so that, to an observer, it would be totally uniform! Random static refined down to infinity becomes total uniformity, a perfect, uniform grey. (It just occurred to me that in a universe in which everything was different from everything else, each unique individual entity would be similar in sharing the same attribute of *uniqueness*. So a universe of complete difference would have to be uninterpreted, without generalities, and thus just as empty of meaning as its opposite.)

So, much as in the beginning of Hegel's logical dialectic with absolute being and absolute non-being, "absolute" sameness and "absolute" difference merge into each other and become indistinguishable. The only way to keep them from melting together is to keep the two opposites distinct, and both present, in relation.

This is how we function psychologically in the phenomenal world. Consider stasis and change, a basic variation on the theme of sameness and difference. The only way that we are aware of something *not* changing is by comparing it to something, if only a clock, that has changed. The passage of time is marked by a sequence of changes. We note that time has passed by noting change, and then compare object X with our memory of it and perceive that it is essentially the same as before, despite the changes in other things, and so we say that it has stayed the same. Contrariwise with change: We are aware of change only in relation to what we consider to have remained the same, even if that unchanging yardstick is nothing more than our own "self." If absolutely *everything* changed from our samsaric point of view (and Buddhist philosophy asserts that everything *is* changing every moment), then we wouldn't be aware of anything meaningful at all, since nothing would have anything remotely resembling a stable and reliable *meaning*. At least the meanings have to remain the same. Even our memories would change, rendering what occurred just a moment ago to be totally different from what replaced it a moment later, or otherwise just totally forgotten. Thus sameness and difference necessarily coexist in a meaningful world; in other words, they *dependently co-arise.*

The philosopher F. H. Bradley, in his monumental metaphysics text *Appearance and Reality*, pointed out a similar co-dependence between qualities and the relations between them, thereby exposing the relativity of relativity itself. A quality, such as "blue," has no meaning unless it is distinguished, and this distinction is a relation with other qualities. But there can be no relation of qualities without the existence of the qualities themselves. This produces a chicken and egg problem of how an entity X can exist at all: its qualities cannot exist unless they are in some relation, yet the relation cannot exist without qualities to relate. And this dual existence incidentally splits X into two distinct aspects anyhow, undermining its very entity-hood. F. H. Bradley discovered Madhyamaka-style dependent co-arising probably without ever hearing of it.

This same kind of paradoxical chicken and egg problem puzzled me years ago with regard to distinguishing an object perceptually and directing one's attention toward it. We couldn't perceive something as a distinct object without directing our attention to it, but we wouldn't know to direct our attention to it in the first place unless we had already distinguished it somehow. It seems that a reasonable explanation is that a perception and the volition directing it *dependently co-arise*. The two are necessarily simultaneous.

Our entire world is created by this kind of paradoxical interrelatedness. It is a psychological and logical system and doesn't *necessarily* have anything to do with any external reality. External reality is essentially a meaningless Void to the extent that it does not come ready-equipped with interrelated distinguished qualities.

It is interesting that, in early Buddhist philosophy, even existence and nonexistence were seen as a kind of dependently co-arising psychological phenomena. For example, in the proto-twelve-*nidāna* theory of *paṭicca-samuppāda* found in the Kalahavivāda Sutta of the Sutta Nipāta, mentioned above, there is a side branch involving this very duality (at the point marked by a small circle on the chart):

In what are founded pleasant and unpleasant?
In what not being do they not exist?
And nonexistence and existence too, whatever that means—Tell

me that in which they are founded.

In stimulation (*phassa*) are founded pleasant and unpleasant;
In stimulation not being they do not exist.
Nonexistence and existence too, whatever it means—
I tell you that they are founded in this.

Again, absolute Being and absolute Non-being ultimately cannot be differentiated, and being and non-being without capital letters are relative, and psychological. They have to exist in order for a meaningful world to exist, and so we artificially create them. This helps me to feel a little less vertigo when coming upon Mahayana texts with words like:

Form is Emptiness; the very Emptiness is Form. (—Heart Sutra)

What is is the same as what is not; what is not is the same as what is. (—Hsin Hsin Ming)

There are no two such things as existence and nonexistence. (—Tibetan Book of the Great Liberation)

Such dependent co-arising exists everywhere; our entire subjective universe is pervaded by it and generated by it. Setting aside such crude examples as beauty depending upon ugliness, up depending upon down, good depending upon evil, etc., consider Dharma practice and wisdom. It is not strictly true that Dharma practice leads to wisdom as a cause leads to an effect, in linear fashion; one could say that the exact opposite is also true: The wiser we are, the more and better we practice. The two dependently co-arise (which causes me considerable skepticism over the Mahasi tradition's assumption that after one becomes an Ariya one can sit back and take it easy, with the "Ariyas" at a Burmese Mahasi meditation center often being the most ostentatious slackers at the place).

And so, dependent co-arising, according to the hypothesis, is a kind of metaphilosophy similar to the philosophy of Kant: it does not describe reality, but rather describes the psychological genesis of unreality, of the samsaric world. A sentient mind, and also the world as we know it, are essentially consciousness filtered through a pattern; and the pattern is produced and stabilized by this very same dependent co-arising. So it's no wonder almost nobody understands it. If some of you would like to answer that I don't understand it either, I wouldn't argue the point.

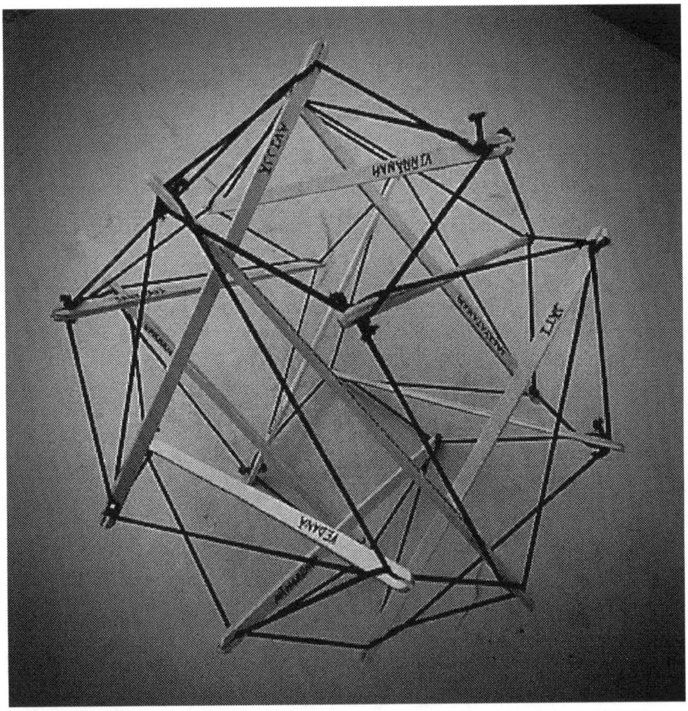

*(A note on the illustration: For many years I have considered tensegrity structures to be a good analogy for dependent co-arising. The whole thing is held together in a stable configuration by mutual forces acting upon each other, with none of the sticks actually touching each other, and if a single piece is taken away, the stability collapses. So I finally managed to build the tensegrity truncated octahedron shown above, which conveniently contains twelve struts, so that in the model each strut represents a link in the standardized 12-nidāna version of the system. I hope someone can appreciate this, because it was a bitch to make. I'll probably make more, though, so it will very probably become*

*easier with practice. Upon showing this to a certain devout Burmese Buddhist a few days ago, he looked at it like a cat looks at a lemon—i.e., totally unimpressed—and then warned me in all seriousness that it is wrong and "dangerous," because the links should all be in a linear, chain-like sequence. But I think for non-Burmese people it can serve as a useful analogy.*)

## APPENDIX: F. H. BRADLEY ON THE DEPENDENT CO-ARISING OF QUALITIES AND RELATIONS

Hence...the qualities [of a thing] must be, and must *also* be related. But there is hence a diversity which falls inside each quality. It has a double character, as both supporting and as being made by the relation. It may be taken as at once condition and result, and the question is as to how it can combine this variety. For it must combine the diversity, and yet it fails to do so. *A* is both made, and is not made, what it is by relation; and these different aspects are not each the other, nor again is either *A*. If we call its diverse aspects $a$ and $\underline{\alpha}$, then *A* is partly each of these. As $a$ it is the difference on which distinction is based, while as $\underline{\alpha}$ it is the distinctness that results from connection. *A* is really both somehow together as $A(a—\underline{\alpha})$. But (as we saw in Chapter ii.) *without* the use of a relation it is impossible to predicate this variety of *A*. And, on the other hand, *with* an internal relation *A*'s unity disappears, and its contents are dissipated in an endless process of distinction. *A* at first becomes $a$ in relation with $\underline{\alpha}$, but these terms themselves fall hopelessly asunder. We have got, against our will, not a mere aspect, but a new quality $a$, which itself stands in a relation; and hence (as we saw before with *A*) its content must be manifold. As going into the relation it itself is $a^2$, and as resulting from the relation it itself is $\underline{\alpha}^2$. And it combines, and yet cannot combine, these adjectives. We, in brief, are led by a principle of fission which conducts us to no end. Every quality in relation has, in consequence, a diversity within its own nature, and this diversity cannot immediately be asserted of the quality. Hence the quality must exchange its unity for an internal relation. But, thus set free, the diverse aspects, because each something in relation, must each be something also beyond. This diversity is fatal to the internal unity of each; and it demands a new relation, and so on without limit. In short, qualities in a relation have turned out as unintelligible as were qualities without one. The problem from both sides has baffled us. (—*Appearance and Reality*, 2nd edition, pp. 31-2)

# THE STORY OF THE ELDER PROTECTOR OF VISION

*(with Commentary, Subcommentary, and Anticommentary)*

The following narrative is the official origin story for the very first verse of the Dhammapada, alias Dh.1, as found in the Dhammapada Commentary. It is one of the best-known commentarial stories in Theravada Buddhism, and I'd guess that most serious, "literate" Burmese Buddhists are familiar with it; although possibly most Western Buddhists, having much less use for the commentarial tradition than their Asian counterparts, have never heard of it. So I include an English translation of it here, because I consider it to be well worth reading.

One reason why it is worth reading is simply that it is an interesting and entertaining story. It is the legend of a hero. However, unlike ancient Western heroes who were fighters and men of action, like Theseus, Hercules, and Beowulf, Cakkhupāla was a spiritual hero, more akin to Christian heroes like the desert fathers and the medieval saints. But, like heroes in general, our hero lived by his own rules, and behaved in ways that common worldlings considered to be unreasonable, or even foolish. Beowulf's comrades considered him to be out of his mind, too, for fighting Grendel naked and weaponless; but Grendel himself fought that way, and Beowulf, being a hero, insisted upon a fair fight. Cakkhupāla is like this, in his own way.

Another reason why it is worth reading is that it shows a kind of Buddhism, and of spirituality in general, that is almost totally alien to what is found in the modern and postmodern West, and so it may serve as a source of perspective, a glimpse of a world more similar to the Buddha's than our own. The Dhammapada commentary is a wealth of information for this kind of perspective, in addition to being much more engaging and more pleasant reading than most of what is in the Suttas.

This is not to say that the story faithfully describes what life was really like in the Buddha's time; the tale is full of exaggerations, anachronisms, and just plain impossibilities (as are some of the Suttas). But that is how stories were told in the Buddha's time, and for centuries afterwards. The ancient world was more surreal, and less objectively precise, than the world we live in nowadays. So despite the mythological flourishes and other presumed inaccuracies, the reader may still see what the attitude of Buddhists could be like in those days. But this is not the place for a subcommentary to the story. That will come after the tale is told.

The translation is my own, based on the Burmese Sixth Council edition of the text. One thing I realized while translating it is just how rusty my Pali is, so I hope I haven't rendered any really gross inaccuracies. But I don't consider translating *dhammā* as "ways of being" to be one of them.

## CAKKHUPĀLATTHERAVATTHU

*manopubbaṅgamā dhammā / manoseṭṭhā manomayā //*
*manasā ce paduṭṭhena / bhāsati vā karoti vā //*
*tato naṁ dukkhamanveti / cakkaṁva vahato padanti //*——

Ways of being are preceded by mind; they have mind as chief; they are mind-made;

If with a defiled mind one speaks or acts,

Then unease follows that person like the wheel follows the foot of the beast of burden.

Where was this Dhamma teaching spoken? In Sāvatthi. In what regard? With regard to the Elder Protector of Vision (Cakkhupālatthera).

It is said that in Sāvatthi there was a landowner named Great Gold, prosperous, of great wealth and many possessions, but childless. One day, having gone to a bathing ghat and having bathed, he was returning home, when along the way he saw a lord of the forest (i.e., a huge tree), laden with leafy branches, and he thought, "That must be inhabited by a very powerful spirit"; so having cleared the base of it he had a fence built around it, had the (enclosed) area strewn with sand, and had streamers and pennants put up; and having bedecked this lord of the forest he placed his palms together in respect and made the prayer, "If I were to obtain a son or a daughter, I would pay great honor to you"; and then he went on his way.

Then, not long afterwards, a child was conceived in his wife's womb. Becoming aware of the conception of the child, she informed him of it; and he performed the rites for preserving her unborn child. After the passage of ten months she gave birth to a son. On the day of his taking a name, the rich man, since his own gain was on account of the protection of the Lord of the Forest, came up with the name Protector for him. At a later time she got another son; this one was given the name Little Protector, with the other being called Great Protector. Upon their coming of age they were bound by the bonds of their own households. Afterwards, their mother and father passed away, and the entire estate was inherited and managed by them.

At that time the Teacher, having set rolling the supreme Wheel of Dhamma, traveling from place to place, was residing at the great monastery of Jetavana—made by the great magnate Anāthapiṇḍika at the expenditure of 540,000,000 (silver kahāpaṇas)—and was establishing a great multitude on the path of heaven and on the path of liberation. Indeed, the Tathāgatha, with 80,000 families of relatives on his mother's side and 80,000 families of relatives on his father's side, spent only one rains residence at the great Banyan Monastery established by twice 80,000 families of relatives; but at the great Jetavana Monastery made by Anāthapiṇḍika he spent nineteen rains, and six rains at the Pubbārāma, made by Visākhā at the cost of 270,000,000 in wealth; so because of the greatness of virtue of these two families he spent 25 rains residences in the vicinity of Sāvatthi. Anāthapiṇḍika and the great female lay disciple Visākhā went faithfully twice a day to attend to the Tathāgatha; and going there, thinking, "The young novices will look to see what's in our hands," had never gone empty-handed. Going before the meal time, they would get staple foods and side dishes, among other things, and go; and after the meal time, the five medicines and the eight drinks. Furthermore, in each of their homes they had always 2000 seats prepared for bhikkhus. With regard to food, drink, and medicines, whoever wanted some was supplied with as much as he wanted.

Yet despite all this, never before, on any day, had the Teacher been asked a question by Anāthapiṇḍika. Thinking, "The Tathāgata is a highly refined Buddha, a highly refined nobleman, who, considering 'This householder is of much service to me' might become worn out with teaching me Dhamma," out of extreme devotion to the teacher, he asked no question. But now at the moment he took his seat it occurred to the Teacher, "This rich man defends me when I have no need of being defended. For a hundred thousand world cycles beyond four incalculable eons I have perfected myself, having cut off my own head, torn out my eyes, torn out the flesh of my heart, renounced my son and wife equal to my life's breath, in fulfilling the Perfections (*pāramiyo*) for the sake of teaching Dhamma." Thinking "He defends me when I have no need to be defended," he spoke to him a discourse on Dhamma.

At that time 70 million people lived in Sāvatthi. Of all of these, 50 million people, having heard the Dhamma teaching of the Teacher, had become Ariyan disciples, with 20 million people still common worldlings. There were two duties for those who had become Ariyan disciples: Before meal time they gave alms; and after meal time they went with scents, garlands, and so on in their hands, and also sending cloths, medicines, drinks, and so forth, with the purpose of hearing Dhamma. So one day Great Protector, seeing the Ariyan disciples going to the monastery with scents, garlands, and so on in their hands, asked, "Where is this great crowd going?" and hearing "To hear Dhamma," he said, "I also will go," and so he went to the Teacher, and after paying his respects he sat down on the outskirts of the congregation.

Now, when Buddhas are teaching Dhamma, they teach Dhamma with regard to the refuges, morality, renunciation, and so forth while being watchful with regard to the dispositions of the hearers; therefore on that day the Teacher, being watchful with regard to this, was teaching Dhamma by giving a gradual, systematic talk. About what? Talk about giving, talk about morality, talk about heaven, and clear explanation of the disadvantage, futility, and defilement of sensuality and the advantage of renunciation. Having heard this, the landowner Great Protector considered: "Going to the next world, sons and daughters, brothers, and possessions do not follow. Even one's own body doesn't accompany one. Why don't I renounce the household life?" At the end of the discourse he approached the Teacher and requested ordination as a renunciant. Now the Teacher said to him, "Is there a relative close to you that you should consult?"

"There is my younger brother, Venerable Sir."

"Then you should consult with him."

Answering, "Very good," he paid respect to the Teacher and, going home, he sent for his younger brother and said, "My dear, whatever is mine in this house, whatever wealth there is, either animate or inanimate, all of it is now your responsibility. You handle it."

"And what are you going to do?" he replied.

"I am going to be ordained as a renunciant in the presence of my Teacher."

"What are you saying, Brother? When Mother died you became like a mother to me, and when Father died, you became like a father. In your house you have a great estate. Even living as a householder it is possible to make merit. Don't act like this."

"Since hearing the Dhamma taught by the Teacher I am not able to live the household life. For, holding up to view the exceedingly fine and subtle Three Marks (of Impermanence, Unease, and No Self), the Dhamma taught by the Teacher is beautiful at the beginning, the middle, and the end. It is not possible to fulfill it by living in the midst of a household. I will renounce the world, my dear one."

"Dear Brother, you are still young. Renounce the world when you are older."

"Really my dear, to one who is old, even his own hands and feet become unreliable; they do not follow his own authority, to say nothing of his family members! So I will not do as you say. I will live to fulfillment the discipline of a philosopher.

> Hands and feet grown feeble with age are unreliable;
> How will he practice Dhamma when his strength is lost?

I will renounce the world, my dear." Despite his (brother's) outcry he went to the Teacher and begged for renunciation, received formal renunciation (as a novice) and full ordination (as a bhikkhu), spent five rains in the presence of a guide and a preceptor, and having performed the invitation ceremony at the end of his (fifth) rains retreat, he approached the Teacher, paid respect to him, and asked, "Venerable, Sir, what are the obligations in this Doctrine?"

"The obligation of texts, and the obligation of insight: these are the two obligations, bhikkhu."

"And what, Venerable Sir, is the obligation of texts, and what is the obligation of insight?"

"Having learned, in accordance with the capacity of one's own wisdom, one or two collections (of texts), or even the whole of the Three Baskets, and the memorization, recitation, and expounding of it—this is called the obligation of texts. And for one living simply, delighting in a secluded dwelling place, having taken to heart the (inevitable) decay and destruction of one's own existence, maturing insight and attaining Arahantship through the power of steadfast endeavor—this is called the obligation of insight."

"Venerable Sir, I have renounced the world late in life and am not able to fulfill the obligation of texts, so I will fulfill the obligation of insight. Please teach me an object of meditation." So then the Teacher taught him an object of meditation capable of leading to Arahantship.

After paying respect to the Teacher and seeking out some bhikkhus to accompany him, he gathered sixty bhikkhus and set out with them, walking on a journey of 2000 yojanas; and upon reaching a large frontier village, he with his companions entered it for alms. The people, seeing bhikkhus endowed with discipline, were uplifted in mind and, preparing seats, invited them to sit, served them with drinks and food, and asked, "Venerable Sirs, where are you gentlemen going?" Upon being told "To a convenient place, lay disciples," some intelligent people, realizing "The venerable ones are searching for a place to spend the rains retreat," said to them, "Venerable Sirs, if the gentlemen were to spend these three months here, we would be established in the Refuges and take the precepts." And so they accepted the invitation, considering, "In dependence upon these families we will make an escape from existence."

The people, receiving their consent, set up a monastery, preparing places for spending the night and places for spending the day, and offered it. They entered that same village regularly for alms food. At that time a healer approached them and made an invitation to them, saying, "Venerable Sirs, in a dwelling place of many people indispositions are bound to occur. In such an event please tell me, and I will prepare a remedy."

The Elder, on the day of entering the rains residence, called the other bhikkhus and asked them, "My friends, in how many bodily postures will you spend these three months?"

"In (all) four, Venerable Sir."

"What now, friends, is that proper? Should we not develop ourselves with uncloudedness of mind (*appamatta*)? Really, we came here having taken an object of meditation in the presence of a real, live Buddha; and it is not possible that Buddhas could approve of cloudedness of mind. They would approve of you only by the beauty of your nature. For the clouded of mind, the four lower realms become like their own home. Be unclouded in mind, my friends."

"And what about you, Venerable Sir?"

"I will spend my time in three of the bodily postures. I will not stretch out on my back."

"Very good, Venerable Sir. May you be unclouded in mind."

Now, for the unsleeping Elder, at the passing of the first month and the arrival of the middle month, a disease of the eyes became manifest. Like a stream of water from a cracked water pot, a stream of tears trickled from his eyes. Having done the work of a philosopher all night, at the advent of dawn he entered his room and sat. The bhikkhus, at the time of walking for alms food, went to the Elder and told him, "Time to go for alms, Venerable Sir."

"Well then, friends, take your bowl and robe." Having taken his own bowl and robe, he went out.

When the bhikkhus saw the tears trickling from his eyes they asked him, "What is this, Venerable Sir?"

"The wind hurts my eyes, friends."

"Weren't we invited by a healer, Venerable Sir? We will speak to him."

"Very good, friends."

They spoke to the healer, and he cooked up some (medicated) oil and had it sent.

The Elder, when he was applying the oil into his nose, did it just in a sitting position; and having applied it he entered into the village. The healer, upon seeing him, said, "Venerable Sir, I have heard that the wind hurts the gentleman's eyes."

"Yes, lay disciple."

"Venerable Sir, some oil was prepared by me and was sent. Did you apply the oil into your nose?"

"Yes, lay disciple."

"How is it now?"

"It's still painful, lay disciple."

The healer, thinking "The oil sent by me was sufficient to cure him with just one application. Why is the disease not cured?" asked him, "Venerable Sir, did you apply the oil sitting, or lying down?" The Elder remained silent; and being questioned again and again, he would not speak. Thinking "I'll go to the monastery and have a look at the Elder's dwelling place," the healer said, "Well then, Venerable Sir, carry on." After sending him off he went to the monastery, and looking at the Elder's dwelling place, and seeing only places for walking meditation and for sitting, and seeing no place for lying down, he asked, "Venerable Sir, did you make the application while sitting, or while lying down?" The Elder remained silent. "Venerable Sir, don't act like this. It is only by maintaining the body that one is able to do the work of a philosopher. Make the application after lying down"; he pleaded with him again and again.

Saying, "Please go, friend. Having taken counsel, I will know (what to do)," he dismissed the healer.

But the Elder had no family members at all there, no blood relations; so with whom would he take counsel? Taking counsel with his kamma-born body he said, "Please tell me, friend Protector: Will you look to your eyes, or to the Message of the Buddha? In the beginningless round of Samsara there is no counting of the times your eyes have been blind; and many hundreds of Buddhas, many thousands of Buddhas are past. And of those Buddhas, not one of them did you honor by practicing his teachings. Now, during this rains residence, I will not lie down for three months; for three months I will exercise steadfast energy. So let your eyes fail, or let them be destroyed, and uphold the message of the Buddha, not eyes." And thus admonishing his physical body, he spoke these verses:

"Let my own eyes waste away,
Let my ears waste away, and the body as well;
Let all of it waste away that is dependent on a physical form;
What use are you, Protector, if you are clouded in mind?

"Let my own eyes wear out,
Let my ears wear out, and the body as well;
Let all of it wear out that is dependent on a physical form;
What use are you, Protector, if you are clouded in mind?

"Let my own eyes be destroyed,
Let my ears be destroyed, and the body as well;
Let all of it be destroyed that is dependent on a physical form;
What use are you, Protector, if you are clouded in mind?"

Having thus admonished himself with three verses, and having applied the nasal treatment to himself in a sitting position, he entered the village for alms. The healer, seeing him, asked, "Venerable Sir, have you applied the nasal treatment?"

"Yes, lay disciple."

"How is it, Venerable Sir?"

"It is still painful, lay disciple."

"Did you apply the nasal treatment while sitting, Venerable Sir, or after lying down?" The Elder remained silent; and being questioned again and again, he didn't say anything. Then the healer said to him: "Venerable Sir, you do not do what is proper. From today onwards, do not say 'That fellow prepared medicated oil for me,' and I will not say that I prepared the oil for you." Abandoned by the healer, he went to the monastery, thinking "Now you've even been abandoned by the healer. Do not give up the bodily posture, philosopher.

"Rejected by the medical art, renounced even by the healer,
Subject to the King of Death, why, Protector, should you be clouded in mind?"

Admonishing himself with this verse, he did the work of a philosopher. And then, at the passing of the middle watch of the night, not earlier, not later (that is, at the very same moment), his eyes and his defilements were destroyed. Having become a dry-visioned Arahant, he entered his room and sat down.

* * *

The bhikkhus, coming at the time for going for alms, said "Time to walk for alms, Venerable Sir."

"It is morning, friends?"

"Yes, Venerable Sir."

"Well then, you go."

"And what about you, Venerable Sir?"

"My eyes are lost, friends."

Taking a look at his eyes, their own eyes became filled with tears. "Venerable Sir, don't worry, we'll take care of you." Having made the Elder comfortable, and having performed the various duties required of them, they entered the village for alms food.

When people didn't see the Elder they asked, "Venerable Sirs, where is our gentleman?" and having heard the news they had rice broth sent, and took alms food and went to the Elder themselves; and paying respect to him, and rolling at his feet and crying, they said "Venerable Sir, we will take care of you. Don't worry," and after helping him to feel comfortable they went away. From then on they regularly sent rice broth and cooked rice to the monastery.

And the Elder constantly exhorted the other sixty bhikkhus. And they, standing firm in his exhortations, at the approach of the concluding invitation ceremony every one of them attained Arahantship with mastery of the discriminative knowledges. And having completed the rains residence, and having become desirous of seeing the Teacher, they said to the Elder, "Venerable Sir, we desire to see the Teacher."

The Elder, hearing their words, thought, "I am not strong, and along the way there is a wilderness inhabited by inhuman beings. They will all be exhausted with me going with them, and they won't be able to get alms food. I'll send them along before me." Then he said to them, "My friends, you go ahead."

"And what about you, Venerable Sir?"

"I am not strong, and along the way there is a wilderness inhabited by inhuman beings. You will all be exhausted by me going with you. You go ahead."

"Don't do like this Venerable Sir; we will go only with you."

"My friends, please don't favor such a course. Your being like this will make me troubled. When my younger brother meets you he will ask about me; then tell him about the loss of my eyesight. He will send someone to me with whom I can come back. With my words, please pay respect to Him of the Ten Powers and to the eighty Great Elders." With that he sent them off.

After asking the Elder's pardon, they entered the village. The people, upon seeing them, had them sit down, and after offering them alms food asked, "What, Venerable Sirs, is there some reason for the gentlemen to go away?"

"Yes, lay disciples. We are desirous of seeing the Teacher."

After pleading with them again and again, and realizing that they still intended to go, they followed after them and, finally, lamenting, turned back.

Eventually they arrived at Jetavana and paid respect, with the Elder's words, to the Teacher and to the eighty Great Elders, and on the next day they entered the lane where the Elder's younger brother was living, for alms food. Recognizing them, the landowner had them sit down, and after attending to them hospitably asked, "Venerable Sirs, where is my dear brother the Elder?" Then they told him the news.

Upon hearing this, he rolled at their feet and cried, asking, "Now, Venerable Sirs, what is to be done?"

"The Elder is waiting for someone to come from here. When he has arrived there, he will come here with him."

"This, Venerable Sirs, is my sister's son, called Protected (*pālita*). Send him."

"To send him like this is not possible; there are dangers lurking on the road. It is better to send him after he has made formal renunciation."

"Then do it thus and send him, Venerable Sirs." Then, having ordained him as a novice, after training him for half a month with regard to handling his bowl and robes and so on, and after explaining the road to him, they sent him off.

Eventually arriving at that village, and seeing an old man at the village gate, he asked, "Is there some forest monastery dependent upon this village?"

"There is, Venerable Sir."

"Who lives there?"

"He is the Elder Protected, Venerable Sir."

"Show me the way."

"Who are you, Venerable Sir?"

"I am the Elder's nephew."

Then, taking him in hand, he led him to the monastery. After paying respect to the Elder and performing various duties and properly tending to the Elder for the span of half a month, he said, "Venerable Sir, the landowner, my mother's brother, is waiting for you to come back with me. Come on, let's go."

"Well then, take hold of the end of my staff."

Taking hold of the end of his staff, he went into the village with the Elder. The people had the Elder sit down, and asked, "What, Venerable Sir, is there some reason for you to go away?"

"Yes, lay disciples, I am going to the Teacher and will pay respect to him." Pleading with him in various ways but not getting their way, they saw the Elder off, going the first part of the way with him, and then turned back, crying.

The novice, going along holding the end of the Elder's walking stick, along the way arrived at a village in the wilderness called Kaṭṭhanagara, near which the Elder had stayed before; and as they came out of the village, in the forest, a woodcutter girl was lustily singing a song. Hearing the sound of a woman singing, he was captivated by her voice. There is no other sound able to suffuse a man's entire body and abide there like the sound of a woman. Thus the Blessed One said:

> *Bhikkhus, I am not aware of any other sound that takes hold of a man's mind and abides there as does, bhikkhus, the sound of a woman. (—from the second Sutta of the Aṅguttara Nikāya)*

The novice, captivated at that point, let go of the end of the staff and said, "Please wait, Venerable Sir. I have something to do." Then he went near her. Upon seeing him, she became silent. Then he accomplished the downfall of his morality with her.

The Elder thought, "Just now I heard the sound of singing, and then the sound of that woman suddenly stopped. And the novice is taking a long time. It must be that he has fallen to breaking his precepts with her."

And that one, having finished his own business, returned and said, "Let's go, Venerable Sir."

Now the Elder asked him, "Have you gone bad, novice?" He became silent; and questioned by the Elder again and again, he didn't say anything. Then the Elder said to him, "Holding the end of my stick is no business for a bad one like you."

Struck with dread, he took off the yellow-brown robes and,

dressing himself in the manner of a householder, said "Venerable Sir, before I was a novice; now I have become a householder again. It was not from faith that I renounced worldly life—I renounced it on account of fear of the dangers of the journey. Come, let's go."

"Friend, a bad householder and a bad novice are both bad. Even when living as a novice you were unable to keep your morality intact; having become a householder what good will you do? Holding the end of my stick is no business for a bad one like you."

"Venerable Sir, the road is a menace of inhuman beings! And you are blind and without anyone to guide you! How will you live here?"

Now the Elder said to him, "Friend, don't be worried like this. Even with this befalling me right now, whether I die or wander lost from place to place, there is no going with you." And having said that, he spoke these verses:

"Oh, my eyesight is gone, and I have come to a desolate path;
Let me lie down and go no farther; there is no companionship with a fool.

"Oh, my eyesight is gone, and I have come to a desolate path;
I will die; I will not go; there is no companionship with a fool."

Having heard him, the other, with dread arisen within him, exclaimed, "Oh, a grievous, horrible, monstrous deed have I done!" flung out his arms and, wailing, dived into a jungle thicket and thus disappeared.

And by the blazing intensity of the Elder's virtue, the Paṇḍukambala Stone Seat of Sakka, King of the Devas—sixty yojanas long, fifty yojanas wide, fifteen yojanas high, the color of a red China-rose blossom, which at the times of sitting down on it or standing up, automatically descends or rises up—manifested signs of heat. Sakka wondered, "Who is it that wants to drive me from my place?" and looking around with the Divine Eye he saw the Elder. Thus it was said by the ancients:

*The Thousand-Eyed One, the Lord of Devas, purified the Divine Eye;*

*While this Protector, censuring the bad, completely purified his way of life.*

*The Thousand-Eyed One, the Lord of Devas, purified the Divine Eye;*
*While this Protector, taking Dhamma to heart, sat delighting in the Doctrine.*

Then it occurred to him: "If I do not go to such a gentleman as this, who censures the bad and takes Dhamma to heart, my head would split into seven pieces. I will go to him." Thus:

*The Thousand-Eyed One, the Lord of Devas, bearing glorious sovereignty over the gods,*
*Coming at that moment, approached Protector of Vision.*

And approaching the Elder, from not far away he made a sound with his foot. Now the Elder asked "Who is that?"

"I am a traveller, Venerable Sir."

"Where are you going, lay disciple?"

"To Sāvatthi, Venerable Sir."

"Carry on, friend."

"And where is the gentleman going, Venerable Sir?"

"I also am going there."

"Well then, Venerable Sir, let's go together."

"I am not strong, friend. You will be hindered (*papañco*) by traveling with me."

"I have no urgent business. And of the ten opportunities for earning merit, I will gain one of them by traveling with the gentleman. Let's go together, Venerable Sir."

The Elder, considering, "He must be a good man," said "Well then, I will go with you. Take hold of the end of my staff, lay disciple."

Sakka did as requested, and by contracting the ground he arrived at Jetavana by evening time. The Elder, hearing the sound of conch horns, drums, and so on, asked, "Where is that sound coming from?"

"We are in Sāvatthi, Venerable Sir."

"Previously when we traveled here, the going took a long time."

"I know a shortcut, Venerable Sir."

At that moment the Elder realized: "This is no human being. It must be a god."

*The Thousand-Eyed One, the Lord of Devas, bearing glorious sovereignty over the gods,*
*Shortened the road, and came quickly to Sāvatthi.*

Leading the Elder, he conducted him to a shelter made of leaves that his younger brother the landowner had constructed just for the Elder's residence; and having seated him on a bench, assuming the appearance of a dear companion, he went to the other and called out, "My dear friend Little Protector!"

"What is it, dear friend?"

"Do you know of the Elder's arrival?"

"No, I don't know. What, has the Elder come?"

"Yes, dear friend—Just now I went to the monastery, and seeing the Elder sitting in the leaf shelter you had built for him, I've come here." Having said this, he went away.

So the landowner went to the monastery, and seeing the Elder he rolled on the ground at his feet and cried, saying, among other things, "Foreseeing this, Venerable Sir, I did not give my consent for you to renounce the world!" Then he made arrangements by having two slave boys set free, sending them to the Elder, and having them ordained as novices, telling them, "Bring rice broth, cooked rice, and so on from the village and attend to the Elder." The novices performed their various duties and took care of the Elder.

Then one day some bhikkhus living in the outer districts, resolving "We will see the Teacher," came to Jetavana and, after paying respects to the Tathāgata and paying respects to the eighty Great Elders, while walking the rounds they arrived at the dwelling place of the Elder Protector of Vision; and they thought, "We'll see this one too." At that moment a great storm cloud arose. Thinking, "Now it's very late, and a storm cloud has arisen; let's go see him tomorrow morning," they turned back.

The rain god sent down rain through the first watch of the night, and during the middle watch he went away. The Elder, being one of steadfast energy, was in the habit of doing walking meditation; therefore during the last watch of the night he went down to his walking meditation path. At that time, with the earth freshly rained upon, many ground mites (called "Indra's cowherds") came out; and with the Elder doing walking meditation, quite a lot of them were crushed. The Elder's attendants did not sweep the place for walking meditation early in the morning. The other bhikkhus came, thinking, "Let's see the Elder's dwelling place," and seeing the killed creatures, asked "Who does walking meditation here?"

"Our preceptor, Venerable Sirs."

They vented their indignation, saying, "Look, friends, at the work of a philosopher! Lying down and sleeping at the time of day when things can be seen, not accomplishing anything, now when no one can see he says, 'I'll do walking meditation' and kills so many living beings! Thinking 'I'll do what is right,' he does what is not right!"

Then they went to the Tathāgatha and informed him of it: "Venerable Sir, the Elder Protector of Vision, thinking 'I will do walking meditation,' has killed many living beings."

"What, and was he seen by you while he was killing them?"

"He wasn't seen, Venerable Sir."

"And just as you did not see him, even so, he did not see the living beings. For those whose encumbering influences are destroyed (*khīṇāsavānaṁ*), bhikkhus, there is no volition to kill."

"Venerable Sir, being so capable of full enlightenment, how did he become blind?

"By the power of his own deed that he had done, bhikkhus."

"And what, Venerable Sir, was done by him?"

"Well then, bhikkhus, listen:

"Long ago, when the King of Kāsi was reigning in Varanasi, a healer was traveling among the villages and towns, practicing his healing art; and he saw a woman with an eye affliction. 'What is your ailment?' he asked her.

"'I cannot see with my eyes.'

"'I will make some medicine for you.'

"'Make it, Master.'

"'What will you give me?'

"'If you are able to make my eyes healthy, I will become your slave, along with my sons and daughters.'

"'Very good,' he said; and he prepared the medicine. With one dose of the medicine her eyes became healthy.

"She considered, 'I promised I will become his slave along with my sons and daughters, but he won't treat me gently and justly. I will deceive him.' When she was visited by the healer and was asked, 'How are you, good lady?' she said, 'Before my eyes troubled me a little, but now they trouble me much more.'

"The healer thought, 'She's lying to me because she doesn't want to give anything. I have no need of her payment. I will make her blind.' Then he went home and told his wife about the matter. She remained silent. Concocting a different medicine, he went to the woman, saying, 'Dear lady, apply this medicine,' and had her apply it. At this, both her eyes went out like the flame of a lamp. That healer was Protector of Vision.

"Bhikkhus, that deed done by my son then followed close behind him. Truly, this evil deed came after him like a cartwheel following the foot of a draught ox pulling a load." And after telling this story and reaching its conclusion, as though stamping with the royal seal a document after the soft clay has been affixed, The King of Dhamma spoke this verse:

Ways of being are preceded by mind; they have mind as chief; they are mind-made;

If with a defiled mind one speaks or acts,

Then unease follows that person like the wheel follows the foot of the beast of burden.

## The Story of the Elder Protector of Vision (Commentary, Subcommentary, and Anticommentary)

*For the sake of completeness, and also for the sake of giving English-speaking people some idea of what the commentaries are like, and thus some idea of the brickwork comprising the finished edifice of Theravadin orthodoxy, I include the* vibhaṅga, *or word-by-word analysis, to the Dhammapada verse itself, as found in the Dhammapada commentary, immediately following the story of Cakkhupāla. Some brief comments of my own are inserted in square brackets and italics...*

> *manopubbaṅgamā dhammā / manoseṭṭhā manomayā //*
> *manasā ce paduṭṭhena / bhāsati vā karoti vā //*
> *tato naṁ dukkhamanveti / cakkaṁva vahato padanti //*

Therein, ***mano*** refers to the type of skillfulness (*kusala*), and so on, of the Sphere of Sensuality, and the consciousness of all of the four levels [*of the Sensual Sphere, Sphere of Form, Formless Sphere, and of the Transcendental, with the Sensual Sphere including this world and everything below the level of Brahmas, and with the Transcendental referring to the consciousness of Ariyas in their transcendence of Samsara*]; and here in this verse it is to be taken as the healer's being led, being bound, being compelled, by the power of his arisen mind, possessed of unhappiness—a mind bound to irritation.

By ***pubbaṅgamā*** is meant being endowed with the state of going first.

With regard to ***dhammā***—virtue, teaching, mastery, and that which is beingless or soulless are called the four dhammas. Of these:

> "Truly, what is Dhamma and what is not Dhamma do not both have the same result;
> What is not Dhamma leads to hell, and Dhamma leads to the attainment of paradise."

This is called the Dhamma of virtue. [*That is, "dhamma" interpreted as righteousness.*]

In "Bhikkhus, I will teach you the Dhamma that is beautiful in the beginning...," this is called the Dhamma of teaching.

In "And here, bhikkhus, there are some gentlemen who thoroughly learn the Dhamma in a discourse or verses for chanting...," this is called the Dhamma of mastery.

With regard to "In this state there are dhammas and there are aggregates...," this is called a "beingless" dhamma, and a "soulless" dhamma is just this also. [*In other words, "dhamma" in this sense refers to elemental qualities that are without self. The passage is a quote from the Abhidhamma Pitaka.*] And with regard to these, in this place, the beingless, soulless dhamma is intended. The meaning of it is the three formless aggregates: the aggregate of feeling, the aggregate of perception, and the aggregate of constructs. So these, having mind coming before them, are called ***manopubbaṅgamā***.

So how, having the same ground with these, having the same supporting stimulus, not arising earlier or later but at the very same moment, can mind be said to go first? By the condition of its arising. Just as, for example, among many bandits working together, if one were to ask, "Who goes first among them?" one would answer that it is he who is the instigator, in dependence upon whom they do their business—"That Datta, or Mitta, [*these being common names in ancient India*] is the one who goes first among them." Thus this account should be understood. So, by the condition of its arising, mind goes before them, and so they are *preceded by mind*. For with consciousness not arisen they also are unable to arise. But mind arises with some mental states not arising. [*The point of this is apparently that although no mental state can arise without consciousness, consciousness itself can arise without this or that mental state—although, according to Abhidhamma and the commentaries, it cannot arise without any accompanying mental states at all.*]

And by means of its dominance it is the chief of them; thus ***manoseṭṭhā***. For just as among thieves, for example, the leader of the thieves, for example, is their chief through dominance, even so, mind is a dominator over them [*that is, over the mental states*], and mind is chief.

And just as these or those objects produced of wood, for example, are called "made of wood," for example, in the same way, those also which are produced of mind are called ***manomayā***, "mind-made."

By ***paduṭṭhena*** is meant defiled by extraneous defects such as greed. For the natural mind is the existence-factor consciousness [*i.e., the bhavaṅgacittaṁ, a phenomenon peculiar to the Abhidhamma literature and not named at all in the Suttas*], and that is undefiled. It is like clear water defiled by extraneous blue dye, for example, and becomes, for example, a kind of blue water; it is no longer fresh water, nor is it the original clear water. In this way also the mind becomes defiled by extraneous defilements such as greed; it is not a fresh consciousness, nor is it the original existence-factor consciousness. Thus the Blessed One said, "This mind, bhikkhus, is shining forth, but it is defiled by extraneous defilements." [*This passage is taken from the Aṅguttara Nikāya, and almost certainly has nothing to do with the hypothetical Abhidhammic bhavaṅgacittaṁ, which is a kind of unchanging subconscious background pattern to the mind and could hardly be said to be "shining forth"; but I've discussed this point elsewhere and needn't belabor it here.*] Thus when he says "***manasā ce paduṭṭhena / bhāsati vā karoti vā***," he refers to one who speaks in accordance with the fourfold misconduct of speech [*i.e., lying, malicious speech, harsh speech, and idle chatter*], and one who acts in accordance with the threefold misconduct of action [*i.e., killing, stealing, and sensual misconduct*]; and even if not speaking and not acting, in one's mind being defiled by greed, etc., the threefold misconduct of mind [*that is, greed, ill-will, and diṭṭhi or wrong view, not to be confused with the similar lobha, dosa, and moha*] is fulfilled. Thus one's course runs in the fulfillment of the ten unskillful actions.

By ***tato naṁ dukkhamanveti*** is meant that due to this threefold misconduct [*presumably of speech, body, and mind*] unease follows that individual; by the unfolding actuality of that misconduct he goes into a dark existence in the four lower realms or in the realm of human beings, with the fruition of that physical/mental unease, based in his body or otherwise, following behind.

How is this? ***cakkaṁva vahato padanti***—like the wheel follows the foot of the beast of burden; like the wheel at one end of the cart shaft follows the foot of the yoked ox at the other end pulling the load. So however he pulls the load, for one day, or two, or five, or ten, or half a month, or a month, he is not able to avoid the wheel or leave it behind; now by moving forwards the yoke chafes his neck from the front, and by backing up the wheel strikes the flesh of his thigh from behind. In these two ways the chafing wheel dogs his footsteps; and in this very same manner an individual, established in a defiled mind, having fulfilled the three (kinds of) misconduct, has bodily and mental unease pursuing him, in places like hell, here and there, in this and that existence, with his misconduct at the root of it.

At the conclusion of the verse, thirty thousand bhikkhus attained Arahantship with mastery of the discriminative knowledges. And for the assembled congregation the discourse was of much benefit, and bearing much fruit.

*The story of the Elder Protector of Vision, the first.*

Thus ends the official commentary to the first verse of the Dhammapada. Now I suppose I should add some of my own comments to the story itself, and, like the commentary itself, end up with the verse.

The conception of Cakkhupāla is attributed to the protection of a tree spirit, or tree-dwelling deva. The reality of tree-dwelling devas is taken for granted in the Pali texts; for example, the rule of monastic discipline forbidding monks from damaging green plants reportedly came to being because a monk had inadvertently maimed a young tree spirit while chopping a tree. Their reality is still taken for granted in places like Myanmar, where large trees are often seen with an accompanying shrine to the resident spirit, and with people occasionally making offerings and prayers. They supposedly are members of the Realm of the Four Great Kings, which is the plane of existence immediately above the human level in the scheme of the 31 planes of existence, being approximate equals to the ancient Greek nymphs and satyrs.

Throughout most of the course of the story, Gotama Buddha is staying at the monastery of Jetavana, or "the Jeta Grove," apparently one of his favorite places. The story of how the rich businessman Anāthapiṇḍika bought it is well known: Wanting to provide the Buddha with a good place near Sāvatthi, and liking the looks of a park owned by a Prince Jeta, he approached the prince and offered to buy it. The prince, being greedy and/or not really wanting to part with the property, told Anāthapiṇḍika that he would sell it for the amount of money required to cover the entire area. The magnate, with price being no object in his generosity to the Buddha, called for cartloads of the standard unit of monetary currency in those days, the silver kahāpaṇa, and covered the entire Jetavana with 540 million of them. (The fact that kahāpaṇas were square rather than round facilitated his completely obscuring the ground with them. If we assume that one kahāpaṇa is one square inch in size, then the area covered would amount to 86 acres.) Thus the prince reluctantly parted with the park, but gladly accepted the money.

The city of Sāvatthi was the capital of the Kingdom of Kosala, in the Buddha's time one of the great powers of northern India, along with Magadha (the latter of which eventually expanded to include almost all of the Indian subcontinent under the Mauryan Empire). But although it was the capital of a great nation, the claim by the commentary that it had a population of seven *koṭis*, or 70 million people, is exaggerated to the point of sheer impossibility. It may be that, at the time, all of India did not have a population that large. And of course, in ancient times, without modern urban planning, sanitation, transportation of food, advanced agricultural techniques, etc. etc., it is hardly likely, to say the least, that a single city could have a population exceeding that of modern New York, Los Angeles, and Tokyo combined. Add to this the claim that 50,000,000 of the population were Ariyas, or Buddhist saints who had had at least a glimpse of Nirvana, and we're smack in the midst of Fantasy Land. I have read that, historically, Sāvatthi was known as a stronghold for the Ājīvakas, an ascetic philosophical school rivaling Buddhism and, in those days, more popular than same. But this claim of 50 million Ariyas in one city may represent not only an exaggeration of heroic proportions but a sign that, early on, the term Ariya (and especially the term *sotāpanna*) had a different meaning than it came to have in the developed system of Theravadin orthodoxy. *Sotāpanna* in particular could have meant simply that a person had entered the stream of a spiritual life and become a Buddhist, not that the person was already almost enlightened and a superhuman being, as it came to mean later. But, again, heroic tales are laden with exaggerations to add to the grandeur of the scale, to make things extraordinary and "larger than life," and to help them be heroic. (Incidentally, I walked over the site of Sāvatthi, "City of Wonders," when I was in India more than twenty years ago, and all that remained of it was a scrubby hill populated by goatherds, goats, and three old temples, two of them Buddhist if I remember correctly, and the other one Jain. Aside from the old temples, and a faint outline of what used to be the city walls, the only other indication that there had ever been a great metropolis there was the fact that the ground, if one looked at it closely, appeared to be composed largely of brick fragments. *Sabbe saṅkhārā aniccā.*)

The account of the "obligation of texts" ("Having learned, in accordance with the capacity of one's own wisdom, one or two collections (*nikāye*), or even the whole of the Three Baskets, and the memorization, recitation, and expounding of it...") is also probably an anachronism, since it is unlikely that, in the Buddha's own lifetime, his teachings were already formulated into a Tipitaka, with scholar monks memorizing it by heart. This is more probably an invention of later scholar monks, who preferred being scholars to being actual serious practitioners of the system. And the finalized, standardized system itself, it should be borne in mind, is more a product of these scholars than of the actual practitioners. The situation in Buddhist Asia remains pretty much the same to this day. The scholars speak with a much louder voice than the people seriously following the system, who often prefer to remain silent. Also, it strikes me as odd that venerable Cakkhupāla would have waited until he had been ordained for five years before asking what the obligations of monkhood are. But stories, and sometimes even scriptures, require a certain suspension of disbelief.

The claim that the Elder and his sixty companions walked 2000 *yojanas* is yet another howling exaggeration, considering that a yojana is somewhere between 7 and 13 miles (depending upon which authority makes the calculations—the Burmese measurement, based upon the commentaries, is 13). The measure is supposedly the distance that a team of bullocks can pull a plow in one day. So if we are to take this seriously, the venerable Elder and his companions walked approximately as far as the circumference of the entire Earth. Burlingame, in his translation of the text, renders it "twenty leagues" instead of 2000, which would be much more likely, and may have been the original figure before some author "heroicized" the details of the story.

The four bodily postures discussed by the monks before the rains residence begins are reclining, sitting, standing, and walking. Elder Cakkhupāla has chosen to avoid lying down as an optional ascetic practice, or *dhūtaṅga.* There are still monks to this day who never lie down. My own teacher, ven. Taungpulu Kyauk Hsin Tawya Sayadaw, for instance, never lay down until he had no choice, during his final illness.

So the reason why ven. Cakkhupāla does not recover from his ailment by using the medicine is that, after putting the nose drops up his nose, because he remains in an upright position the medicine simply drips back out his nose, and has no effect. It would be easy to point out that he could have just tilted his head back, so that the medicine would stay up his nose…but Cakkhupāla was a hero, and heroes don't play by our rules. If they did, they wouldn't be heroes.

Why does the Elder so obstinately keep his mouth shut when the healer questions him about how he took the medicine? This is another aspect of *dhūtaṅga* practice. The Visuddhimagga, for example, exhorts bhikkhus to keep their *dhūtaṅga* secret, like a thief conceals his hidden treasure. In fact according to that text he should inform only his own teacher of it, or some other respected Elder before whom he declares his intention. There is a story of two monks sharing a cabin. One of them is a practitioner of "the sitter's practice," and the other is not. One night there is a thunderstorm and, during a flash of lightning, the non-sitter sees the other sitting upright in the middle of the night. He asks him, "Do you do the sitter's practice, friend?" Whereupon the other, who had not been horizontal in years, immediately lies down and says

"No." Then the very next night he starts the sitter's practice again. So Cakkhupāla, although stubbornly silent with the healer, was a bit lax in his practice by informing all of his companions about his resolution for the rains retreat.

The healer's struggles to talk some sense to the Elder represent one of the more interesting and poignant themes in the story, in my opinion. The theme in question is that of worldly common sense butting heads with saintliness. First it was the Elder's brother trying to talk him out of his rash decision to throw his wealth and worldly life away, then it is the healer trying to get him to lie down for the sake of his health, and later on in the story it is the nephew trying to persuade the Elder that by not continuing on his way with him he is practically committing suicide. But to a saintly being like Cakkhupāla, such common sense is seen more as an obstacle and hindrance to the Goal than as anything else. It is a kind of paradox that in order to have what it takes to be a genuine saint, essentially a superhuman being, one must have at least a touch of irrational, wild-eyed fanaticism; being purely *sensible* is just too lukewarm to make the grade. While reading the story it struck me that the younger brother, the healer, and the nephew speak with the most *modern* voices in the story; modern people probably can relate to them better than to someone like Buddha, Cakkhupāla, or the faithful villagers. Cakkhupāla in this sense is reminiscent of Dostoyevsky's Idiot, who exasperates modern readers by being so damn christlike—simply forgiving people who try to swindle or even kill him, and continuing to love them like brothers. Favoring worldly common sense has become very much the fashion in modern times, which helps to account for why genuine saints have become such an endangered species. Worldly common sense has evolved into an overwhelming juggernaut.

When it is said that the Elder became a "dry-visioned" arahant, what it means, primarily, is that he became an enlightened being not endowed with psychic powers such as the ability to remember his own past lives. Traditionally it is Vipassana meditators who make this attainment, with cultivators of jhāna getting the psychic powers. But also, of course, it's a kind of play on words, since a blind man is "dry-visioned." I'm not sure about Pali, but in Burmese the word for the eyes going blind is the same as the word used to describe a well or stream going dry in the hot season. So we have some poetic imagery here. Also, I may as well point out that it would appear that the Elder became enlightened while practicing walking meditation. Walking meditation should not be neglected.

Another significant and somewhat poignant theme of the story, for me anyway, is the faithful support, often *extreme* faithful support, of the lay community. Although the tale is rife with exaggerations, the laypeople begging monks to stay, doing all they can to support them, and rolling on the ground in tears when they go, is not necessarily an exaggeration. To this day there are still devout Buddhist laypeople like this living in Asian villages. On the other, more cynical hand, it does appear that the praise of very supportive laypeople like Anāthapiṇḍika, the occasional assertions that they attain great prosperity and happiness, even sainthood, as a result of their merit, and the contrary assertions for those who are lax in their support, could be seen as a kind of monkish propaganda. A predominant theme of the text Petavatthu, or "Ghost Stories," for example, is the rather propagandist idea that you will be reborn as an afflicted spirit if you do not conscientiously and unfailingly support the Bhikkhu Sangha with all that it needs, and that you may become a deva if you do. Such teachings are also staple fair for Burmese laypeople listening to the sermons of Burmese sayadaws. But still, it's not entirely a bad thing. Rather than excessive, zealous, unquestioning support for monks in the West, practically the opposite situation prevails there, so that if Asian immigrants suddenly stopped supporting the Bhikkhu Sangha in the West, it would probably collapse, and very quickly. From what I have seen, the generosity of American lay communities is insufficient to provide a single monk with a daily bowl of food. This, combined with the aforementioned worldly common sense that is in fashion, has contributed to make Western bhikkhus another endangered species, with the total population amounting to only a few hundred throughout the world—fewer than mountain gorillas. So, better too much generous support than not enough. If you support monks you may be reborn as a deva.

The "concluding invitation ceremony" mentioned twice in the story is a formal act of the Sangha called *pavāraṇā*, held on the last day of the three-month rains residence, in which all the monks who have spent the residence together invite each other to admonish them with regard to their lapses in monastic discipline. This ceremony has degenerated into a meaningless formality in Burmese monasticism, with, as an unspoken rule, nobody answering each other's invitation, since the proportion of Burmese monks who actually try to follow the rules of monastic discipline is somewhere around 2%, with the corresponding proportion of Burmese monks in the West, from what I have seen, being approximately 0%. Many of them do take the "obligation of texts" very seriously, though; and many Burmese monks are phenomenal scholars, with very few Western Buddhists capable of rivaling even a mediocre Burmese monastic scholar. They are very dogmatic by Western standards, and don't exercise much critical thought, but they know the texts forwards and backwards, including even the rules of discipline that they don't follow.

When it is said that monks are fully enlightened with "mastery of the discriminative knowledges" (*paṭisambhidā*), the meaning is essentially that not only are they enlightened, but they also understand Dhamma systematically and in fine detail, so that they are able to expound it fully. This detail is a hint of the predominant intellect- and system-orientation of the commentarial literature.

One interesting problem which the story brings up is the case of Arahants, fully enlightened beings, who are *desirous* of seeing the Buddha. Wouldn't an Arahant be without desire? There are various ways of looking at the issue. It is my understanding that, according to orthodox tradition, an Arahant may still have *good* desires, such as a desire to pay respect to the Buddha, but no longer has unskillful or *bad* desires, such as a desire to hit somebody, have sex, or put sugar on one's cereal to make it taste better. But as I see it, desire is desire, and wanting to see the Buddha is still desire, which an Arahant should have risen above. So I consider one plausible explanation to be that, an Arahant still experiences all sorts of feelings, in accordance, perhaps, with brain physiology or the momentum of past karma, but that, being perfectly mindful, the karmic power of those feelings is neutralized. They feel the desire, but they do not identify with it or allow themselves to be attached to it. Another explanation of the enlightened beings being *desirous* of seeing the Buddha is that this story is just a legend. The desirous Arahants might fit into the same category as the 50 million saints living in Sāvatthi.

With regard to Him of the Ten Powers and to the eighty Great Elders, the One of Ten Powers is of course the Buddha. I'm really not into lists, so if you want to know what those ten powers are you'll have to find it elsewhere, like in some other Buddhist book. I will say, though, that the first power, allegedly, is omniscience. The eighty Great Elders are the eighty monks who were the most eminent of the Buddha's disciples, not including the two *Chief* Disciples, vens. Sāriputta and Mahā Moggallāna. Each of them was foremost in some regard or another; for example, ven. Mahā Kassapa was foremost in *dhūtaṅga*, or ascetic practice, following all of them at the highest level, ven. Upāli was foremost in mastery of monastic discipline, and ven. Sivalī was foremost in fortuitously receiving requisites. (Consequently, images of the fortunate Sivalī are common in Burma, and I think in Thailand also, as talismans of good luck. He is always portrayed as standing and holding a fan, alms bowl, and walking stick.) Most of the good monks mentioned in the Pali texts are members of this group, with the group itself presumably being an anachronism, developed with the growth of legend.

*a "good luck charm" representing ven. Sivalī*

Speaking of Elders, I may as well point out that, technically, the venerable Elder Protector of Vision was not really an Elder, since an Elder, or Thera, is a monk who has been ordained for at least ten rains, and, by the time of the end of the story, ven. Cakkhupāla had completed only his sixth. But he was a saint, and a great hero besides, so the title is probably honorary.

Sakka, King of Gods, owner of the levitating Paṇḍukambala Throne, is none other than Indra, star of the Rig Veda and patron deity of the early Indo-Aryan proto-Hindus. His profound change of heart and conversion to Buddhism is pretty obviously a supreme example of machiavellian religious propaganda indulged in by the early Buddhist systematizers—but we needn't dwell on that. The point of the throne heating up is that, evidently, when someone performs an act of *tapas* or spiritual austerity so intense that no ordinary being could accomplish it, the throne, by some invisible connection, becomes so hot that Sakka/Indra cannot sit on it in comfort. So in such a case he is bound to help that person, if only so he can sit down again. Although in this case he is given the further incentive of not wanting his head to split apart.

One little point in the story which is of interest to the biologist in me is the little *indagopaka* bugs that the venerable Elder steps on while doing his walking meditation. The bugs are red, and come out of the ground after a heavy rain. Now, the climate, flora, and fauna of upper Burma is very similar to that of the ancient Ganges Valley, and in Burma the only creatures that fit this description are not insects but a kind of large, velvety, vermillion-colored ground mite which the Burmese call *nat thami po* ("goddess bug") or *nat thami khun thwei po* ("goddess betel spit bug"). At the beginning of the rainy season they come out in great numbers and can be seen slowly bumbling all over the place. If this is the right creature, however, then the story is guilty of one more, minor, anachronism, since the Elder steps on them at the end of the rainy season, whereas, as a rule, they come up out of the ground only at the beginning of the monsoon. But I'm pretty sure that's what Indra's cowherds are supposed to be. Despite being arachnids, like spiders, they're totally harmless and kind of cute, in a creepy sort of way. I like them, and bless them when I see them. May they be well and happy.

On the one hand this story is a kind of fairy tale replete with gross exaggerations, blatant anachronisms, and flat-out impossibilities, from a modern, Western point of view; but then again, that is the style of ancient heroic legends, and besides, the story also is an interesting one with some subtlety as well as genuine wisdom. With regard to characterization, for example, there are some well-known personality types met with even today: the proud, pedantic doctor who considers his word to be law for his patients, the cocky, borderline-rude youth (the Elder's nephew), the stern old fellow of few words that the nephew meets at the city gate, and at the end of the story the group of busybody monks wanting to play the tourist and stirring up trouble, this time by "tattling" on another monk to the Buddha. All in all, though, I would observe that the bulk of the story really doesn't fit the context of the verse very well, at least not the commentarial interpretation of it, and I would guess that the story was fitted to the verse some time after the fact. The first verse of a Pali text is an important one, and the commentators needed a suitably good story to accompany it, so it may be that they chose this one regardless of whether or not it was really the inspiration for the verse. Technically, the Dhammapada is not considered by critically-minded scholars to be particularly ancient anyway, and is certainly not included in the oldest "core texts," so most of the Dhammapada itself may not represent what the Buddha actually taught—not in his own words anyway. But it doesn't matter. Authenticity, and even objective truth, let alone worldly common sense, are really not the point. The point is this: Does it help you to Wake Up?

And now back to the word-by-word exegesis of "Dh.1" that started this post. This part is the "anticommentary" I warned you about. Most of the explanatory stuff has already been inserted, in brackets and underlined italics, but there is one longer observation I will make here, and that is with regard to the commentarial interpretation of the word *dhammā*, as in "*dhammā* are preceded by mind."

The reader may have noticed that, after defining the word *dhammā*, or "dharmas," in the verse as the three aggregates of mental states (in Abhidhammic jargon, *cetasikā*)—perceptions, feelings, and every other kind of mental state—the commentator then has to explain why the Buddha would say such a thing as "mind precedes mental states" when technically it isn't true, considering that mind and mental states do not occur one after the other but simultaneously. The verse is interpreted to have the meaning that consciousness is more important than mental states, which seems rather odd, and which appears to have nothing to do with the story of Cakkhupāla. I accept that it is possible that this is the originally intended meaning of the verse, but being a critically-minded Westerner I have little choice but to be skeptical.

It is true that the commentary provides other possible meanings for *dhamma*, i.e. virtue, practical philosophy, and mastery of Buddhist literature, but there are still more possible meanings for the term. In fact *dhamma* is one of the vaguest terms in the Pali language, and can mean just about *anything.* Literally it is related to the verb *dharati*, meaning to bear, to support; so *dhamma* literally means something along the lines of that which bears or holds up.

One of its earliest, pre-Buddhistic meanings was "law," possibly in the sense of that which holds up society, or that which must be upheld by the individual living in society. As a Buddhist philosophical term it came to mean, like Spinoza's *substance* or "substance," that which stands under and holds up the apparent qualities of experiential phenomena. So *dhamma* can mean something as general as "phenomenon" or "thing." Add to this that, as I have read somewhere or other, *dhamma* interpreted as "mental state" as opposed to consciousness itself appears to be a Buddhist innovation, and may not have originated with the Buddha himself, and it becomes more plausible that the first verse of the Dhammapada was originally saying something quite different from what the commentator would have us believe.

If *dhammā* is interpreted generally as "phenomena," or, as I have it, "ways of being," then what we've got is a more radically idealist interpretation, which is also more in harmony with the origin story. Even the most traditional, orthodox Theravada Buddhism admits that karma is a mental state which conditions everything pleasant or unpleasant that we experience in life; so in this sense our own mind creates our destiny. But Abhidhamma, which according to non-Burmese authorities did not come directly from the Buddha himself but gradually arose over the course of a few hundred years, adopted materialist ideas that were commonly accepted in ancient Indian philosophical circles; and since Abhidhammist interpretations and jargon permeate the commentarial literature, the idea that the world is an outward projection of our own inner "issues" was largely downplayed in favor of a more materialistic, more mechanistic, more classically "scientific" explanation of Samsara. Mind is still a major player of course, but it must stay in line with all of the other "ultimate realities" posited by Abhidhamma. But if *dhammā* in this famous verse really means worldly phenomena and not just *cetasikā*, then the message of the first two lines is not merely a technical quibble over the relationship between mind and mental states, but an overt assertion that we are creating our own reality; that we make our own bed, and then we lie in it.

One moral of this story—not the story of venerable Elder

Protector of Vision, but the story of commentary—is that there is some benefit to be had from reading the commentarial literature. Many of the stories are fascinating, and provide a kind of cultural atmosphere for the philosophy found in the suttas. In order to understand something, it is good to learn as much about it as possible; and stories like the ones in the Dhammapada commentary contribute to a comprehension of Buddhist culture much in the same way as the stories of Samson and Delilah or Lazarus rising from the dead themselves constitute significant bricks in the edifice of Western culture. Also, if one is reading a Pali text and comes across a strange word or incomprehensibly convoluted sentence, the commentaries may help. Sometimes their guess may be no better than yours, but sometimes they get it right. On the other hand, confusing Buddhism with Buddhaghosism can be a serious stumbling block for someone wanting to understand what the Buddha really taught. A real understanding of Dhamma doesn't come from books, not even from the Tipitaka itself.

# THE GREAT SCHISM

*(This is not about Christianity's split into Catholicism in the West and Orthodoxy in the east, nor about anything else particularly western or Christian. It is an attempt at a short and simple history of how Buddhism got divided up into different sects. Not too surprisingly I suppose, the splits began shortly after the Buddha's disappearance from this world, with the first preliminary cracks appearing during his very lifetime. Such is humanity.)*

This could be a relatively scholarly article, with translations from the Pali and lots of end notes and references, but I'm lazy, and furthermore I need to write several articles by the end of the month, as I intend to be in retreat during December, won't be writing then, and need four articles to be posted automatically by Google's artificial intelligence while I am occupied. So following will be some relatively unscholarly reflections, based mainly on memory, of some very early Buddhist history. It's still well worth reading though, probably.

According to the Pali texts, the first schism in Buddhism occurred during the Buddha's lifetime, and was instigated by his cousin and brother-in-law Devadatta. Theravadin tradition portrays Devadatta as a murderous villain, considerably worse than the archetypal Christian villain Judas Iscariot, as Devadatta allegedly attempted to murder the Buddha more than once, and, after impressing Prince Ajātasattu of Magadha with his jhanic psychic powers, persuaded the Prince to murder his own father and become King himself. Yet ironically, the schism in the Sangha is said to have arisen over Devadatta's insistence upon greater strictness in monastic discipline. He insisted upon five points, namely:

1. That all monks should be forest dwellers, with staying in a village being considered wrong;
2. That monks should not accept invitations for meals, but should eat only alms food collected by (silent) begging;
3. That monks should not accept donated robe cloth, but should wear only robes made from cast-off rags that they had picked up and sewn together;
4. That monks should not live under a roof, but only under trees; and
5. That monks must be vegetarian.

The Buddha replied that all of these are optional practices for members of the Sangha, but would not be made obligatory. Allegedly, Devadatta knew in advance that the Buddha would disagree, and insisted on these five points only as a pretense to make himself look good. Then he talked 500 monks into becoming his followers and left the presence of the Buddha with them in tow. When the 500 soon afterward went back to the Buddha, Devadatta is said to have become so frustrated and mortified that he vomited hot blood, dropped dead, and plunged straight into hell.

So the attempted schism was presumably an abortive one. But the details provided by tradition may not be very reliable, partly because it is hard to believe that Devadatta could be so monstrously evil as portrayed in the texts, and partly because his sect or "reform movement" may have continued for centuries. I remember long ago reading an account of one of the Chinese Buddhist monastic pilgrims who traveled to India may centuries after the time of the Buddha; and he claimed that near the Jetavana monastery there was a monastery of monks who professed to honor all Buddhas *except* Gotama, and that the founder of their movement was Devadatta. But even if this is true, Devadatta's sect never amounted to very much in the history of Buddhism, and it eventually died out.

The first *big* schism in the Buddhist Sangha, the one that really got the schismatic ball rolling, is said to have occurred about one hundred years after the Buddha disappeared from this world. It is associated with the second Buddhist great council, the details of which are given in the same book—the Vinaya Cullavagga—that describes Devadatta's most egregious attempts at stirring up trouble. I have read that other ancient schools of Buddhism, some of whose texts still survive, also gave similar accounts of this council.

The Theravadin version of the story gives the account of a monk named Yasa from the western districts, who was traveling through the region of Vesālī farther east. He happened to come to a monastery where the monks collected monetary donations from laypeople; and when they tried to give him his share of the "take," he refused, stating, in the presence of the laypeople, that handling money was improper and against the rules of monastic discipline. This naturally outraged the Vesālī monks, so they conducted a formal act of reconciliation against him (a formal act which, as far as I have ever heard, has not been conducted in Burma for centuries, if ever), requiring him to apologize to the laity for speaking so offensively. So the monk Yasa went to the laypeople and made things even worse by explaining the rules of discipline to them, including a little poem attributed to the Buddha, but, as far as I know, not found in any Pali sutta:

*Some philosophers and priests are defiled by lust and aversion,*
*Men enveloped in ignorance, delighting in pleasing forms;*

*They drink ale and wine, they indulge in sexual relations,*
*And they consent to silver and gold, the ignoramuses.*

*Some philosophers and priests live by wrong livelihood;*
*These are called defilements by the Buddha, kinsman of the sun.*

*Some philosophers and priests, defiled by these defilements,*
*Are not bright; they do not shine—they are impure, dirty animals.*

*They are wrapped in darkness, slaves to craving, led on by their own inclinations;*
*Their sole fulfillment is an awful one—the cemetery—and they take yet another existence.*

The result of this debacle should be easily predictable: The outraged monks of Vesālī decided to conduct a much more severe formal act against him, an act of suspension from the Sangha. So Yasa ran away before they got the chance, went back to the west, and told the stricter monks there about what had happened. Representatives of the two factions, east and west, convened to settle this controversy, and the meeting became known as the second great Buddhist council.

The primary issue was the legality of monks handling money, although other, less serious matters of monastic discipline were also addressed, such as whether or not it is allowable for a monk to keep salt for the sake of seasoning his food, and whether it is allowable to use a sitting cloth without a proper border. The western, proto-Theravadin side reportedly got its stricter way on all counts, and I have read that some records, at least, on the other side agreed that the western faction won the debate, although of course they didn't cast as dim a light on their own side as the Pali authors did for them. (I do consider it somewhat ironic, or like dark comedy, that the descendants of the victorious stricter side mostly handle money nowadays, not to mention keeping salt to season their food.)

But recently I read that some non-Theravadin texts, especially a text of the Mahā Sanghikas (descendants of the eastern faction) called the *Śāriputraparipṛcchā*, claim that the westerners were innovators trying to add new Vinaya rules to the ones already established, with the eastern side actually being the conservatives. The fact that the easterners were the larger faction (hence the name Mahā Sanghika or "of the Great Sangha"), situated in the traditional homeland of Buddhism, and the alleged fact that the Mahā Sanghika Vinaya contains fewer rules and appears to be more primitive, would seem to lend some circumstantial support to this claim. Also it is fairly obvious that the rules of the Theravada Buddhist Vinaya do not all date to the first council. They were added in layers, so to speak, with essentially two different sets of rules: the Pāṭimokkha, and everything else. And some rules in the "everything else" category even prescribe the proper conduct with regard to monks of other sects of Buddhism, which of course didn't exist at the time of the first council, or even the second—unless we assume that Devadatta's sect was intended.

The details of exactly what happened around the time of the second council are unclear, and some scholars claim that the council took place only about seventy years after the time of the Buddha, with the schism itself occurring approximately thirty years after that. This would explain why some eastern texts admit that the westerners won the debate at the council. It would also make more plausible the textual claim that a former disciple of the venerable Ānanda attended the council. In fact some accounts by the descendants of the eastern Buddhists say that the actual split occurred over matters of Dharma, not Vinaya—with the most famous issue of contention being the question of whether or not an Arahant could backslide and become unenlightened again. (I also seem to remember something about arguments over whether or not an enlightened being could have a wet dream.) The eastern side said Yes, and "our side" said No. If this is true, then it is a little sad that only one hundred years after the time of the Buddha they could already no longer find an Arahant and just ask him or her.

Disagreements over monastic discipline apparently had something to do with the breakup, or *sanghabheda*, between the *Mahāsāṁghika Nikāya* in the eastern homeland of Buddhism and the *Sthavira Nikāya*, or proto-Theravada, located mainly farther west, in districts more recently converted to Buddhism. In fact nowadays scholars theorize that Pali is an ecclesiastical language which developed as proto-Theravada moved westwards across northern India, picking up elements of western dialects as it was gradually displaced farther east. So pretty obviously geography was also a significant factor in determining the schism. Travel and communications were slower and more difficult in those days, and thus the cultural evolution of Buddhism moved in different directions largely as a result of isolation of various groups, and slightly different emphases taking precedence and growing into major distinguishing tenets. This kind of isolation serves as a factor in the evolution of religious organizations as well as in the evolution of species of biological organisms.

The breakup continued within both of the original factions, so that within three centuries of the time of Gotama Buddha there were said to be 18 different sects of Buddhism. One of the more influential and well-known on the Sthavira side were the Sarvāstivādins, who may have been the "non-Buddhist heretics" allegedly purged from the Sangha in the Pali commentarial account of the third great council, conducted during the time of the emperor Asoka.

Despite the disagreements, it is heartening that the ancient Buddhists evidently did not abandon their peaceful ideals, as I am unaware of any sectarian violence erupting between the followers of different sects at this time. If it happened it didn't make history. In fact, monks of different sects could be found studying together and debating at the same monastery compounds and Buddhist universities, although they did carry out their formal acts of the Sangha separately. Sometimes the debates could grow vitriolic, but there is no comparison with what happened in Western Christianity a few centuries later, with blood flowing in the streets from violent altercations over, say, whether Christ had two natures, divine and human, or only one, or whether the Holy Spirit emanated directly from the Father, or from the Father but *through the Son*.

Vinaya and geography may have been the original factors catalyzing the division of the Sangha, but by the time of the "18 Schools" the primary source of disagreement had become philosophical theory. The two main groups, *Sthavira* (Sanskrit for *Thera*) and *Mahāsāṁghika*, including their respective subgroups, began moving philosophically into practically opposite directions in certain respects, which resulted in an interesting polarity arising to distinguish the two. In fact it is this polarity which is actually the main reason why I wanted to write about this in the first place.

The monks of the Great Sangha and associated schools tended toward *absolutism*, or an emphasis on a transcendental Ultimate Reality. They also stressed the importance of the intuition of the individual, and favored elaboration of philosophical views, including the view of No View. Mahayana arose mainly from this side of the fence, with one of its high points being manifested in the

Prajnaparamita literature, the "Perfection of Wisdom."

The Sthaviras or "Elders," on the other hand, favored philosophical conservatism, and adherence to doctrinal orthodoxy. They also tended to favor the view that Ultimate Reality is not so transcendental that it cannot be understood intellectually. This latter tendency reached its zenith in the various Abhidharma literatures of the various schools. Rather than mystical monism they preferred objective pluralism, with arguably the most extreme school in this regard being the Sarvastivadins, who were extreme atomists. They considered the elemental atom, or individual *dharma*, to be the ultimately real unit of samsaric reality, being itself unconditioned and eternal, with only the combinations of these atoms being subject to impermanence—or so I have read. Various sects of the "Elders," including Theravada, came up with their own philosophical elaborations in the form of some kind of Abhidharma, but after this phase of getting everything suitably explained they adhered rigidly to their explanations, making minor adjustments here and there but disapproving of innovation.

Thus Buddhism diverged, very generally speaking, toward the two polar extremes of traditional dogmatism vs. progressive "liberalism" of thought and intuition, which polarity forms two horns of a dilemma. But the dilemma is compounded if one considers that each of these two poles—traditional dogma and subjective intuition—bears its own dilemma of mutually negating positive and negative aspects. I have observed before that a strength tends to carry its own weakness, as a flip side of the same coin; and this observation tends to be borne out if one observes the paths taken by the two main branches of ancient Buddhism.

Which is better: spiritual conservatism or spiritual liberalism? Well, as the Bible says, "The letter killeth, the Spirit maketh alive." And there can be little doubt that in traditional Theravada there is quite a lot of killeth. The established tradition has ossified to such an extent that even explaining some aspect of Dhamma in one's own words, instead of the words of an authorized text, may be seen as Wrong. The notion that an intellectual system really can explain Reality, and even be the *only* correct explanation, has resulted in some famous Theravadins, for example the English monk Nyanavira and the Burmese Pah Auk Sayadaw, asserting that anyone who disagrees with their particular interpretation is so wrong as to have no hope of liberation. On the other hand, a common illustration of a fool in the Pali suttas is one who says, "Only this is true! Anything else is wrong!" But a dogmatist would reply that the fool says it with regard to a pernicious Wrong View, but that saying it with regard to orthodox dogma is Right. So spiritual conservatism can result in adherence to dead words and abstract concepts replacing genuine, living inspiration.

On the other hand, "progressive" freedom of interpretation may result in the seeker wandering away from the main point entirely, as arguably could be said of the Pure Land traditions that arose in some of the Great Sangha schools at the beginning of the Mahayana movement. Freedom from dogma is certainly no guarantee of wisdom; and without that wisdom one may throw away any valid guidance contained in the dogmatic tradition. (Dead words definitely have their limitations, but, like a dead hammer or saw, if used as a tool may not be entirely useless.) Consequently, Mahayana has diverged to the extent of being all over the map, ranging from the ridiculous to the sublime; and although Theravada has its own fair share of ridiculous as well as sublime, still it seems to have remained consistently closer to the original message. Mahayana over the centuries may have had more living inspiration, but it has also had more of everything else, with the inspiration often being overwhelmed in the flood.

So a limitation of conservatism is that one may become attached to somebody else's words, and fail to move beyond them into one's own genuine realization of the Way. A limitation of liberalism is that one may wander completely off the track and wind up in La-La Land. Both approaches have their strengths and their weaknesses. It's a multiple dilemma.

But of course, Buddhist Dharma teaches a Middle Way, so one good solution would be to steer a middle course between relying on a map (without mistaking it for the terrain) and trusting one's own intuition, inspiration, and experience (without disdainfully dismissing the map).

Another way of looking at it is to consider that strengths and weakness inevitably cancel each other out, so that the universe can remain in some semblance of a stable balance. Anything with strengths and corresponding weaknesses is a samsaric phenomenon which negates itself; and true Dharma is neither positive nor negative. It is purely neutral, and beyond strengths or weaknesses. It cannot really be negated, or confirmed either. So let the pluses and minuses cancel each other out, attaching to neither, and keep your heart and mind as wide open as possible. Be wide awake, be careful, follow your deepest sensitivity, respect teachers regardless of whether they teach anything you can use, and know that the blessings of gods and saints are upon you. And good luck.

# VIPASSANA: INSIGHT, REFLECTION, OR MINDFULNESS PRACTICE?

I am writing this as a response to numerous communications made to me regarding Vipassana, and what it is, as there seems to be a modicum of confusion on the subject. Some people ask me about Vipassana practice, or "doing Vipassana." A few practitioners of the Goenka method have mentioned Vipassana to me and have been surprised to be informed that Goenka-style body sweeping is not standard Vipassana straight out of the Pali texts, that that's not simply what Vipassana is. The fact is that, as with other Buddhist terms like "karma" or "jhāna," many more people use the term than know quite what it means—or at any rate what it used to mean. Usage by the masses determines the meaning of words, so I'm not trying to be a linguistic hard-ass here. Everything, including a definition, is impermanent. But still, in the ancient Theravada Buddhist texts, *vipassanā* generally does not refer to the kind of meditation techniques that are called by that name in the West, and sometimes also in the East.

Frankly, I don't even like to use the word "vipassana." "Insight" is a perfectly adequate English rendering, and there are other adequate English words for other possible meanings of the Pali one. "Vipassana" may be, in common usage, so vague as to be almost meaningless. Consequently, in order to clarify the situation a little (just a little), to untangle the tangle somewhat, I'm writing about it, even though I don't much like using the "v" word.

The Pali word *vipassanā* is a compound of the prefix *vi-* and the verbal noun *passanā*, the latter meaning, quite literally, "seeing." *Vi-* literally means something like "apart," so that *vipassanā* could theoretically mean something like "seeing apart" or discriminating; but *vi-* is also frequently used simply as an intensifier. For example, *mokkha* can mean "liberation"; but the final liberation of enlightenment is more frequently stressed as *vimokkha.* Similarly, *suddhi* means purity, but *visuddhi* is used in a sense to stress complete purity in a spiritual sense. So the Pali word *vipassanā* can be said to mean something like "deep seeing"; and thus "insight" really is not a bad English equivalent.

The thing is that, technically speaking, you really don't DO Vipassana. It is not a bodily action, nor is it intellectual, or even particularly volitional. (The act of *looking* is volitional, but simply *seeing* may be assumed to be otherwise.) Vipassana, or at least *vipassanā*, is, strictly speaking, an intuitive insight which arises spontaneously, often, but not always, as a result of meditation. Insight may also be triggered by such events as hearing a discourse or by experiencing some profound shock, even by the experience of dying. It is a prerequisite for enlightenment (whatever that is), so anyone who attains enlightenment experiences liberating insight; and it appears pretty obvious, judging from the literature, that not everyone who becomes enlightened is practicing meditation at the time.

Furthermore, even when insight does arise from meditation, the meditation is not necessarily what is commonly referred to as "Vipassana meditation"—so I suppose I should discuss, very briefly, the two main types of meditation in Buddhism. We may ignore for the moment the fact that they are usually distinguished as *samatha* and *vipassanā.*

The two main types of meditation in Buddhism, or at least in Theravada Buddhism, are based upon *samādhi* or "concentration," and *sati* or "mindfulness." Concentration here involves the quieting and simplifying of the contents of the mind, the unification of mind. Mindfulness, on the other hand, involves being wide awake in the present moment, in the seen only the seen, and so forth; it implies living up to Ram Dass's old motto of *Be Here Now.* These two modes of meditation are not mutually exclusive, and can be practiced beautifully together—in fact they can supplement each other. Fourth jhāna, which is often considered to be the highest level of concentration, is identified in the texts with "purity of mindfulness." A clear, still, quiet mind makes intent awareness much easier, and *vice versa.* This clarity, stillness, and quietness can rightfully be called *samatha,* or "tranquillity." But neither of these two forms of meditation, strictly speaking, is the same as *vipassanā.*

One of my favorite examples of how liberating insight can arise is a description found in the Small Discourse on Emptiness in the Majjhima Nikāya (M121). In this case it arises from extreme *samatha* practice. A meditating monk progressively empties his mind through solitude and highly refined concentration until he goes beyond fourth jhāna and attains "the formless concentration of mind," or *animitta cetosamādhi.* This presumably represents the absolute limit that a meditating mind can reach, the highest possible meditative state. After inevitably coming out of that state, and seeing that even this highest state is not enlightenment, he realizes thus:

"This signless concentration of mind too is conditioned and volitionally determined; and whatever is conditioned and volitionally determined is impermanent and subject to cessation." And knowing thus, seeing thus, his mind is liberated from the encumbering influence of sensual desire, liberated from the encumbering influence of the momentum of existence, liberated from the encumbering influence of ignorance. In the liberation there is the knowledge "I am liberated." He realizes, "Finished is birth, lived to fulfillment is the Holy Life, done is what needs to be done. There is no more of this or that state of existence."

This realization is a poetic description of liberating insight, *vipassanā.*

Partly because of textual accounts like this, I suspect, hyperintellectual Buddhist systematologists of ancient India interpreted *vipassanā* as a kind of exercise of reflection, and elaborated upon it mightily. Thus orthodox tradition tells us that Vipassana is a training to be developed along with the other trainings of morality and concentration. The cultivation of this Vipassana is declared to occur in a five-stepped sequence beginning with insight into corporeal form and ending with the application of the Three Marks (of *anicca*, *dukkha*, and *anattā*) to the interacting duality of mind and matter as conditioned by Dependent Co-arising. There are claimed to be nine stages, and eighteen chief kinds, or Great Insights. All this shows that, far from remaining a spontaneous, non-intellectual realization, *vipassanā* evolved into a very non-intuitive technical term. Insight turned into an intellectual discipline—but even this is not the same as what is usually called "Vipassana meditation" nowadays. Actually, I'm not quite sure how Vipassana came to be identified with *satipaṭṭhāna* or mindfulness practice, unless maybe it was incorporated into *dhammānupassanā*, the fourth factor of *satipaṭṭhāna.* With regard to technical matters, I suggest that the one technicality that may be genuinely useful to know is that insight, in order for it to be *liberating* insight, must involve, according to tradition, the application of the Three Marks to one's experience.

(Also I will add, in parentheses, that the aforementioned nine stages of *vipassanā*, the so-called insight knowledges, starting with *udayabbayānupassanā-ñāṇa*, or "the knowledge of the reflection on arising and passing away," form a kind of theoretical backbone to certain Burmese mindfulness techniques such as the Mahasi method. One may be required to experience these insights, in the proper sequence, in order to be recognized as an Ariya. But enough of technical lists.)

Consequently, bearing all this in mind, it is clear that a person may practice *samatha* meditation and experience liberating insight; or, on the other hand, one may practice mindfulness till one is blue in the face and still be very far away from it. So again, you don't really DO genuine insight. Nyanatiloka's Buddhist Dictionary, before diving into a swamp of technical gobbledygook, defines *vipassanā* as "the intuitive light flashing forth and exposing the truth of the impermanency, the suffering and the impersonal and unsubstantial nature of all corporeal and mental phenomena of existence." Or, to be even less technical than that, it can be defined as simply a kind of "click" which allows one, suddenly, to see Reality more clearly. That click can be evoked by clear mindfulness, and it can also be evoked by jhāna, or the prodding of a teacher, or even a blow to the head. Mindfulness definitely helps, though.

But seriously, call it whatever you like, and continue being a member of an Insight Meditation group which endorses the practice of Vipassana meditation in the form of mindfulness—it's quite all right by me. But do please bear in mind the discussion above if you wish to discuss Buddhist meditation with me, as I'm fussy about the "V word" and its usage. I'd appreciate that. Be mindful, good luck in your practice, and may you experience genuine insight.

## SPECIAL CONFUSING APPENDIX

*Just for the niraya of it I used Google's automatic translation gadget to translate this essay into Bosnian, then Japanese, then Swahili, and finally back into English again. Following are the first two paragraphs, followed by the last two paragraphs, processed, of the preceding essay. Artificial intelligence apparently has a ways to go before surpassing human beings in certain language skills.*

### Vipassana Insight, meditation, or mindfulness practice?

Why am I me of Vipassana, of this writing, depending on the number of contacts. There seems to be little respect to the subject of confusion. Some people, "do Vipassana." Did you ask me about Vipassana practice, the body sprinkled with some of my on Vipassana mentioned pentachloride practice of law and was surprised but style pentachloride, Vipassana rate, that is not just what is Vipassana, provide information that is not directly from the text of the Pali. In fact, like other words Buddhist as karma and Jhana, the more people use it with a long, but it is, what they are is being used for it, at least mean - Do you know the exact amount of the expenditure, since determining the meaning words, I'm here. I'll try not to be the butt of a hard language throughout. All of them, including definitions, are temporary. But still, in the ancient texts of Theravada Buddhism, Vipassana, in general, Western countries, sometimes to the east It does not apply to the type of meditation that is called by that name.

In fact, I do not know if that also use the words "Vipassana." "Insight" is very correct English words, there are other suitable English word for other possible fire 1. It may be "Vipassana", in normal use, it is controversial because many meanings. I but finally there is a lot, such as using the word "V", obviously a little (just a little) the situation, in order to elucidate more tangled, and I will write upon him....

Consequently, to hold all this in mind, a person makes Samatha meditation, it is clear that you can experience release awareness. One is blue in the face, until still has far too much, or, on the other hand, will be able to perform calm. So, once again, truly original insights. Nyanatiloka The Buddhist dictionary, before jumping in a pool of shit technical, Vipassana is flashing "bright light and are defined as follows, etc. and impermanency, both physical and mental existence and suffering and to expose the truth about the nature of the grounds of faceless phenomenon . "Otherwise, it is true that the technical compliance, it only can be defined as a form of" click "which may be one, suddenly, please you to see clearly the truth. Click on this, you can clear the memory is caused by, and Jhana or interesting teacher or even to the head, can be induced to blow,. Mindfulness But definitely helps.

But seriously, you can take what you want, still a member of the group to consider supporting the awareness of the practice of Vipassana meditation in the form mindfulness fine is only for me. However, to use it as a "search", if I was nervous, please bear discussion and I say Buddhist meditation. I appreciate it. Please note Fortunately fact, you really are generating awareness.

# TECHNICAL MATTERS: VINAYA RULES EVEN STRICT MONKS BREAK

## *or: How to Follow Strictly a Corrupt Tradition*

First of all, I would like to specify that the kind of rule-breaking I intend to target in this post is not the kind in which a monk breaks a rule, sees the offense, confesses it, and expiates it. Most strict monks, and almost all "exemplary" ones, do break Vinaya rules in this way regularly, however, so I may as well discuss the matter a little before moving on to the target.

There are very many Vinaya rules for monks, I'd guess somewhere between two and three thousand. Many of them are obsolete or otherwise difficult to break (e.g. offering food with one's own hands to a naked non-Buddhist ascetic, using an alms bowl made from a human skull, eating lion meat); but there are plenty than can be broken easily, even by strict monks. For example, the rule against drinking alcohol is worded in such a way that even if the monk drinks something alcoholic accidentally, he still breaks the rule. Thus on one occasion long ago I was offered some herbal medicine stuff that I was assured contained no alcohol, but when I tried a sip of it, it tasted like it was about 80 proof. Or on a few other occasions I was offered some drink that, in the hot Burmese weather, had started to ferment spontaneously; I'd take a drink and the stuff would taste like wine. So in such cases one takes the hit and confesses it.

Also, some rules can easily be broken in a moment of careless unrestraint. For example, unnecessarily looking up in a public place (as monks are supposed to look down in public). Or making a humorous reference about somebody else while talking. Or using water while suddenly entertaining the doubt that maybe there are living creatures in it. Such offenses can occur rather often, especially if a monk is not Vinaya-obsessed, and again, the thing to do is simply to confess it, and the ecclesiastical reset button is pushed, clearing the offenses.

Then there are rules that even a serious monk may break deliberately, considering *not* breaking the rule to be more objectionable than breaking it. For example, it is against Vinaya for a monk to practice medicine on laypeople. The purpose of this is partly to prevent monks from working for a living like "householders who enjoy pleasures of the senses," with people going to them for health issues rather than Dhamma (with such monks consequently practicing Dhamma less and teaching it less), and another reason is that, if the monk messes up and the person gets worse or dies, then people may blame the Sangha for it. Anyway, when I was living in a very remote forest area of Burma a supporter of mine, really a good guy who I liked as a friend, told me that his daughter had had malaria for several months. (Malaria is endemic in this area, and potentially deadly.) I had some state of the art malaria cure; so, even though it was against the rules I considered it to be better to break a minor rule than let a person remain very ill and possibly even die. So I gave him the pills for his daughter, and she got better. Another example of arguably "righteous" rule-breaking occurred long ago when a young and very serious American man wanted to be ordained as a bhikkhu under venerable Taungpulu Sayadaw, but he didn't have the permission of his parents to be ordained, as they were devout Christians who disapproved of such a course. Taungpulu Sayadaw ordained him anyway, saying, "The Sangha is willing to make the sacrifice." That is, they were willing to break the minor rule of ordaining a man without his parents' consent, for the good of helping him to live the Holy Life. Afterwards they confessed the offense.

Then again, there are rules the breaking of which is practically unavoidable. For example, it is against Vinaya to enter a toilet with one's upper robe on; one should strip to the waist before entering an outhouse. At the same time, it is against Vinaya to remove one's upper robe in a public place. So any monk who has to use the toilet at a public place just has to choose which rule he prefers to break by taking the pee, since he breaks one either way, yet his back teeth are floating, he has to pee so bad. So in all these cases, when a monk breaks a rule, he just makes confession to another monk, in accordance with other Vinaya rules designed to deal with the situation. It's all built into the system. Almost all monks break rules like this. There are a very few bhikkhus who are so conscientious, or fanatical, or whatever, that they would actually let a girl drown rather than break a rule by swimming out and saving her, or who never unnecessarily look up in public for that matter. Such are rare specimens.

But, as I say, this kind of rule-breaking, with the monk committing, seeing, and expiating the offense, is not the kind of rule-breaking that I intend to discuss here. The kind I intend to discuss is with regard to rules broken chronically and habitually, sometimes even as a matter of monastery policy or venerated tradition, with no acknowledgement of the offense, and consequently no confession or other expiation. Because of this phenomenon even many strict and "exemplary" bhikkhus never have a single day of pure Vinaya restraint or pure morality in the entire course of their life as a monastic.

This sort of thing is common in religious systems, I think. It's common in the human race. Conformity is seen as essential, even if it is conformity to a corrupt tradition. The idea seems to be, "If everyone else is breaking the same rule, then it's all right"—but this is essentially a bovine herd instinct, and not Dhamma.

The issue of conformity arose at the second Buddhist great council, in ancient times. Monks had started handling money and breaking other rules, and one topic of debate at the council was whether it was right to follow one's teacher with regard to Vinaya interpretation and practice. The Theravadin side argued that sometimes it is and sometimes it isn't—implying that following one's teacher is valid only if one's teacher's conduct is in harmony with real Vinaya. The Theravadin side won the debate. So regardless of whether breaking certain rules is justified and universal in a tradition, technically it's still breaking rules. Following are some examples.

**Clothing (including shoes, hats, etc.):** With regard to robes, I may write someday a more technical article than this discussing the originally correct manner of sewing and wearing them, as well as their correct size, although here I'll skip the manner in which robes are made, the proper materials, etc., and will just mention one thing about size. According to the 92nd pācittiya rule of the bhikkhu pātimokkha, a monk may not wear a robe as big as or bigger than the Buddha's upper or outer robe, which was nine handspans by six, according to the size of the Buddha's own hand. The Vinaya commentarial tradition has decreed that the Buddha's handspan was 3½ times the length of an ordinary man's handspan, thereby causing the rule to mean that a monk may not wear a robe more than seven meters in length, which of course is no rule at all, since nobody would even want to wear a robe that large. Assuming that the Buddha's hand was not much bigger than that of the average monk, and certainly not three and a half times as big, then the size of the average monk's robe nowadays is about twice the allowable size. If one reads the texts one may see that in the Buddha's time monks wore relatively small robes; and two of the most influential Vinaya texts in English, the *Vinayamukha* translation and Ajahn Ṭhanissaro's *The Buddhist Monastic Code*, point out this very fact that monks' robes should be much smaller than the ones usually worn. But if you see a picture of either of the venerable authors of these two books you will see that, more than likely, they also are wearing big robes which they admit are in violation of the rules of Vinaya. Why? Conformity. But that doesn't make it any less against the rules, even though the author of the *Vinayamukha* was a Thai Sangharāja.

The ironic thing about this for me is that monks living in the temperate zone, like in Western countries, continue to wear robes in conformity with a corrupt South Asian tradition, which then serves as a justification for breaking more rules. They continue to wear robes suitable for a hot, tropical climate, with thick cloth being too thick to wear in the peculiar Asian way, especially in the Thai manner with part of the robe wrapped around one arm most of the time. So this difficulty is seen as a sufficient reason for breaking the rule against keeping and wearing extra clothing also.

According to the first nissaggiya pācittiya rule of the pātimokkha a monk is allowed to own and wear three robes (lower, upper, and outer), with any clothing in excess of this to be relinquished (given or thrown away) within ten days of acquiring the excess. Any piece of cloth larger than eight finger widths by four finger widths (according to the Buddha's hand again) is counted as robe cloth, i.e. clothing, unless determined for some other use, such as a towel or bed sheet. Thus the rule includes not only robes, but also underwear, shirts, sweaters, coats, socks, stocking caps, and Mahayana Buddhist-style pajamas. All of this technically is against Vinaya, yet almost all monks living in the West, including the "exemplary" ones, violate the rule without compunction, and do not confess it—which wouldn't work anyway unless they relinquished all the extra clothes beforehand, which they do not want to do. The stocking caps, underwear, socks, etc. are also layman's clothing, the wearing of which is in violation of another rule.

One important point to bear in mind, it seems to me, is that, according to the Pali texts, it was during the coldest time of year in the ancient Ganges Valley that the Buddha decided that three robes are enough for any monk. It is stated that at this time of year (in ancient times before global warming kicked in) the temperature got down to around freezing. Also, allowed in the Vinaya texts is a kind of woolen felt blanket called a *santhata*, also called a *pāvāra* or *pāvuraṇa*, which may be worn as a cloak. I can assert from my own experience that three small, thick robes and a felt blanket are plenty for staying warm in environments that are freezing cold. Western monks dressing like Eskimos in temperatures above freezing is simply a case of bovine conformity, wimpiness, or both. At temperatures well below freezing, however, some "righteous" rule-breaking may be in order. But still it would probably count as breaking rules, and something to be confessed.

One way that ostensibly strict monks avoid the rule about extra clothing is by determining all extra clothes (and sometimes the regulation three robes also) as "accessory cloth," i.e., cloth not used as clothing, but kept for other uses. But what the hell is that, if not lying? There are two ways in which a monk may determine cloth for this or that use: by speech and by physical action. It is stated that if a monk determines a robe to be "accessory cloth" by physical action, he just holds it and waves it around a little while mentally determining it as whatever. But what more obvious way of determining a robe physically than by just putting it on and wearing it! If one wears it as a robe, then it's a robe. If it looks like a duck and quacks like a duck.... Seriously. By refusing to acknowledge that they are in fact breaking rules, monks creep into the realm of dishonesty, or just following and believing corrupt nonsense, refusing to see the obvious.

This very same approach could be used to avoid all sorts of rules. Want to drink whiskey? Call it medicine, or "accessory liquid." Want to use money? Call it "accessory paper." Don't want to admit that something is what it is? Call it something else! It wouldn't count for diddle at a real trial at a real law court, as such reasoning is obviously bogus, but no matter. The situation reminds me of the old Burmese monastic saying, "If one is skillful in Vinaya one may kill a chicken." Skillful in all the lame loopholes, that is.

With regard to shoes, only certain kinds of sandals which leave the toes and heels open are allowable. Some strict-ish monks break this one in the temperate zone, but *most* of them break a different one: A monk is not allowed to wear shoes at all in public places, unless he is unwell. The danger of frostbite in subzero weather would presumably count as a valid reason for wearing shoes in town, but that usually is not a present danger. Again, bovine conformity and wimpiness prevail over Vinaya.

*three ways of wearing robes*

**Food:** Non-strict monks may break all sorts of food rules, such as eating food that wasn't properly offered (which includes a monk touching a huge table that he couldn't lift while laypeople intending to offer the food on the table also touch it or group-lift it), eating food stored at the monastery, eating before dawn (possibly going with some chart that claims dawn has dawned when meanwhile the sky remains totally dark), eating food that they cooked themselves, and so on. But strict monks from Thai traditions notoriously eat cheese and dark chocolate in the afternoon...which on the face of it appears to be eating food at an unallowable time. Now, there is nothing inherently *immoral* in eating a piece of cheese in the afternoon. What is at least verging on immorality, however, is the cheesy justifications given for breaking the rule by eating it. Venerable Ajahn Ṭhanissaro, in his first book on monastic discipline, actually suggested that eating cheese in the afternoon is all right because cheese is not substantial food, but is actually a kind of butter, which is allowed as a medicine. Almost needless to say, this strikes me as blatant sophistry of a rather base sort. (I call it "backwards logic": starting with the conclusion one wants to arrive at—that eating cheese in the afternoon is allowable—and then working backwards, cooking up the most plausible rationalization for it.) Of course cheese is substantial food; it is a meat substitute for vegetarians, right? It's almost pure curd...although it can't be *called* curd by the monks who want to eat it, because curd is considered to be substantial food in Vinaya and thus must not be eaten in the afternoon. So they can say what they like, but strict-ish monks who eat cheese in the afternoon are doing it because of 1) conformity and 2) weakness or else a simple desire to eat something. The only Burmese monks who would eat cheese in the afternoon would also eat rice and curry in the afternoon—and I admit there are quite a few of those.

Dark chocolate is a slightly more subtle issue. One argument I have heard is that dark chocolate (with no milk, as milk is considered to be substantial food) is actually a kind of congealed juice, and juice is allowable in the afternoon. What to me sounds more plausible is that dark chocolate is not substantial food, and is medicinal in some way. Even if it is congealed juice, because it contains a significant amount of sugar in solid form it is to be treated as medicinal. (Yes, sugar is medicinal. It's good for you.) So only monks who are *unwell* are allowed to eat it in the afternoon. Unfortunately, however—or fortunately, depending on how one chooses to look at it—the medieval commentarial tradition states that a monk who is tired or just hungry may consider himself to be unwell. So a monk can't eat chocolate in the afternoon *as food*, but he can eat it because he's *hungry*. My question here is, What's the difference? How many people think things like, "I'm not hungry right now, but I want to eat this in order to replenish depleted nutrients," eh? Not very many. And even if they do, they'd probably be more likely to eat spirulina tablets than chocolate in such a case. It's just more traditional corruption and sophistry which is very convenient for monks to follow. I've been told that at Wat Pah Nanachat the monks pass the afternoon treat tray around the sangha three times, with the monks sitting there eating the most expensive designer dark chocolate, "like householders who enjoy pleasures of the senses."

This condition that medicinal substances like sugar be eaten in the afternoon only if a monk is not feeling well applies not only to chocolate of course, but also to hard candy and other treats. But the main reasons why it is indulged in are conformity, weakness, and a borderline-dishonest desire for it not to be against the rules. Unless you sincerely believe that feeling hungry is the same as being unwell.

**Money:** There is one Vinaya rule concerning money that may be virtually impossible to follow correctly, with *very* few monks succeeding, especially in the West, and that is the rule prohibiting monks from handling the stuff. The thing is that a monk is not only prohibited from handling it, he is prohibited even from *consenting* to someone else keeping it or handling it on his behalf. The rule states that if someone expresses the intention of having some money kept in a fund for a monk's benefit, if the monk doesn't like the idea at all he may remain silent, thereby allowing it to happen, but if he likes the idea he is required to tell the person not to do it. If they stubbornly persist after he forbids them, then it is allowable. I have found that the most viable way to follow this rule is to live in some remote forest area of tropical Asia where people have little money, and to avoid monasteries; or at the very least to live in a deeply Buddhist culture where monks are supported, and to avoid having anything at all to do with money. But in the West especially it can be damn near impossible.

Some strict-ish monks don't actually touch money, but they not only consent to it being kept for them, they also tell supporters or monastery attendants what to do with it. Endorsing a check is a similar case: although technically it may not be handling money, it is still endorsing an order to "pay to the order of," which is still handling money indirectly. So that also is against the rules, and an extremely convenient one to break for abbots running a monastery especially. Much of this kind of rule-breaking is by monks conscientiously trying to follow rules but being unaware of all the technical complications in Vinaya. It requires careful study to avoid breaking rules, and most monks, even most conscientious ones, don't do enough of that. And even if they do, conformity to the corrupt tradition is considered to be more important than conformity to the original rule, which behavior is totally in conformity with human nature.

**Some Miscellaneous Ones:** The mythological measure of the Buddha's allegedly giant hand results in several other broken rules even among strict monks: for example, the legs of a monk's bed may not be more than eight finger widths long, or about 15cm. Also, quilted bedding, like sleeping bags, are against the rules. Some rules with regard to human females are very easily broken, especially in non-Buddhist countries, and are broken by many "exemplary" monks, such as traveling by arrangement with them or sitting alone with them (and whether or not a door is open is irrelevant, as a rule is still broken if no other male can see and hear them). Even using a full-length toothbrush is technically against Vinaya, as there is a rule that a monk may not use a tooth-cleaning stick longer than eight of his own finger widths (or shorter than four). I still have a habit of cutting off part of the handle of my toothbrush, which I have retained from my extremely strict days. So again, almost all monks, including strict ones, are breaking Vinaya rules all the time, generally without acknowledging them or confessing them. And, as I pointed out in a previous essay on Vinaya, even the way they confess their offenses is usually against the rules.

Towards the beginning of Ajahn Ṭh.'s first book on Vinaya he called for reform...and then throughout the rest of the book he pretty much ignored genuine reform and endorsed an amazing quantity of lame loopholes from the medieval commentaries and Thai tradition, as well as cooking up a few new ones. That was disappointing, especially as my hard-ass strictness was going full blast in those days. Really, though, Western Theravada Buddhist monasticism seems to be blowing a golden opportunity for some really beneficial reform, since there is really no call for importing traditional Asian corruptions along with Dhamma/Vinaya. But not only have the old corruptions been maintained, new corruptions (like the arctic expedition gear unnecessarily worn by so many bhikkhus) are being added. And this in addition to the almost mandatory luxury of life in modern Western civilization.

If Western monks really do not want to follow ancient Vinaya rules, it seems to me that one obvious choice is to develop a new order of renunciants in the West, not officially bhikkhus but something else, with rules adjusted to fit a new world order. This would also allow for a genuinely equal order of nuns to be established—although that will be a topic for the next post.

Which is better: breaking a rule, acknowledging that one has broken it, and expiating the offense in accordance with Vinaya itself, or breaking it and refusing to admit that one has broken it at all, and furthermore justifying the act with absurdly flimsy rationalizations? Or in other words, which is better: to be straightforwardly lax, or to rig the game so that one can consider oneself to be strict? The first option may seem more shameless, but it is also more *honest,* with oneself as well as with others. But do as you like. That's what I do too. (I laugh)

# APPENDIX ON BHIKKHUNIS AND EQUALITY

In the previous essay I discussed the phenomenon of Theravada Buddhist monks "strictly following a corrupt tradition," that is, breaking the rules in the texts without acknowledging the fact by following later corruptions of those rules. In a different essay I mentioned having seen two of the somewhat controversial new bhikkhunis, the first two I've ever seen. And what I noticed is that these bhikkhunis were evidently conforming to the same kind of corruption of monastic discipline as the aforementioned "strict-ish" bhikkhus (for example, neither of them was wearing the regulation clothing of a bhikkhuni), in addition to simply ignoring some of the other rules specifically pertaining to bhikkhunis (for example, with regard to sitting in the presence of a bhikkhu). So the present discourse is a kind of appendix to the previous one—a logical continuation of the same theme, although moving in a tangential direction. The big question herein is: Why revive an ancient order if those who revive it are unwilling to follow the code which defines that ancient order?

The following discussion may turn out to be very politically incorrect. I'm not deliberately *trying* to be politically incorrect, although I do freely admit that I consider political correctness to be insane bullshit. Furthermore, cutting through bullshit is one of my callings in life. So mainly I'm just trying to cut through some bullshit here, so that somebody might see a certain situation with a little more clarity, or at least from a different angle. *Fair warning*

How many new bhikkhunis sit crosslegged, say, when they meditate? Guess. Probably most if not all of them, right? I figure that's probably the case. But did you know that it is against the code of monastic discipline for a bhikkhuni to sit crosslegged? She is required by the Pali Vinaya to sit with both feet tucked in to one side, the way demure Burmese women traditionally sit. Almost every Vinaya rule comes with an official explanation for why the Buddha established the rule in the first place, and the official reason for the prohibition on nuns sitting crosslegged is to prevent them from "consenting to the touch of the heel." I. B. Horner, the translator of the Pali Text Society's English version of Vinaya, included in her translation a quaint, innocent little note discussing the question of whose heel these nuns were consenting to. Based upon an ignorance of the lotus position and/or of human anatomy, combined with some old-fashioned maidenly naïveté, she concluded that bhikkhunis sitting in a group were causing distraction by having their protruding heels rubbing against other bhikkhunis. Personally, however, I don't think her theory is correct. Long ago, before my ordination, a female friend told me that as a young girl she learned how to masturbate by sitting on her heel and rocking back and forth; and I'm pretty sure that that's what "consenting to the touch of the heel" really means. So the rule which probably nobody follows is intended to prevent nuns from turning their meditation into a masturbatory experience.

It may be that most of the new bhikkhunis are simply ignorant of the existence of this rule, although ignorance is no excuse for breaking it. Even if they find out, I'd guess that they'll continue to sit crosslegged, possibly without seeing it as an offense. It could be argued that the rule shouldn't be followed because it discriminates against women: monks are allowed to sit crosslegged, and nuns are not. On the other hand, some rules are less strict for nuns than for monks, but that is not used as an excuse for monks to ignore their own rules. For example, masturbation itself is a much more serious offense for monks than for nuns; but monks don't refuse to do penance for masturbation using this discrimination as an excuse. Besides, the rule against bhikkhunis sitting crosslegged is due in large part to the biological fact that female genitalia are designed differently from that of males; and there's not much that can be done about that. (Vinaya distinguishes between males and females anatomically, not psychologically.) So again, women want to be acknowledged as bhikkhunis, but they don't want to follow the ancient discipline required of bhikkhunis. This strikes me as a serious stroke against the credibility of their cause.

It isn't just "lesser and minor rules" either which may be seen as discriminatory against ordained women. Bhikkhunis have twice as many pārājika rules—the most serious rules, which result in automatic excommunication if broken—as bhikkhus have; and anyone who understands how Vinaya works knows that there is no way in hell that that is going to be changed. It can't be changed, unless maybe via some extraordinarily radical decree of an international Great Council of the Sangha of the Four Quarters, which is very unlikely to happen. Also, the ordination procedure discriminates against women, for example by the embarrassing personal questions asked of a woman before she is ordained; and changing these rules would no doubt be seen by many conservative traditionalists as simply rendering the ordination invalid, thereby worsening the situation.

Many politically correct individuals, especially in the West, vehemently insist that the bhikkhuni order must be revived *and* immediately modified, not caring about such quibbles as technical validity or even democracy, for the sake of gender equality—despite the plain fact that inequality is built deeply into the system of the Bhikkhuni Sangha. In this case political correctness trumps obvious facts and also the will of the majority, the majority here being the majority of Theravada Buddhist monastics, almost all of whom are Asian. The whole situation is quite a dilemma.

So again, the big question is: Why go to the trouble of reviving an ancient system that pretty much nobody really wants to follow, and then immediately overhaul it so that it is no longer the ancient system, but is something else? Why try to reinstate an extinct order defined by Vinaya, and then reject much of the same

Vinaya which defines it? The answer seems pretty obvious: Mainly what these folks want is the *name*, the official status, the worldly recognition of women being genuine bhikkhunis, which is largely a desire to make a political statement, to assert an idealized social principle. The trouble with this is that names, official status, and worldly recognition (let alone political statements) are part of the very same worldliness that a true renunciant is supposed to renounce. It has nothing to do with genuine Dhamma. It is a symptom of Western mentality that social issues, political correctness, and other superficialities take precedence over what is truly essential. What is truly essential often isn't even on the radar.

I have suggested before (and I still think it is a good idea) that an obvious solution to the dilemma of reviving an ancient system that pretty much nobody wants to follow is *to start a new order*. Maybe two orders could be started—one for women, and one for men. The founding members could establish whatever rules they considered to be appropriate for a modern world, with female and male monastics being completely equal, so that presumably it would be a matter of seniority and nothing else that would determine who bowed to whom, and who got to go through the doorway first. Technically it wouldn't amount to full ordination as bhikkhunis and bhikkhus, but so what; I do not believe that official ordination into a particular ancient tradition is necessary for enlightenment anyway, and enlightenment is supposedly the main purpose of the whole thing. Furthermore, this way would not amount to real schism, so long as the women and men were not claiming to be really ordained bhikkhunis and bhikkhus. The Japanese Buddhists and the western Catholics already have something like this. I would guess that the officially ordained Theravadin Sangha would even allow the existence and affiliation of a kind of quasi-Sangha more suited to the West. Possibly the biggest problem with this scheme, if it were really to become manifest, is that politically correct Westerners might make a deliberate show of disrespecting the older monastic system as remaining incorrigibly sexist...which could then warrant dissociation from Theravada proper. We would then have a new sect—Navakavada, or "Doctrine of the Newcomers"—which might still manage to avoid the stigma of schism if its members just minded their own business and did not consider themselves to be officially ordained bhikkhunis and bhikkhus. They could call themselves anything else they liked, however. I think it could be a really good idea, and one more likely to be without sticky problems than reviving the official bhikkhuni order, or just controversially attempting to revive it, and then mutating it, in the face of opposition of the majority and lack of official recognition.

But of course, this scheme would not provide what many appear to consider the essential point of the thing: the absurd crap of worldly status, which crap of course the new renunciants ideally should be renouncing. It's the name "bhikkhuni" that seems to be the primary issue for some. Trying to reconcile Dhamma/Dharma with the Western point of view is really a dilemma. Dhamma just doesn't fit into Western society without it being dismembered and the pieces that fit stuck in around the edges.

In Buddhism it is taught that it is the inner state that is most important; the outward form of things is of secondary importance at best. Good and bad, right and wrong, just and unjust, are mental and volitional, not external, physical phenomena. And even the Pali texts show the Buddha freely admitting that women are the spiritual equals of men, being equally capable of enlightenment. So really, if women are not equal to men NOW, they never will be, unless maybe genetic engineering or some such changes one or both biological human genders. What is on the inside is what really matters, and what is on the outside is supposed to be mindfully let go of by a renunciant. If you think that artificial laws, social patterns, and political correctness will somehow make women equal, and that they are not equal already, then you are more worldly, superficial, and sexist than I am. But maybe more about this some other time.

If there are any women who read this who want to be real bhikkhunis, then I respectfully suggest that you follow the real rules for bhikkhunis, and not an amputated, mutated version of same. On the other hand, if you don't want to subject yourself to such discrimination, which is understandable, then please *create something better.* Something different. I know you are equal, and I'm really on your side, and am willing to help. At least I feel like I'm on your side. *appamādena sampādetha.*

## APPENDIX TO THE APPENDIX: MASTURBATION RULES AND THE ORIGINS OF THE BHIKKHUNI MONASTIC CODE

In the foregoing discussion I mentioned that the rules against masturbation in the pātimokkhas for monks and nuns differ between the sexes. There are more rules in place for preventing bhikkhunis from playing with themselves *at all*; yet masturbation all the way to orgasm bears a much stricter penalty for bhikkhus, requiring them to do six days and six nights of penance, followed by a large, inconvenient reinstatement ceremony. In fact nuns' masturbating to orgasm is not mentioned in the Pali, and thus carries no stricter penalty than simply the insertion of a finger past the second knuckle. My explanation for "complete" masturbation being a saṅghādisesa offense for monks and only a medium-severity pācittiya offense for nuns is this: The puritanical celibate Elders who came up with the rules did not know that women are able to have orgasms! Otherwise, there can be little doubt that they would have penalized it severely.

Now, I would assume that Gotama Buddha, being an extremely wise person, would at least be aware of this relatively important aspect of female sexuality. After all, he had lived a sensual life before he renounced the world, and had a wife, and maybe even a harem of slave girls. Consequently I consider this masturbation rule business to be one of several bits of evidence that the Buddha himself did not devise the bhikkhuni pātimokkha—and possibly not the bhikkhu pātimokkha either. Some very ancient texts actually warn against a renunciant subjecting himself to systematized rules; and it is fairly clear that a primary purpose of the first Great Council, convened after the Buddha's death, was to formulate a monastic code.

There is circumstantial evidence in the Pali texts that some Elders did not like the idea of having a Bhikkhuni Sangha; and the texts themselves have the Buddha himself asserting that instituting it was a bad idea which would greatly shorten the lifespan of the Sāsana in this world. (See "On the 500-Year Lifespan of Buddhism," at the beginning of this volume.) But that assertion, plus much of the negative discrimination, may have been added by the aforementioned unsympathetic Elders who participated in the formulation of official Doctrine. It may be that the Buddha really did allow an order of ordained nuns; but the extant monastic code for these nuns (and maybe for monks too) may not have been his idea.

Therefore, I consider this to be another argument in favor of spiritually-oriented Buddhist women today simply creating a brand new order more sympathetic to the needs of women. In order for it to work, pretty much all that is required is to avoid that one contentious word "bhikkhuni," since technically a bhikkhuni is defined by the same monastic code which is designed in part to drive women away from the Sangha, and possibly back into the arms of insensitive husbands who don't even know that they can come.

# ABOUT THE AUTHOR

## John David Reynolds (Alias Paññobhāsa)

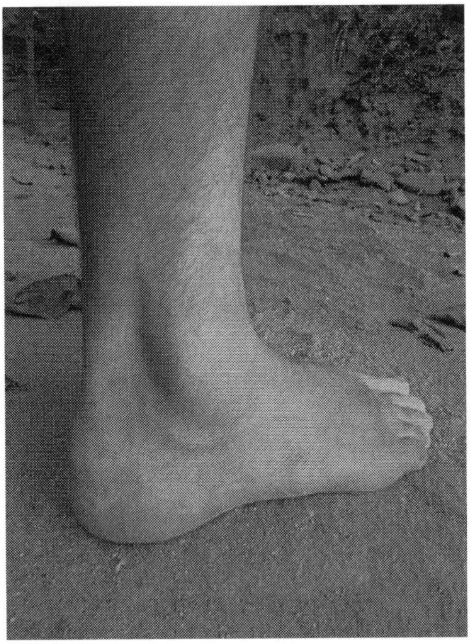

David/Pannobhasa is an American (of mostly English ancestry) born in Alaska and raised in the Pacific Northwest of the USA, with a degree in Marine Biology and a lifelong mystical and philosophical streak. He was ordained as a Theravada Buddhist monk in 1991, and eventually disrobed back down to nobody in particular in 2021, after thirty years in robes, more than twenty of those years spent in Burma/Myanmar, and most of that spent living alone in caves in forests. America (and the west in general) not being nearly so conducive to living a reclusive monk's life, and David genuinely wishing to be of some service to others in their path to awakening, he has begun teaching and sharing his knowledge with a wider audience, including the good person holding this book.

He currently lives in South Carolina, and may be contacted at the link on his website, nippapanca.org.

# REFERENCES


Basham, A. L. (1954). *The Wonder That Was India.* London: Sidgwick and Jackson.

Bradley, F. H. (1906). *Appearance and Reality: A Metaphysical Essay.* New York: MacMillan.

Mon, Mehm Tin (1995). *The Essence of Buddha Abhidhamma.* Yangon: Mya Mon Yadanar.

Nyanatiloka (1991). *Buddhist Dictionary.* (Third revised and enlarged edition, edited by Nyanaponika) Singapore: Singapore Buddhist Meditation Centre.

Pande, Govind Chandra (1983). *Studies in the Origins of Buddhism.* Delhi: Motilal Banarsidass.

Rhys Davids, T. W., and Stede, William (1999). *Pali-English Dictionary.* Oxford: Pali Text Society.

Schopenhauer, Arthur (1969). *The World as Will and Representation.* (Translated by E. F. J. Payne) New York: Dover.

Vicittasārābhivamsa, Bhaddanta (1992). *The Great Chronicle of Buddhas.* Translated by U Ko Lay and U Tin Lwin. Rangoon: Ti=Ni Publishing Center.

Wallace, B. Alan (1996). *Choosing Reality: A Buddhist View of Physics and the Mind.* Ithaca: Snow Lion Publications.